THE BI

NIALL MURTAGH was born and grew up in Dublin. After graduating from University College Dublin in 1979, he travelled slowly across Europe, Asia, Australia and Latin America, working along the way but taking time off to earn several degrees, including diplomas in Japanese and French and a doctorate in artificial intelligence. He has lived in Japan since 1986, initially as a Japanese government-sponsored student, then as an ordinary employee of Mitsubishi for 14 years. He recently escaped from the corporate world to work as a writer and consultant, based in Yokohama, Japan.

THE BLUE-EYED SALARYMAN

From world traveller to lifer at Mitsubishi

Niall Murtagh

P
PROFILE BOOKS

This paperback edition published in 2006

First published in Great Britain in 2005 by
PROFILE BOOKS LTD
3A Exmouth House
Pine Street
Exmouth Market
London EC1R 0JH
www.profilebooks.com

10 9 8 7 6 5 4 3 2 1

Typeset in Minion by MacGuru Ltd
info@macguru.org.uk

Printed and bound in Great Britain by
Bookmarque Ltd, Croydon, Surrey

A CIP catalogue record for this book is available from the British Library.

ISBN-10 1 86197 789 1
ISBN-13 978 1 86197 789 2

For my parents, Martin, now gone, and Angela;
and for Miyuki, the salaryman's wife.

Acknowledgements

For several years I hesitated to write about my career in Mitsubishi, holding back in respect of the privacy of my colleagues. At the same time I felt there was a need to show what life is like as a foreign employee in one of the big conglomerates of east Asia, particularly now as economic and demographic trends compel them to employ more outsiders. Finally I decided to hit the keyboard, my solution being to create composite characters, using pseudonyms and altering some situations in order to protect the confidentiality of those who were generous and helpful to me, both within Mitsubishi and the other companies and universities mentioned. To them I owe a debt of gratitude.

Although I have worked in more than one Mitsubishi company over the years, the corporate culture was always similar and so I combine the organisations here and refer only to Mitsubishi. By describing what I encountered as honestly as I can, my hope is that this book may give some positive guidelines and perhaps act as a stimulus for change.

I have been helped by many people in putting my experiences on paper. I would like to express my gratitude to my agent, John Pawsey, for guiding my vague ideas in the right direction, to Andrew Franklin of Profile Books for his insight and encouragement, to Penny Daniel for polishing the manuscript, and to Ruth Killick, Benjamin Usher and Kate Griffin, who helped put the book on the road. Finally, a word of thanks to Brian Burns and Masaki Tanioka for their comments and enthusiasm.

1

郷に入っては郷に従え

Go ni itte wa, go ni shitagae
When you enter the village, obey the village

So you're gonna become an ant, said straight-talking Thomas that day, many years ago, when I told him about the job.

– Me? An ant? Course not. I'm just gonna see what it's like, then move on.

He was not convinced.

– Off to work in the crowded train with a little briefcase, back home before midnight.

– Hey, it's not lifetime employment. Call it a new experience. See how the other half lives.

– Well, enjoy the experience, he said and gave me a funny look, a look that said, Man, you gotta be crazy.

Even today I remember that look whenever I ask myself the question, Do I still enjoy being a salaryman after all these years? Or am I crazy?

I remember the interview back in 1990, the plush meeting room with the polished table and swivel chairs in one of the Mitsubishi office blocks just west of Tokyo Station. I remember the three Mitsubishi men with the overtime smiles who said they were internationalising and had to start somewhere. Could I work with them two or maybe three years? Could I work as an engineer or researcher or whatever fancy job title I like, because titles and work are flexible? Could I support the factories and write some state-of-the-art software or come up with brilliant new ideas for intelligent robots, smart elevators, spiral escalators, undersea cables, civil aircraft, steel bridges, sports stadia, nuclear power stations, speed control systems for the *shinkansen* – the fastest train in the world – or any of the hundreds of things they made? I tell them I can work a year or maybe two, though I don't have any brilliant ideas for any of those gizmos.

– No problem, they say. The specifics of the job can be decided later. You will be based in the plant just outside Yokohama, an hour from here.

I sign up because I feel this is the next thing for me to try. I've already been here a while, studied in the salaryman prep school, got a grip on Japanese. Let's see if I can handle the real world, where this country has become an economic superpower, about to overtake America. It won't be one of the usual jobs they give to foreigners, hired as cultural specimens for language practice and letter writing, told to sit in a corner, shuffle papers and look cosmopolitan. I'll be an ordinary employee, the same conditions, the same ups and downs as all the others. And if I can handle the downside, if I can swallow my individualism just a little and do some compromising, something useful might come out of it all. It's worth a try.

I think back to the first morning at the company, that hot September morning, the inevitable crowds at the station, the feeling of apprehension at the start of something new and unknown. I stared out the train window, watching the platform flash past, wondering where my life was headed. It's only for a year or two, I told myself. How wrong I was.

I thought about Thomas. He would never do this. He studied with the locals like me, but he left to return to Austria, where the only ants are the little ones on the ground.

Ants. Little creatures that rush here and there, following unspoken orders, loaded down with no time to stop or rest. Will it be like that? If so, I'm going back to South America or India or anywhere. If I can't stick it, I'll save a little money and hit the road again. But first I'll conform a bit, work a reasonable number of hours and no more, go for a drink if I feel like it but not if I don't, and perhaps learn a few things I didn't pick up on the road. I've come this far. I may as well go a little further.

After a few stops, I squeeze off the train, up the stairs, out into the morning sunlight. I stop and wait at the traffic lights even though there are no cars coming, because there's a crowd of people around me, watching what I do, approving or disapproving without saying anything or doing anything. In another time and place I wouldn't care whether they approve or not and I'd already be on the other side of the street, but this is different and I'd prefer their silent approval because these people are probably my future colleagues and they'll remember a foreigner who ignores the traffic rules right in front of them. Someone who doesn't obey the traffic rules probably won't obey other rules either. The lights change and I follow the crowd. The crowd goes down the first side street, past the 7-Eleven shop, the flashy *pachinko* hall, the cram school and the huge Mitsubishi sign, towards the white steel gates of the company, everyone wearing the same salaryman white shirt and grey suit, carrying the same salaryman briefcase, and I'm thinking about ants. I walk though the gate to become a salaryman.

A security guard looks on, dressed in navy blue uniform, the red three-diamond Mitsubishi logo on his peaked cap. He stands with legs apart, hands behind his back like an army officer, looking at each face passing through the gate. Army vibes already. If this continues, I'll soon be a deserter. This is peacetime. Deserters won't be shot.

The security guard shouts good morning at each face because it's official company etiquette to greet your colleagues enthusiastically in the morning, though many people don't say anything, they're not in the mood, and those who do merely grunt because it's hard to be enthusiastic early in the morning after commuting from the outer suburbs of Tokyo or Yokohama with twelve hours of work ahead.

The few trees near the entrance give way to corrugated-steel-walled factory buildings on one side of the company road. On the other there's a small Shinto shrine to keep the manufacturing gods on our side. Next to the gods' little home is my building, a sleek, new office block, eight storeys high, housing the research centre and offices. The receptionist tells me to go to Personnel, where they give me booklets about company history, rules, benefits and employee obligations. They give me a company jacket, an ID badge and a cloth cap with the three-diamond company logo. What's the cap for?

Kawaii-*san* is in charge of kitting out new recruits. She says it is a safety cap because you never know how or where you might bump your head. Then she adds that if you're not working in the factories you don't have to wear it.

I tell her I don't think I'll wear it too often. I'll be careful not to bump my head.

– But you must wear the ID badge at all times. And at no time should you walk around with your hands in your pockets.

What's wrong with walking around with my hands in my pockets? There must be a reason, but I'd better go easy on the questions for now.

She brings me to the photo studio. The photographer gives me a blank number plate and helps me pick out the digits of my personal man-number from a box of magnetic number strips. Everyone has a man-number, even the women. He arranges my man-number on the plate and tells me to hold it in front of my chest.

– Up a little higher, please, otherwise your man-number won't show. Look straight ahead. Try not to look so serious. It's not a prison, you know.

He takes my mug shot with man-number for the company files and I go back to Personnel with Kawaii-*san*.

– Please introduce yourself with a little speech, she says. All the new employees do it.

The busy Personnel people look up from their desks and stop working for a moment or two. I stand up straight, look at the desk in front of me because no eye contact is necessary yet, and say something – my name, where I'm from, what else? An apology. Apologies always go down well. It doesn't matter what the apology is about, anything will do. Please forgive my poor Japanese. Please correct my mistakes. An apology breaks the ice. He can't be that bad if he starts off with an apology. Almost like one of us. My speech continues – what I did before arriving in the company, how I studied hard in graduate school and got my degree like any new recruit. I don't mention my career as accidental sailor and intercontinental hitchhiker, drifting whichever way the wind was blowing and ending up here because it happened to be blowing east.

I continue my little speech by telling my new colleagues what they want to hear, how pleased I am to be joining the company, even if I'm not sure, and how I look forward to getting to know everyone and have a lot to learn, please teach me about company life, that's all for now, thank you very much. I finish with a nod that will have to do for a bow, everyone returns to work and I'm part of the organisation already. The right stuff.

The first thing I notice in my new department is the quietness, except for the hum of the computers. Diligent salarymen in the Mitsubishi corporate laboratories are not the noisiest in the world. People do more thinking than talking here, which is fine, as long as you don't come to work to socialise. Later, when I work for a boss who thinks aloud so that all on the floor know his thoughts, I realise not everyone is quiet. But that boss spent years in one of the factories, where the atmosphere is different from the research lab.

There are over a hundred grey steel desks on our open-plan floor, with dark-brown cloth-upholstered swivel chairs and dark heads bent over keyboards or papers, hardly moving the whole day long. The desks are laid out in traditional style: lines of four or five pairs, each pair head to head, stretching from a central passageway almost as far as the windows, with the manager's desk at the window-end of the line, perpendicular to the others. Employees sitting at one of these phalanxes of desks form a section or group. Where the group is large, it may also include a few desks in a neighbouring phalanx. There are usually between three and five groups in a department, and a couple of departments on each floor. In our building, chest-high partitions separate the pairs of desks so you don't have to stare into the face of the person opposite, although in Administration and Personnel, which are more traditional, there are no partitions. The desks are arranged in order of seniority, with new recruits sitting closest to the central passageway and older employees closest to the manager. Every desk has a large monitor, made by Mitsubishi or Sun, with a computer unit beside it or on the floor under the desk. I'm impressed at the sleek Mitsubishi monitors till

I discover later they are manufactured by Hewlett Packard and repackaged for sale in Japan under the Mitsubishi label. Besides the computer, each desk has a few books, journals or manuals, with one telephone for every two desks. On the senior salarymen's desks you might see the latest issue of the *Nikkei Sangyo Shimbun* (*Nikkei Industrial Newspaper*) or the *Nikkan Kogyo Shimbun* (*Nikkan Industrial Newspaper*). I never saw a *manga* comic anywhere in the Mitsubishi offices, although salarymen often read them on the train. I assume my colleagues are careful about keeping them out of sight while at work.

Along the central passageway there are white panel boards for each group, listing the names of group members, with magnetic markers saying where they are – desk, meeting room, library, business trip, day off. It's a relief to see *day off* unashamedly written in bold letters. It means the official twenty-five days' leave we get is not just theory. Add those twenty-five to the thirteen national holidays and the seven Mitsubishi holidays, and my calculations tell me I won't die from overwork, even if I'm a good salaryman and only take half the leave. I'm glad I didn't join a smaller company where they only get three days off a year – if they're lucky.

The floors are of dark-grey carpet tiles that can be pulled up to add new cables to the ducts below. The ceiling has rows of fluorescent light strips, smoke and heat detectors, emergency water sprays, speakers from which bells ring out several times a day, and a few large air-conditioning ducts that blow deliciously cool air between mid-June and mid-September. Along the central passageway are a few potted plants with leaves that look green and natural, though they're only plastic. The windows have blinds to block out the strong sunshine that might reflect off our computer screens and make them hard to work at. If you go to the window and pull back the blinds you see a warehouse, a factory building with grey wall cladding and a zigzag roof, and workers in blue overalls walking or cycling along the company road below. From the top floor of our building you can see beyond the industrial buildings and nearby houses to the Tanzawa mountain range on the western horizon and on clear days the magnificent peak of Mount Fuji, snow-capped from September till late June.

Unlike Head Office and Administration, salarymen in the lab are permitted to dress casually, under the Mitsubishi jacket. Some of the younger ones with no meetings to attend never wear a tie, and footwear standards are relaxed. When they arrive in the office, most salarymen swap their shoes, which are always black leather, for slippers or sandals. Your footwear lets everyone know how at home you feel. Those who do the longest hours have the most casual footwear: slippers they could sleep in. Later, I notice that one of my bosses goes around in his socks. He always works late.

On our floor there are a few OLs, a Japanese term derived from the English *office lady.* Their official role is to carry out simple clerical tasks and make tea when a visitor comes, but their real task is to add colour to the office. They are always polite and never seem to be stressed, unlike many of the salarymen. The OLs wear a neat company-issued navy blue apron, but otherwise do not have dress restrictions. Since they don't work late, their footwear is on the formal side; they never wear slippers like the salarymen.

There are a few female engineers and researchers who are not OLs and could be described as honorary salarymen. They have Mitsubishi jackets, like their male colleagues, but their footwear is formal, like the OLs. They have little chance of being promoted beyond lower management level, but, in recompense, are not expected to work as late as the real salarymen.

Beyond the phalanxes of desks on my floor are a couple of alcoves partitioned off for the department managers. Near the stairway is a locker room with the narrowest lockers I've ever seen. Mitsubishi salarymen do not put posters of any type on the locker doors, although there are some posters on the walls – colourful Mitsubishi posters with slogans about quantum leaps in quality or with the company president's mug shot. The president is not holding his man-number.

Shinsetsu-*san* is the manager of my group. He welcomes me with a smile and shows me my desk, which is midway between the junior desks near the central passageway and the senior desks closer to the manager. This means I am ranked by age rather than years in the company. He tells me not to worry about all the rules and formalities; they are just to make life easier for everyone and I'll get used to them. He introduces me to the group members in a voice loud enough to be heard across our phalanx of desks but not so loud he might disturb the neighbouring groups. Everyone in our group stands up. I give another little speech as before, with a couple of apologies just for politeness.

– Now, to work, Shinsetsu says. We are undertaking a new project this year for the elevator factory – the lifts, as you call them. Can you write some software to help our engineers design their elevators? Please tell us what you can do in a report to be completed in about three months. Is this possible?

– Yes, I think it's possible, I say, although I've no idea, but it's good to be positive.

Maybe my colleagues can help me decide what is possible – the accessible colleagues who feel comfortable speaking to an alien like me, probably the first they've ever worked with.

Riko-*san* seems comfortable with aliens and he knows about elevators.

– Mitsubishi holds the record for the fastest elevator in the world, he tells me. And do you know that our elevators in the new Landmark Tower in Yokohama will be so smooth you'll be able to put a ten-yen coin standing on its edge on the elevator floor when you enter and it will still be standing on its edge when you reach the seventieth floor after zooming up from ground level at world record speed?

I want to tell him that most people keep their coins in their pocket. But that is not the point. The point is that Mitsubishi elevators are the fastest and the smoothest in the world and we have to support the elevator factory outside Nagoya because if we don't Hitachi and Toshiba will be breathing down our necks and maybe we'll even have the foreign companies like Otis and Kone on our heels. It's tough being a front-runner.

– We have to stay ahead of our competitors and that is where your work will help. You can see the elevator-testing tower when we visit the factory next month. You can also see the Mitsubishi spiral escalator and the only elevator in the world with a glass window that looks down on the rice paddies.

Majime-*san* sits two desks away from me. He doesn't work with speedy elevators or spiral escalators but he knows everything about connecting computers and printers to the network so he's a useful person. He is always looking at his desk or his computer screen. He never looks up to see what's going on or to look at me and I fear I make him feel uncomfortable. I'm sure he's scared of aliens but I can't help it, and besides the eyes and hair I'm not that weird. I'm about average height and weight in the department and don't have a loud voice like some aliens. I even apologised twice in my introductory speech but that doesn't make up for the hair and alien-contoured face. When I ask Majime-*san* about the printer and the network, he doesn't look at me but mumbles an answer I can't hear to his computer screen.

One day I achieve eye contact with him, just a fleeting glance before his gaze returns to the screen, but I still can't hear most of what he says. I change tack. I desist from my aggressive attempts at blatant eye contact and when I ask him something, I look only at the computer on his desk so that he feels more at ease, can answer without feeling scared and I can hear most of what he is saying. Even if his answer is to the computer screen, the message is to me and we've found a way to talk to each other and be friends, or if not friends, at least co-workers capable of communicating with each other. It just takes time and patience.

Kawaii-*san* gives me the *Guidebook for New Employees* – please read it when you have time and please ask your colleagues if you have trouble reading the characters or understanding the difficult words. New employees are assumed to be starting their first job and are expected to know very little. They'll learn everything they need to know after entering the company. But I'm different. I've already seen and done a lot and assume the *Guidebook* doesn't apply to me, that it can be stuffed away in a drawer when no one is watching. I've a deadline coming up in a few months. But when I meet Kawaii-*san* in the corridor she asks me if I understood the booklet. I tell her I'm working my way carefully through it, page by page. I decide I'd better dig it out of my desk and read it right after lunch. I open the *Guidebook for New Employees* and start reading about a salaryman's life in one of Japan's greatest multi-nationals.

The company was founded by Yataro Iwasaki in 1870, underwent a couple of name changes before becoming *Mitsu-bishi,* meaning three rhombuses or diamond-shapes, and quickly grew into the greatest of the *zaibatsu* – the industrial and financial conglomerates of the late nineteenth and early twentieth centuries. There are 139 independent companies in the Mitsubishi Group, with twenty-nine core members whose presidents meet once a month in one of the Mitsubishi buildings near Tokyo Station. The group includes the largest trading company in the world, several of the largest banks and insurance companies, the top beer-, camera- and glass-makers in Japan, and manufacturers of aircraft, ships, cars, train systems and power stations. It includes companies in real estate, construction, chemicals, steel, rubber, paper, energy, textiles, warehousing, transport and agriculture, and they still find time for philanthropy, environmental protection and lots of good things. I suppose I should be proud. But not yet. The booklet says Mitsubishi is a great organisation to work for. Then it says what is expected of new recruits.

A smiling photograph of the company president on the inside cover congratulates you on becoming a Mitsubishi man. The booklet tells you how to bow, from the lightweight stuff to the heavyweight fifty-degree bows reserved for expressing deep gratitude or apologies: bow from the waist, back straight, and the eyes have to bow too. This bowing stuff is hard to take, like the rule about not walking around with hands in your pockets. I've got by on three-degree nods up to now and they will have to do from now on. Even for the company president.

The booklet tells you to always have your business card ready because, otherwise, people won't know your position nor how to treat you and they won't remember you. I understand this as company existentialism: *I have a business card, therefore I exist.*

Before a meeting, you must find out how many people will be there and have extra cards ready, just in case. If one person is scheduled to attend, you should have three cards ready; if two people, have six cards. Recite your department and name as you offer your card, which should be done with the right hand extended at about chest height. When you receive a card you should accept it with the left hand, look at it carefully for a few seconds and then place it lightly on the table with your right hand. Never write any notes on the card while people are watching because it's as if you are telling them you will forget them immediately. It's all right to write something on the card after they've left. The company existentialism is saying: *the business card is a piece of your soul so handle it with care.*

A proper telephone manner is important. When you speak on the phone you should not forget to smile and keep your back straight. Always pick up the receiver the moment it rings and give your company and department name before asking who the other party is. Do not speak in a loud voice, say unnecessary things, nor mumble your words; use concise, accurate and respectful language. Always wait till after the other party has hung up before quietly putting down the receiver.

I know about the next section in the booklet because Kawaii-*san* has already told me all about titles and how to address my colleagues and superiors. Forget about the titles people might use in the world outside, *san*, *Mr* or even *Dr*. Mitsubishi is more advanced than the average company where they have long-winded titles like section manager (*kacho*) and sub-section manager (*kakaricho*). Mitsubishi uses English letter titles, short and international. I should call my boss Shinsetsu-GR, not Shinsetsu-*kacho*, GR meaning group leader (for linguistic reasons *l* and *r* are often confused in East Asia). Riko-*san* is Riko-T because he's a *tanto* – in charge of something. In charge of what? Nothing really, except his work. It's company-speak. I'm a T as well. Muruta-T, I'm pronounced.

Ts are usually in their twenties or thirties. I learn later that an employee who reaches forty or fifty and is still a T clearly has limited abilities, is hard to get on with, or is an OL and therefore not meant to rise up though the ranks. The few foreigners I met over the years in Mitsubishi were always T-class. Normally, an employee takes a test in his early thirties and is promoted to *shuji* or C-class, C standing for chief, although in practice *shuji* just means senior staff. A few years later he takes a more difficult test for promotion to KS-class, KS standing for *shukan* or manager. During the high economic growth period up to the 1980s, most *shukan* would sooner or later be given a group or project to lead and become GRs, although this has changed in the last two decades and, as I discovered for myself, a KS is no longer sure of becoming a GR. Above the KS and GR level is the B-class, B meaning *bucho*, or department manager. A young department manager would be in his mid-forties, although most are in their fifties. The salaries go up a little at each promotion, but not a lot, since compensation is based mainly on length of service and age. More important than the small salary increase is the status implied in each promotion. This is emphasised by the strict use of company titles when formally addressing colleagues at meetings, in emails and in all written documents. The exception is when you are talking about your fellow employees to an outsider, a non-Mitsubishi person, in which case respectful or honorific language or titles should *not* be used, even for your superiors. You should say Tanaka, not Tanaka-*san* or Tanaka-GR. The company is like family, and you would not use titles for family members in front of outsiders, would you?

The *Guidebook* then tells you how to sit. Before you take a seat at a meeting, wait! Never take a seat before your superiors have taken theirs and never stand up till after they have done so. Sit with your back straight leaving a tiny space between your back and the chair. You may not choose where you sit because as a new employee you have a very low rank and the person of lowest rank should always sit closest to the door because, as I found out later, in medieval times that was the seat most likely to be attacked if a ninja burst in with a dagger. The person of lowest rank, the most expendable, should sit there ready to be sacrificed, if necessary, for the sake of his boss, as any loyal employee should do.

The rules are hard to learn and even harder to take seriously. But a few months later I enter a restaurant after a meeting and because I'm first I take the seat farthest from the door. One of my bosses, who is schooled in old traditions, shouts, What's this here? Muruta-T doesn't know his table manners. He thinks he's a manager already! Come on, change your seat. Our guest and I should be on the inside, not you.

The next section deals with the delicate subject of encounters with foreigners, who probably have all sorts of strange customs and need to be treated with caution. When meeting a foreigner, you should stand up straight, don't look at the floor, look at the foreigner eye to eye, don't bow or bend your head.

The booklet tells you how to greet the foreigner. Normally, a superior will be first to hold out his hand for a handshake, always with the right hand. You should offer your business card and give a good impression of your company. You should not be reserved just because the person is a foreigner.

If you have a meal with a foreigner, do not take a seat before him and do not stand up after the meal till he has done so. Make sure you never put your finger or a matchstick in your mouth, nose or ear. Such habits are especially frowned upon by foreigners, who are strictly taught not to do so from a very young age.

The booklet says we should be neither ashamed nor overly proud of our national customs and our company. We Japanese have our unique culture and traditions but other countries have theirs too. We should have a quiet and restrained pride in our country and company.

I'm not sure if I'm ashamed or proud to be part of the company because it's so different from what I did before. Am I selling my once-adventurous soul for a business card stamped with Mitsubishi in big blue letters?

The *Guidebook for New Employees* finishes on a lighter note with the lyrics and music score of the 'Employees' Song', to be sung in marching style, *con vivo.*

*Technology Always**
The world so wide, east, west, north, south
Together, working, advancing
In cities and towns of our country
New products for the world
Oh-oh techno-life
Mitsu-bishi wu wu wu

Working, reaching out, no looking back
With new ideas for the consumer
Throughout our nation and the world
Techno-living is for us all
Oh-oh techno-life
Mitsu-bishi wu wu wu

I look at all the busy people, Shinsetsu-GR, Riko-T, Majime-T and the

---

*Lyrics written by the author, based on his translations of various Mitsubishi company songs.

others, wondering if they've memorised the words, if they hum the tune in the bath, because I'm not sure I feel comfortable working for an organisation with an official song that goes *oh-oh techno-life Mitsu-bishi wu wu wu* even if I'm wearing the company jacket and ID badge, with my man-number and mug shot, looking as close to being a true blue Mitsubishi man *wu wu wu* as ever a blue-eyed foreigner could. Did I really leave behind all my non-conformist adventurous past, wandering through almost half the countries in the world, and come to this faraway place, struggle with the beautiful but terrible language, study my ass off through graduate school, to end up working for an organisation with an anthem that goes *oh-oh techno-life Mitsu-bishi wu wu wu*?

2

井の中の蛙大海を知らず

I no naka no kawazu taikai o shirazu

A frog in a well knows not the ocean

Where did it all begin, this salaryman life? I grew up in Dublin in the sixties and seventies, venturing overseas only twice by the time I was twenty – both times to England. After university I saved a little money, and in the autumn of 1980 I set off for a year of living free while I had the chance, because you only get the chance once and there would be plenty of years for a normal, everyday job later.

I hitchhiked from Paris to Istanbul, sleeping in parks, in hostels to get a shower, on the beach, partly to save money and partly to see how rough and how far I could go. Turkey was under martial law and the army was on the streets. Iran was at war and the consulate in Istanbul had stopped issuing transit visas. The only ride I could find going east was with a busload of pilgrims on their way to Mecca. The bus conductor put business before religion and didn't mind an infidel on board.

– You pay me dollars, I let you off at Jeddah, he said. No problem.

I didn't mind paying – I wasn't expecting freebies for ever – but I felt there was a problem. I felt his business instincts would not delay the pilgrimage for me if I got stuck at some border crossing, and an Irishman without a visa or a prayer mat on a Mecca-bound bus would surely arouse the suspicions of the border police.

– Come with us young man, they'd say, and we will find out if you really mixed up Mecca with Rome!

No, I wasn't going to get stuck so soon. After a day on the pilgrim bus

I let them go their way and took a plane to India, where it was peaceful. I met gentle people, going nowhere, taking life as it comes. For a moment I thought I could join them, read the *Upanishads* and find enlightenment. But I realised I couldn't sit all day watching the Ganges flow at Varanasi or meditating in the Himalayas. The Western work ethic was there in my baggage telling me how to act, telling me I had to be doing something – standing on the side of the road waiting for a lift to anywhere, learning a language, even working. So I left the enlightened people, travelled on and worked – in a camp for Bihari refugees in Dhaka, on a construction site in New South Wales, in a pacifist school in the mountains of Fukushima. I even dug out a clean shirt and trousers from my rucksack and got a proper job for a while, just to stay in touch with the conventional world and keep that work ethic satisfied.

By the time I reached China I had done nearly everything there was to do in the East and it was 1983. The year on the road had become two and then three, and I was beginning to feel some travel burnout. I took the slow train back to Europe, wondering what happens when the big trip is over. Do I just melt back into the society I left as if I had read everything in a big book? The train trundled westwards through the white Soviet winter and for the first time I wasn't really sure where I was headed.

I spent an unsettled year in graduate school, wondering what I would do, studying hard so I could finish early. I applied for some faraway jobs but didn't wait around for replies that might be negative. The pull of the open road was strong, and in 1985 I set off again because I seemed to be able to think more clearly when I was on the road. This time I went down to Africa, with a plan to go from top to bottom or as far down as I could, maybe to Kenya, maybe to Cape Town. Something would turn up along the way and I would know what to do next.

Something did turn up, but, as always, not what I expected. In Casablanca I met a carpet-seller, a friendly chap, and we talked all day in a café in the old town. He showed me around and invited me to dinner. I was his guest.

– Why don't we go to my farm south of Marrakech for a few days, where the mountains meet the desert, the real Morocco, so different from big city Casa?

Why not? He was a friendly chap. I was his guest. And his farm south of Marrakech was my type of place, not Casablanca.

– We will go there tomorrow. Let us meet at the Café de Safi, early morning.

But we never met at the Café de Safi and we never went to that farm where the mountains meet the desert because the friendly chap knew very well how solo travellers with adventure in their eyes and naivety in their rucksack can be stung. After that long day of tall tales he had urgent business to attend to, a carpet to be picked up, the bank was closed, *merci* for helping him out, *merci* for the loan, and he didn't come back in ten minutes, didn't come back in a hour, left me sitting in the café feeling silly, my pride and funds at a low ebb. I wanted to leave big city Casa and the memories of the carpet-seller behind as quickly as I could and travel where I wouldn't need much money.

I bumped into a couple of French sailors about to set off in their home-built ferro-concrete yacht to some distant place, they didn't know where yet.

– Depends on the trade winds, said Gilles, the captain, who was only twenty-two. If they blow, we'll do the crossing – the Atlantic. We need another deck hand. You'll come?

– I'll come.

I'd never sailed anywhere before and I'd never heard of a yacht made of concrete, but what the hell, Gilles and Benoit were friendly chaps, they weren't selling carpets and I just wanted a ride out of Casa. Anywhere would do.

Gilles picked up his girlfriend, Isabel, before we sailed. That persuaded me he wasn't planning to sink in mid-ocean, although I had doubts about doing the crossing on a home-built boat that had no life raft nor radio. We'd have to guess the weather as we went. But I was just an amateur and I wasn't planning to start a mutiny over matters I knew little about. The trade winds blew and we made good progress for a week. Then we hit the doldrums and bobbed up and down without going anywhere for three days. I learned how to determine our position with an old sextant, went swimming in the afternoon heat, read books in the evening about Sinbad the Sailor, who after one trip always wanted to go off on another. I sympathised.

The winds picked up and we meandered on – slowly, because concrete boats don't run. I looked forward to the night watch under skies with a million stars, picking out a constellation here and there. I liked watching Orion as we splashed through the darkness. Then the weather grew stormy and I wondered what would happen if something went wrong, because things can go wrong at sea – broken masts, injured crew or even worse. I told myself that if this boat got us across to the other side it might be a good time for me to give up this wandering life and find a more settled existence somewhere, anywhere. The winds kept blowing and the old boat got us across. Four months after Casablanca I was sitting under the palm trees of Martinique, savouring the gentle breezes of the Caribbean and the good feeling that comes after doing something uncertain that works out in the end. Gilles was preparing to set sail for Argentina and I was on my own again. I'd done the ocean, seen the islands. Now it was time to move on and find my settled existence. After the months on the Atlantic, I knew I didn't want to be a sailor, not a real sailor who sails off into the sunset again and again. The carpet-seller in Casa made me realise I didn't have what it takes to be a businessman, not a real businessman who can suss out anyone he meets. What was left? A steady salaried career in Dublin or London? No, that was out of the question. Even America looked conventional.

I got word that one of the applications I sent off before leaving for Africa had come through. I had an offer of a place on a foreign student programme in Japan. The Japanese Embassy people probably selected me because I was the only candidate who could mumble a few words of their language at the interview six months before. And I was a diligent student – when I wasn't on the road. The thought of going back east again felt good, something new to try, though I had doubts about the lifestyle, which seemed too regimented and group-oriented for me. But the Western lifestyle also seemed too regimented and group-oriented for me. I was going to have problems wherever I went but at least I would find somewhere different to live.

It was early in 1986. Japan was on a roll and looked a good long-term bet, even for non-conformist foreigners. I would have to learn a bit of the language and go to graduate school; in return I would receive a few yen to keep me from starving. Learning a bit of the language and getting a few yen every month sounded fine, and even if I had doubts about graduate school, there was nothing in the letter about how many hours a day had to be spent studying, whether I had to pass exams, or what I had to do after it was over. On the beaches of Martinique I came to a decision. For good or for bad, my settled existence for the next few years would be in Japan. Forget the lifestyle for now. I would think about that when the time came. If it was too much to take, I'd find somewhere else to go.

I got the airfare forwarded to me, flew home and prepared to go east. I stuffed a suit and a few books into my rucksack because I knew I would have to do a bit of compromising and conforming this time.

The language course is low-key and relaxed, a few months in a university called Osaka Gaidai in the green hills north of the city. I learn about the grammar, the scripts and the daunting lists of Chinese characters. I learn about respectful, humble and plain language and then forget them all because any old language will have to do if you're not far off thirty, trying to learn a new way of speaking and even of thinking. All I want is to be semi-literate and semi-cultured in the local ways and I don't even know if I like the country or not. But at least it's different and that is something.

With a bit of the language in my brain, I move to graduate school in the Tokyo Institute of Technology, or Tokodai, as they call it here – a crowded cluster of five- to ten-storey buildings surrounded by car parks, apartment blocks and busy shopping streets all squeezed together without much room to breathe. The students look laid-back, though they are not like students in other countries because they dress too well and are too quiet. People tell me that Tokodai is a prestigious place where hardworking students prepare for the elite company jobs that await them because in this country your career is determined by the university you graduate from. They say that Japan's technological might is nurtured here in Tokodai, but for a blow-in like me it is a dubious privilege. I don't want my career determined so surely and safely. I'm not interested in a company job, elite or otherwise. I just want to stay put for a while, do something useful and see what life will throw up next. But I don't have options now. It is this prep school for budding salarymen or nothing. My supervisor will be Professor Erai, or

Erai-*sensei*; I will study with seven grad students and six undergrads in his laboratory, attend a few lectures, do some research, maybe get a degree for my trouble, and after that who knows? I will sleep in room number 309 of the international student dormitory and commute to the campus, taking the train on the Denentoshi Line every day. It's all decided.

There are no courses for reforming adventurers or intercontinental vagabonds trying to come out of orbit and back to everyday life on earth. If I could, I'd like to study more of the language, the culture or maybe some ancient Japanese poet like Basho, who was a bit of a traveller himself, bumming all around the country in the seventeenth century in between writing *haiku*. I think I'd learn a lot from him. But the programme I'm on doesn't allow it because this is the 1980s and I am down as a techie. I became a techie because I was told years before that techies could travel and work anywhere, and it's true, to some extent. Languages, culture and writing are like travel and the open road – for enjoying, not for making a living, unless you are lucky. If Basho were alive today, he would probably have to combine his travels and writing with being a techie because he'd never make a living as a poet writing *haiku* all day long.

I look through the study options permitted and choose artificial intelligence because it's new and might even expand the mind a little. If I manage to get some sort of a degree from this famous institute in the booming East, I'll be able to wiggle into the conventional world of salaries and staying put for a while, even if I'm not sure that's what I really want. But I can't live on fresh air and freedom for ever.

Erai-*sensei* is more like a company director than a professor – cool, grey-haired, intelligent, busy. The good thing about him is that he leaves us grad students alone most of the time. Our lab is less formal than other labs, and I like it that way. It's very different from Li's lab on the floor beneath us. Li is from Beijing and he thinks it's weird because his *sensei* behaves like he is running a primary school. He checks on everyone everyday and wants an explanation if Li arrives after nine in the morning or leaves before ten at night. The lab is home now and the *sensei* is responsible for study, living and almost everything else. The students have to consult him before making any decisions.

Once Li didn't do this and his *sensei* got very angry. Li had a Chinese girlfriend, who was also a student in Tokodai. One weekend they got married, just like that, but he didn't ask his *sensei*'s permission and didn't inform him till two weeks later.

– Why didn't you tell me? Don't you know I am responsible for your actions while you are here?

Li thinks it's all stupid, especially if you look at the situation from a Chinese point of view. I agree.

– We think the same. We're both outsiders here, he says. That's why it's tough. But let's keep in contact.

– Yes, let's do that. We're both outsiders.

The only problem with my lab is that Erai-*sensei* doesn't give any advice. I don't know if my studies are pushing forward the boundaries of oriental science or re-inventing the rickshaw, but at least I'm not in Li's lab. Nobody is telling me how to live and what to study, and I'm doing something that might be useful for making a living some day, which is better than traipsing forever through Asia, Africa and across the ocean on a concrete boat that might sink.

Erai-*sensei* comes into our study room once in a while and eyeballs the students.

– How is the study? Any progress? Any earth-shattering new discovery?

He smiles when he asks about the earth-shattering discovery because he's not expecting one.

Matsuno, Otake and the other undergrads due to graduate next spring slide textbooks over the *manga* they've been reading. They tell him they're studying hard. Liars. But what else can they say?

– Keep it up, he says. Write a good report.

And he leaves. He just wants to keep an eye on things.

For a few weeks he is away at conferences and we don't see him. Matsuno and the others spend less and less time in the lab, then don't come at all. When Erai-*sensei* returns he looks into our room one Monday. Where is everyone? He pops in again on Tuesday and Wednesday, looks around, doesn't say anything. The next day notices are posted on the walls of the study room.

It has been noted that certain students are regularly absent from the lab. Continued absence will imply that a student has withdrawn from the graduation class. If a student is absent from the lab for more than one day, he must submit an explanation in writing. You will recall that one student, who was absent for extended periods last year, was not permitted to graduate.

M. Erai

The news hits the grapevine. Matsuno and the others are back in the lab next day, looking at the notices and discussing strategies. They know about the student who didn't graduate last year. Kitano was his name. He had the Honda 400. He toured as far as Hokkaido in the summer, Izu when the weather got cold and had a great year. But he didn't come to the lab much, Erai-*sensei* didn't let him pass his exams and what he is doing now is anyone's guess. He will never be an elite salaryman if he can't get through this prep school and there is not much else to aim at in this country besides being an elite salaryman.

– Not showing up in the lab. That's what did it for Kitano, says Matsuno. He wrote a good report. I saw it. But he didn't show up often enough.

– The afternoon, says Otake. That's when Erai-*sensei* comes. We have to be here then. It's no good just popping in between lectures in the morning.

In the days and weeks that follow, Matsuno and his friends are in the lab every afternoon. They work away, consulting the piles of *manga* for inspiration, discussing the state of the art in game technology, the baseball scores and the best places to go in Shibuya. Sometimes they even study a little. Erai-*sensei* looks in once or twice, sees that his notice has had the right effect, and leaves without saying anything.

I know Matsuno doesn't do much in the afternoon besides chat and consult the piles of *manga*, but he does a lot at night because when I arrive in the morning the blinds in the small meeting room are often drawn. I hear snores and I know he's sleeping in. The lab has a foldaway bed for emergencies and he is making good use of it. Poor guy. He's working so hard, trying to make up for the time he wastes in the afternoon. His apartment is far away and he must be working too late to catch the last train home. I close the door quietly and leave him to his slumber. He gets up before noon, pulls open the blinds, folds up the camper bed, washes and shaves at the sink in the corner and goes out for a late breakfast, ready for the afternoon in the lab.

– Aren't you working too hard? I ask him.

– No, no. I skip the morning lectures. But yes, I am busy at night. Many commitments.

– The library?

– No, no. The evenings are for student life. Tennis club meetings on Mondays, festival preparation meeting on Tuesdays, movie night on Wednesdays. On other nights I have to go to Shibuya to meet friends. But there is no choice. This is a busy year for me.

– Why not wait to have a good time next year after graduating?

– Next year? I will be in a company next year. Salarymen cannot sleep late. They have to work at night. I want to be a good salaryman, so I must enjoy this year.

He has it all planned, clever guy. Collect those fond memories of a carefree youth, Matsuno, something to look back on when life gets serious, because if you've nothing to look back on, then what've you got?

It's different for me and Li. We're grads, supposed to be older and wiser, writing papers and dissertations. We are not supposed to be collecting fond memories in the bright lights of Shibuya, at least not on weekdays. I don't need to collect fond memories anyway. I have plenty, haven't I? And I'm not planning to be salaryman. The salaryman life is for the locals.

In the lab I don't collect any fond memories, especially at the weekly study meetings when we present our work to the other grads. There's a snotty young *sensei* who criticises and picks on people during the meetings like he is trying to show how strict a teacher he is.

– Your research report won't make a paper, Kibishi-*sensei* says. It's pretty useless.

I don't care about what he says, but I hate him for saying it in front of the others, their eyes glancing at him, then at me. I have no good answer, especially in his language. When the meeting is over I tell him to lay off the heavy stuff, but it's not much use because he's the type who just says what he thinks.

I get a letter from France. The old yacht never made it to Argentina. They sailed as far as northern Brazil but the customs men in Fortaleza demanded that taxes be paid. Gilles told them where they could shove their tax papers – in French, not Portuguese, so they didn't arrest him. He told them the tax was higher than the value of the boat. They could take the boat and shove it the same place as the tax papers. He and Isabel would go back to France and build another. The customs men in Fortaleza shoved and Gilles went back to France.

When I get letters from far away I sometimes ask myself what I'm doing here. I'm free to leave anytime, go anywhere, am I not? But I'm not free. I've started something here. I want to see it through. Like hitching to Istanbul or doing the Atlantic, I can't stop half way. I decided in Martinique that my settled existence would be in Japan, for a while at least. If I don't get some results, I'm wasting my time and might suddenly find myself back in a conventional country working in an ordinary job with an easy but boring life ahead. I don't want that.

There are good times too. On Sunday afternoons I wander through the crowds in Shibuya to meet Miyuki, who'll be waiting in Hachiko Square, the busiest street corner in Tokyo. We talk of faraway places and different lifestyles. Miyuki says she's heard that Tokodai is a dull place, too much of a prep school, preparing for a dull existence to come – at least that's what Li told her before he introduced me. Li doesn't have time to come join us. He's working too hard.

Miyuki talks of India, where she went one long summer, Madras and Calcutta in the monsoon time, Sri Lanka one winter, and I feel that maybe she is right about Tokodai. But I will be finished in a year or so, won't I? The night is falling cold on the city, the crowds thin. We'll meet again soon.

I work away, throw together my half-baked ideas. Erai-*sensei* begins to say positive things.

– A little more work here, a little more there.

Thanks, Erai-*sensei*. He makes me feel more comfortable. Forget Kibishi-*sensei*. Erai-*sensei* is more important. One day he says, Okay, you've done enough, write your final dissertation and have five bound copies on my desk in three months' time. I have the copies on his desk three months later. All that is left is the oral examination.

I go to the presentation room with slides and notes in Japanese and in English too, just in case I forget what I'm talking about. It's mid-afternoon and the professors look like they have listened to too many presentations already. I don't mind if you're not listening. Just don't ask awkward questions. Only one of them asks an awkward question. I'm sure he is the only one who has read my dissertation. I waffle an awkward answer. It's that sleepy time of the afternoon and my answer is enough. I give a little bow and exit. Next day Erai-*sensei* tells me I've passed. All that remains is to write a research paper in English and send it off to some American journal he recommends.

Soon it will be March, graduation time. The time in salaryman prep school has gone fast. It wasn't so free and easy after all, too much to do, no time to go slowly. I should be glad to leave it all behind, find another rhythm of life elsewhere. I should be, but I'm not. I've got used to this town Tokyo, the crowds, the lingo, the life, summer escapes to quiet lakes where fireflies flash over black water in the night and cicadas cackle in the heat of the day, and Sunday afternoons in Shibuya with Miyuki. I don't want to leave it all behind. I might even work here. Just for a while. With my degree from Tokodai, I could get a job as a lecturer or teacher. I ask Erai-*sensei* about it because I'd need his recommendation.

– Would it not be better if you returned to your home country? Foreign students are visitors. Visitors should not stay too long in faraway places or they will forget to go back.

I've stayed too long in many places. I've long ago forgotten to go back, but he doesn't know. He's treated me well during my time in his lab. I don't want to push him about a job. I'll find my own way. There are plenty of jobs around, just there for the taking, although those jobs are in the local companies, the big corporations, and not everything I've heard about them is positive. There's always a catch.

Matsuno and the other students are doing the company rounds, Sony and Toshiba this week, then NEC, Hitachi and Mitsubishi. I begin wondering what it would be like to work for them. Would it be as bad as they say? I start collecting information.

Sony is a relatively young company. It began in 1946 in a makeshift workshop set up by Masaru Ibuka in central Tokyo. Ibuka persuaded his friend, Akio Morita – who was about to become a lecturer in Tokodai – to join him as demand for radio repairs increased. Ibuka declared that their little company would use the latest technologies to make products the large corporations could not match. Sony still uses the latest technologies but their little company now has over 160,000 employees.

Toshiba is about the same size as Sony and is an important member of the Mitsui Group, at one time the largest *zaibatsu* and the main rival of the Mitsubishi Group. It began as Tokyo Shibaura in 1939 when two old electrical companies merged and set up headquarters in the Shibaura area of the city. NEC is a little smaller than Toshiba in employee numbers and is linked with Sumitomo, the third of the old *zaibatsu.* It was set up as a joint venture with Alexander Graham Bell's company, Western Electric, in 1899, the first such venture between a Japanese and foreign enterprise.

Hitachi, like Sony, is not related to any of the old *zaibatsu* and has its own group of companies. It started out in 1910 making motors and has become the biggest manufacturer in Japan, with over 320,000 employees in the Hitachi Group, even larger than Matsushita, owner of the Panasonic brand. My lab in Tokodai has strong links with Sony, Toshiba, NEC, Hitachi and Mitsubishi, but not with Matsushita, Sharp or Sanyo because they are based in Osaka, 500 kilometres away.

Other labs in Tokodai have connections with the car companies, particularly those in the Tokyo–Yokohama region, like Honda and Nissan. Honda has always been the most independent of the auto-makers since it was founded in 1946 by Soichiro Honda. He disliked the old *zaibatsu* and their friends in the powerful Ministry of International Trade and Industry (MITI). In the 1950s MITI tried to merge the numerous car-makers into two major companies: Nissan and Toyota. They did not succeed, partly because of Honda, who defied them by moving into the car business in the early 1960s. Honda has done quite well in spite of its less-than-perfect relationship with MITI and the *zaibatsu*.

Nissan began producing cars in 1933 in Yokohama and has a company group of its own, but no links to the old *zaibatsu*. Toyota, headquartered in Toyota City near Nagoya, was set up by Sakichi Toyoda, based on his invention of an automatic loom. His son moved into automobile production in 1937, and although the company had connections to the Mitsui *zaibatsu*, it maintained its independence.

The links between the members within each of the former *zaibatsu*, Mitsui, Mitsubishi and Sumitomo, are much weaker now than in the early twentieth century. Although member companies still hold each other's shares and pool economic information, they are free to do business with anyone. When I joined Mitsubishi I was told to open an account for salary payment at the local bank, which is a Mitsui one, not Mitsubishi.

Nowadays, the corporate groups are generally called *keiretsu*, and the companies have relatively horizontal relationships, unlike the vertical chains of command in the old *zaibatsu*, which had a single family at the top. The former authoritarian leadership has been replaced by democratic boardrooms in the different companies, where the president is often a titular head chosen more for his abilities to balance competing demands from different business segments than for strong leadership. This system works well when all divisions are of similar strength, but not when one or more should be shut down or sold off.

The students in my lab say Sony is the most international corporation, though I'm more interested in the old traditional ones, like Hitachi, Mitsubishi and Toshiba. The grapevine in Tokodai has it that there is little difference between them in corporate culture and working style. They have a tacit agreement not to hire people who leave one of the three, because if you don't fit in here you probably won't fit in there. It is possible, however, to move to or from other companies. I later met one Mitsubishi colleague who switched from Matsushita at the age of thirty and another who moved from Sony. When I asked why they moved, the former Matsushita man said he wanted to get away from Osaka, where Matsushita have their main operations. The ex-Sony man wanted to work in the satellite business where Mitsubishi is strong.

But the vast majority of new recruits stay for life. The conventional explanations put this down to loyalty and dedication to the company, but in reality salarymen stay because it doesn't make economic or career sense to move. The implied commitment of the company to provide a job till retirement, together with promotion and compensation based on length of service, makes switching companies an unlikely option. Many of my Mitsubishi colleagues accept this system without question, although some, particularly the younger ones for whom the chances of promotion are slight, look with envy at the Western system where people are freer to change jobs, even if they are freer to lose them as well.

I tag along with the students of Tokodai on their visits to the big companies. Toshiba invite us to a reception in their shining new headquarters in Shibaura, overlooking Tokyo Bay. It is an intelligent building with intelligent doors, window shades and even intelligent toilets that know what you're doing and when you're done. Mitsubishi talk about their space satellites that will be launched next year. They say the space business is where the future lies, even if the satellites they built last year came to a watery end when the rockets launched from Tanegashima went splat into the ocean. But Mitsubishi only built the satellites, not the rockets, and they say the satellites would have worked perfectly if only the rockets hadn't gone splat into the ocean. Hitachi invite us to Hitachi Laboratories in Hitachi City, two hours north-east of Tokyo on a train called the Hitachi Express; they give us Hitachi lunches in Hitachi lunch boxes and it's almost too much Hitachi to swallow in one day. For scenic views from the offices and intelligent toilets that know what you're doing, Toshiba win hands down. For travel expenses and brand name hard-sell, Hitachi are tops. For space-age sushi, beer and satellites with short lives, Mitsubishi tastes good. But otherwise there is not much difference.

All the companies say they welcome graduates from Tokodai and a foreigner would be welcome because it would make them feel modern and cosmopolitan, even if they are conservative and traditional. They introduce us to OBs – the old boys who are Tokodai graduates and now have important positions in the companies. There are one or two OGs but the old girls do not have important positions. The OBs and OGs tell us the good side of working in these corporations. We listen and believe them, more or less. The companies are not as bad as I thought: exciting work on state-of-the-art technology, twenty-five days' leave per year, and they pay a salary too – something I wasn't used to.

A few of this year's Tokodai students opt for the electrical companies. Matsuno prefers Honda because they pay more and Otake decides to become a securities analyst with Nomura. Most of the foreign students will leave for greener fields elsewhere. Li tells me he has found a job in a small company in Kawasaki, which won't be run like a primary school. And what about me? I'm thinking about it.

◆◆◆

Although it's still March, the graduation day is warm and sunny and the cherry trees look as though they will blossom soon. The campus auditorium walls are draped with red and white bunting, the colours of celebration, rows of seats are marked to show who sits where, and a special desk is set up on the stage where the conferring will take place. The small orchestra bellows out a welcoming tune as the chancellor of the university and deans arrive, and everyone stands up. The chancellor begins his speech, telling us to get in touch with Tokodai fraternities in the companies we join, not to forget our *sensei* and please try to attend the annual reunions.

The speech continues and everyone listens, no one moving, everyone quiet. Then it is payback time and we get our pieces of paper. They call out our names and we approach the podium, one by one. The native students stand a big distance, maybe two metres, from the man with the papers. They stretch forward their arms as they bow deeply, probably more deeply then they have ever bowed before. I think they might fall over but they don't. The man with the papers looks like he's too far away to give them the degree but he makes a deep bow too and just about manages. When the students rise from their bow their arms are still held out in front and they're holding the degree. They slowly lower their arms, turn around and walk back as if they have just met the emperor. My turn comes. I bow a reasonable bow but I don't stand two metres away from the man with the papers because I'm not going to fall over – it's only a piece of paper, isn't it? I take my degree, thanks for the memories, and walk back to my seat admiring the calligraphic script and trying to read what it says. The piece of paper says I'm a *hakase*, which means PhD. I should be pleased, but now that I have this paper I realise I don't care much for fancy titles and I'm worried that it might tie me down. I don't want to build my life around a piece of paper. Still, I have to get a job in the conventional world sometime.

I'm in contact with Hitachi, Mitsubishi and Toshiba. It seems that one or more of them will offer me a job and I'm wondering if I should accept. Erai-*sensei* thinks that foreigners should go back to their home countries, not stay here. Li and other friends think that foreigners should work for foreign companies, not Japanese ones. The common wisdom is that I shouldn't join a big Japanese company. But I like doing contrary things.

Mitsubishi ask me to come for another interview. They are among the oldest and most traditional of the big corporations and if I'm going to see what company life is like, then I'm going to jump in at the deep end, no half-ways. If it doesn't work out, I'll find something else, or I'll take Erai-*sensei*'s advice and leave.

The job interview is easy because the Mitsubishi personnel manager doesn't care much about what I did before I came to this country – a foreigner is almost expected to have an unusual history, and having the degree from Tokodai makes up for the vague career gaps. They will even pay me more because I bummed around university so long and collected those pieces of paper. The manager says they will put me in the research division, so I won't have to wear a suit everyday.

– But I would mention that general conditions will be the same for all new recruits, whether in the research labs, the factories or Head Office.

– Okay. I'm not expecting any special treatment.

He shows me a video about the company. It starts off with the Mitsubishi three-diamond logo glowing red over a modern Tokyo skyline, then fades to Osaka in black and white in the nineteenth century when only the castle was more than a couple of storeys high. The video describes how an ambitious young man called Yataro Iwasaki went into business in the 1860s, but decided he wouldn't get far if he stayed in his home on the island of Shikoku. He moved to Osaka, where he set up a shipping enterprise, and from there the Mitsubishi legend grew.

Unlike the modern Mitsubishi, at that time all decisions were taken by Iwasaki himself. He realised the importance of having friends in high places, moved his head office to Tokyo in 1874 and earned government favour by providing transport for a military expedition to Taiwan. On his death in 1885 his brother, Yanosuke, became company president. He moved aggressively into banking, mining and warehousing, to make Mitsubishi one of the four great *zaibatsu*, along with Mitsui, Sumitomo and Yasuda. The Mitsubishi conglomerate was controlled by various members of the Iwasaki family until 1945. At the outbreak of the Pacific War, the video says, Koyata Iwasaki reminded his staff they had worked with Americans and other foreigners before and would become friends again when peace returned. The video does not mention the great work they did building the *Musashi*, the world's biggest battleship, and the Mitsubishi Zero, the most effective Japanese fighter aircraft of the war.

When the Allied forces ordered the disbanding of the *zaibatsu* in 1945, Mitsubishi alone resisted but was eventually forced to comply. Most of the companies dropped the Mitsubishi name and were dissolved into small enterprises with new management. But the disbandment was only temporary. With the outbreak of the Korean War and the Cold War in the early 1950s, the American administrators realised the benefits of having a strong industrial base in the East and the pre-war industrial groups were allowed to reform into the modern *keiretsu*.

I sit there listening to this company history, and think, Yes, joining Mitsubishi is a risk. I know I don't conform as easily as the other students from

Tokodai and I certainly don't conform as much as my Western friends. I wonder if I've changed during the years in Tokodai. I must have, because I would never have dreamt of working in a Japanese company four years earlier, and look where I am now. But I haven't really changed, not deep down. I still dream of the open road, going places I've never been, sleeping under the stars, waking up in the morning not knowing where I'll be by night. In the meetings I've had with the Mitsubishi people I've noticed how enthusiastic they are to have me and I've been thinking I can wangle a little time off before I start. I'm sure they'll be obliging and I'd just love to try that open road once again. A few months should be enough. It will be my reward for studying hard over the previous years. After playing it safe and steady for so long, I need some variety and even a little bit of danger. A trip far away will do me good, help me get things in perspective. Yes, it's true I thought the African trip that became the Atlantic trip would be the last. But another taste of freedom won't do me any harm, will it?

The video is over and the personnel manager is talking to me.

– As I mentioned, general conditions will be similar for all new recruits. Can you start with everyone else, the first Monday in April?

It's time for some bargaining.

– It may be a little difficult for me to start then. I wonder if I could start a little later.

He's surprised, but he wants to be nice to me. Otherwise, I might still go to Hitachi or Toshiba.

– I have to visit some places overseas, you see. I have to, eh, clear up some things.

– It is unusual for new recruits from the local universities not to start at the beginning of April. But if you have to clear up some things then, yes, it can be arranged. How long do you need? A week? Two weeks?

– Well, I was hoping for a couple of … months.

– A couple of months? Okay. We can make an exception. Till June?

– It's very humid in June and almost summertime. A bit after June.

– July?

– Or August.

– Okay. August.

– How about September?

– Well … Okay, then. We'll make it September. Can we say mid-September?

I'm about to say October, but I stop myself. I've gone far enough. He might start wondering if I really want to work for Mitsubishi at all.

– Please take care and come to the company on 16 September, he says, relieved he has a starting date.

The big Japanese companies can be flexible when they want to. I've got some special treatment already. A Western company would have wanted me to start next week, if not sooner, and there would have been no special treatment. They'd be only thinking in the short term.

I walk out of the interview feeling better than I have in years, excited at the prospect of a few months of going where I want, doing what I want, without the uncertainty about how I find a job afterwards. Now I can get drunk on the freedom of the open road just one more time. After that I'll go dry. I promise.

I've already done Eurasia, left to right and back again; Africa top to bottom didn't work out. I'll try Latin America top to bottom this time. When I tell Miyuki my plans she is interested, but when she hears the main plan is that I've no plan, besides wandering through a couple of war zones, across a desert or two, over a few mountain ranges, and down at least one big river, she has second thoughts. Her parents might be worried. I understand. I wouldn't go off with someone like that myself – unless the someone *is* myself, of course.

I take a cheap flight to Los Angeles, get a bus to Mexico and slowly head southward. The Spanish I speak is a mix of French verbs, English nouns and Japanese adverbs. The French and English easily pass for Spanish because they're practically the same language, but the Japanese doesn't come across well and the Mexicans give me funny looks – what sort of mixed-up gringo is he and what sort of gringo takes buses from Los Angeles to Tegucigalpa?

The buses become trucks in Nicaragua, rumbling past blown-up bridges and bullet-riddled police posts, but Reagan's war is over, the Americans are gone and it's not dangerous anymore. Panama City is more dangerous because it is only a year since the Americans invaded. Maybe I'm staying in the wrong part of town but the streets look awfully mean. Everyone looks like an impoverished ex-GI with nothing to do but hang loose and look mean. I shouldn't be here. I should go somewhere safe – like Colombia. But before I do, a heavy-handed ex-GI grabs my arm, rips the wallet out of my pocket, rips away half the pocket as well and I'm flashing a bit of hip flesh at the mean streets of Panama. But it's only a decoy wallet with three dollars inside – the rest is safely stashed in my money belt. The ex-GI skips off. I know he won't be pleased when he counts his spoils. I quickly get myself to some busier streets and lie low in a McDonald's restaurant that has an armed guard sitting inside the hardened glass doors who doesn't mind gringos flashing hip flesh.

From Caracas I take buses to the Orinoco, then along the red mud track down to Manaus. They don't make roads like this in Japan and I wouldn't mind if they did, for a change. Riverboats along the Amazon to Belém, then buses to Rio. As I slowly go southwards I blow away the doubts I feel about the job awaiting me in September. I begin to get back that confident feeling I had when I was on the road before, doing things the hard way and liking it. Whatever comes next I'll take in my stride.

Four months after Los Angeles, I reach the end of the overland trail. I'm at the bottom, in Tierra del Fuego, with only Cape Horn and the Southern Ocean beyond. It's windy, freezing and empty but it feels good to finish something. I watch the waves of the grey Pacific crashing on the rocky shoreline. I'm 15,000 kilometres from Japan but could be a million miles away. For a moment I can imagine that the place doesn't exist, that it's just a mixed-up dream of pretty mountains, pretty faces, wooden temples, concrete cities, crowded trains, study and work. Yet if it weren't there anymore, I'd miss it. I've finished this trip, got rid of the wandering bug for now, but I'm not finished with Japan. And my funds are low, as usual. Time to turn around and head northwards. I'm as ready as ever to try the salaryman life.

3

住めば都

Sumeba miyako

Wherever you live, it is the capital

I heard bad things about the company dormitories for new recruits. They were short on space and long on rules, with wake-up calls and double-calls to make sure no one was ever late for work, house managers who felt free to wander into the residents' rooms while they were out at work and sometimes while they were home, checking that sheets had been changed, the air conditioning set at the correct temperature and nothing dubious stored in the closet, like a girlfriend's nightclothes or a forgotten sandwich. If something were found, you would be required to write an explanation, marking it with your personal stamp – the oriental equivalent of a signature – and submit it to the house manager next day. Perhaps you should do something about the girlfriend's nightclothes or the sandwich too, within a few days, but the paperwork and the personal stamp must not be forgotten on any account. Attitude is most important. As a new employee you would not complain. You would be grateful to the company not only for the steady job in a world-famous corporation, probably for life, but also for giving you a good salary, a roof over your head and cheap meals in the dormitory canteen.

I think about where I'm going to sleep at night. I may have stayed in dingy rooms in cheap hotels over the previous months but that was a different world I was just passing through. Now I'm back in the workaday world and I want a little better.

I don't need much space. I haven't many possessions and much of my baggage is gone anyway, lost on the flight back through Moscow. I can manage without most of it, though I miss my old rucksack – my trusty companion that served me well over ten years on and off the road, through mountains, jungles, seas and deserts – and dangerous airports where it finally went out of my life. Now it's probably in a flea market somewhere in Moscow about to earn a few roubles for a poor airport baggage handler. At least I hope he's poor. I wonder if it was just chance that I lost it before starting this job. Or is this a sign that my wandering days are finished? I don't want to think about such serious matters. I'll forget the rucksack.

I begin negotiations with Anshin-T, who is in charge of making sure all employees have a proper place to live.

– As you know, the company will pay for your hotel for one week, he says. After that you can move to a dormitory.

Before I can tell him that dormitory life would be difficult for me, we are on our way to visit the Mitsubishi bachelor residence a few minutes' walk from the company. We have to watch out for cars and bicycles as we step off the narrow pathway that is blocked every ten metres by thick concrete poles for the telephone and power lines. We pass a mom-and-pop shop selling every food that can be wrapped in plastic; then we come to the bachelor residence – an elongated, four-storey box, with concrete walls painted white like a cheap hotel.

We take our shoes off at the entrance and squeeze them into the pigeon-hole shoeboxes built into the wall. Most of the boxes have numbers corresponding to the rooms, 1 to 160, a shoebox for every resident, but there are a few boxes marked *visitor,* where we put our shoes and take the plastic heal-less slippers provided. Beside the shoe-changing area is a large wall mirror so that residents can check how they look as they rush off to work in the morning. We step up into the hallway. A panel of room number plates is set on the wall next to the reception window so that everyone can see who is at home and who is out. A notice nearby reminds you to switch off your air conditioner and slide your room number plate to *absent* whenever you go out.

The house manager appears and Anshin-T explains that this recently arrived foreign employee may be moving in. The house manager looks alarmed for a moment, then recovers and suggests we take a look at one of the empty rooms upstairs. The room has a reasonably sized bed, a closet, a small desk and a chair. There is an air conditioner above the window and a fluorescent light on the ceiling to brighten the half of the room the window light doesn't reach. I tap the walls to confirm they are thin plasterboard. I understand the importance of the sign in the corridor that says, *Quiet, please. Think of your neighbours!*

– The rooms are very, er, compact, I say.

– Yes, says Anshin-T, but they used to be more compact. When I joined the company a few years ago, there were two people to a room and we had only futons, no bed or desk.

– Before that it was four to a room, says the dormitory manager.

It seems like we are moving into one of those *when-I-was-young* conversations. I resist the urge to make any more comments.

We visit the common bathroom. The changing room has rows of boxes along the wall where you place your clothing and towel. I slide the frosted-glass door open and look into the bathing room: a row of taps and showers so that a dozen people can wash at the same time; little plastic seats where you sit as you scrub; and a very large communal bath like the ones I'd seen at hot-spring resorts in the mountains. A notice at the door says the bath is only available in the evening, although showers may be used at any time.

We have a look at the relaxation room on the ground floor: a large Mitsubishi TV, three couches surrounding a low table, and a bookcase with newspapers and magazines. The cafeteria next door has a list of the week's menus, with the calorie count for each meal and the hours during which food is available. You have to take at least one portion of vegetables, rice, fish or meat, pickles and fruit. A colleague tells me later that if you try to skip your vegetables or rice, the cafeteria staff will *remind* you to eat one portion of each. It is their duty to ensure that all residents are properly fed.

The dormitory manager says I can move in any time and he gives me a sheet of rules before we leave.

As we head back Anshin-T tells me the dormitory is very cheap and convenient – only ten minutes' walk to work, good healthy meals every weekday morning and evening, and laundry taken care of. He recommends that I stay there.

– Yes, it is convenient, I tell him. But I'd like to study the rule sheet first. I'll contact you later.

Back at my desk I look through the sheet of rules:

No food to be eaten in the rooms.
No visitors after 7 p.m.
No females at any time.
No noise after 10 p.m.
Rooms to be kept clean and tidy.
The dormitory manager is to be informed if you plan to stay out overnight or travel anywhere.

I tell Anshin-T dormitory life would be very difficult for me.

– I can't eat rice and miso soup at seven in the morning. It would affect my work performance. Can I live in my own apartment?

Anshin-T frowns and scratches his head. He's wondering if I can look after myself, all alone in the big, bad world, far from home and kin.

– Is this your first time living in a foreign country? Oh yes, I remember. You went to university in Tokyo, right? But can you get up early in the morning, eat right, pay the utility bills, pay your rent on time, separate the combustibles from the other rubbish and put it out on the correct days, be nice to the neighbours?

– Yes, Anshin-T, I can.

– Okay. You can live in your own apartment. But please inform me when you have selected a place. I will come to see it and stamp the papers.

– Thanks, Anshin-T.

I set off apartment-hunting the first evening after work. Shinsetsu-GR tells me not to wait till five, go early and don't worry about work because there will be plenty of time later. The real estate agents look surprised when I walk in, eyes wide open, sometimes mouths open too – would you look at what the evening commuter tide has just washed up? Their faces silently shout, A foreigner, what will we do? Does he speak our language? Do we have to speak his? What will happen if the landlords don't want foreigners? Who will be his guarantor?

I put them at ease, somewhat, by speaking their language, and before they can tell me it might be hard to find an internationally minded landlord here in the boondocks of Yokohama, I drop the magic words: *I'm a new employee at Mitsubishi.* Their facial expressions change for the better. With a big company that will act as guarantor it will be much easier to find an internationally minded landlord. They pull out maps and pictures of this apartment and that, all high class and just right for an employee of Mitsubishi. Who cares how high the rent is and what's a little signing-on fee, equal to four months' rent, to an international employee of Mitsubishi, who probably has such a huge salary he can't find enough ways to spend even half of it? I explain more and their happy faces return to normal as they realise I'm not an expatriate employee with a fat expense account, I can't afford the top of the market, and I'm just a new company recruit looking for a place to sleep when I'm not working, a place big enough to invite a friend around at weekends, with enough space outside to park a bicycle. They understand. They can still help. They find me the perfect little apartment, not too expensive (72,000 yen a month), not too small (two rooms and a kitchen), not too far away (five kilometres from the company), and a landlord who is not afraid of foreigners, provided the company acts as guarantor.

Anshin-T takes a taxi with me to view the place. The apartment occupies half the ground floor of a typical two-storey timber-framed house with a gently sloping slate roof. It fronts directly onto the street and has low block walls separating it from similar neighbouring houses. It even has a backyard, though it is only sixty centimetres long. We step up from the street into a small porch. There are two doors, one for each apartment on the ground floor, and a steel stairway leading up to two apartments above. Anshin-T pulls open the front door – the doors always open outwards to maximise the space inside. We slip off our shoes and step onto the timber floor of the kitchen, then look at the other rooms, which have the traditional *tatami*

floors – neatly woven straw mats bordered with embroidered cloth, each mat about the size of a beach towel. The low ceilings are of imitation cedar and the walls decorated with off-white rice paper. It seems to meet with his approval. He walks through the kitchen and looks at the bathroom.

– Well, Anshin-T, does it comply with company standards?

– Yes, it is fine – except for the gas heater. It is made by Toshiba, not Mitsubishi. Maybe you need a new gas heater.

But I see he's smiling. I'm allowed to use the Toshiba gas heater.

Buying a new fridge, air conditioner and TV is no joke. Does Mitsubishi have a few spares I can borrow?

– No spares. But there is a discount for employees. Please go to the showroom tomorrow.

I visit the showroom, but before buying I check the local discount store and discover that Sanyo have the best-value TV, Hitachi, the best-value fridge, and Sharp, the best-value air conditioner. I'm not a loyal Mitsubishi man. The special employee discount is not worth much, Mitsubishi is stingy, and Sanyo, Hitachi and Sharp will do just fine. I recall hearing that in some companies in the Mitsubishi Group it is almost compulsory to buy company products. If you work for Mitsubishi Motors you'd better not ask for a parking space outside the company housing if you have a Toyota. But an electrical appliance is not a public statement like a car is.

I settle in to my new home. Very few cars use the street outside, the neighbours in the next house seem quiet, even the dog up the street barks quietly. It's a place where I can rest after a hard day's work in the company, recharge my batteries and write letters to friends far away.

But within a few days I discover I'm wrong.

The noise begins the second night. As I'm cooking my microwave dinner, the ceiling above begins to shake and it is not an earthquake. It could be a sumo wrestler waddling across the room, but sumo-*sans* live in special training stables, not here in the suburbs of Yokohama. I switch on the TV and forget about the big guy upstairs till it is time for sleep but he doesn't stop. He takes a little rumble across the room every few minutes, sleepwalking or going for a pee, and I can't sleep till the rumbles stop after midnight. They start again soon after dawn, but the early morning thuds don't bother me because I have to get up. On the way to work I look at the post-box outside to see who is living upstairs but the name plate – Keiryo – doesn't tell me much. I decide to wait a few nights before doing anything.

The next night is the same. I lie on my futon staring at the dark ceiling above, quietly shouting, Please stop sleepwalking or going for pees, Keiryo-*san*, among other polite requests because I don't know any swear words in the language. I'm going to do something. But what? I could start learning swear words but first I'll have a chat with Anshin-T. He might be able to help.

Anshin-T, consultant on residential problems for employees, listens to my story, nods in appreciation of the situation, but doesn't look like he has a solution.

– It is not that your neighbour is heavy, he says. It is because of the building. That's the way the ordinary houses are built here. Timber-framed buildings are not noise-proof, but if you live there a few weeks, I think it will become normal and you won't even notice it.

I doubt it but what can I do? Anshin-T is just hoping I won't ask to be put back in a hotel at company expense, because he would have to say no, or that I won't ask him to search for another apartment and stamp more papers with the powerful seal of Mitsubishi. The powerful seal would get less powerful if it is used here, there and everywhere. It would mean more overtime for Anshin-T, telephoning real estate agents, visiting apartments and catching up on other work when he should be home with his family. I don't want to ever be responsible for making a salaryman colleague work more overtime just for me. I head back to my desk and forget my unsettled home life for a while.

Early in my salaryman career I learn about the group, or *gurupu*, as we pronounce it. In Mitsubishi a group is made up of anything from four to fifteen members, with an average of about ten. The group leader or manager spends most of his time at meetings or making visits to the factories or Head Office and has little time for discussing problems. Within the group he may be backed up by one or two *unit leaders*, who have the KS title. They have the same seniority as himself but they do real work and don't spend their days at meetings. Below the KSs are a few Cs and the rest of us are plain old Ts, the bottom of the pile. The group manager, in consultation with the department manager, makes decisions about who will work on what, but the work itself is often proposed by the KSs or Cs, or is in response to requests from the factories. Everyone seems happy with his position and title, which is based on age, length of service, attitude and ability, or some combination of these. I sometimes thought this was not a bad system. In Western companies it may be easier to get ahead and climb above the others if you are aggressive and ambitious, but this can cause unhealthy competition, office politics and friction. There is little sign of office politics or friction in Mitsubishi.

I was never quite sure how groups came into being. Some of them seemed to exist from time immemorial – perhaps years before, although the group names, members and work content change quite frequently. The groups in our department are named after current technologies – network interfaces, multimedia, signal processing, machine intelligence. These names change every year or two, depending on what technology is in fashion. Groups in other departments have less fashion-conscious names that don't change, like FEM2 and GA3.

Occasionally people are assigned to groups because their expertise is required, but in most cases the assignments are made to balance out the ages or numbers of personnel. I never hear of anyone asking to change group. Things decided by high-up people are not questioned.

If a group does not seem to be producing any useful results, its members will gradually be reassigned elsewhere and the group will eventually be absorbed by a more productive one. If a group manager is not up to the task, he will be shifted sideways to the planning or administration department but will not be demoted. Since promotion is based on age, attitude and connections, rather than ability alone, once you go up, you can be pretty sure you will never go down again.

For me, the most important thing about the group is that it is easy to talk to fellow group members, even quiet types like Majime-T. If you want to ask someone in a different group a question, you should convey the message via your group manager, who will ask the other group manager, who will pass the question to the relevant person. Being a foreigner allows me to bypass this system, particularly if the person I wish to consult is an internationalist, which normally means someone who likes to speak English. There are a few internationalists on my floor. Most of my group colleagues, however, are not, and speak only Japanese, but if I ask them something they are generally helpful.

Our group leader, Shinsetsu-GR, tells me I can write my reports in English because he thinks I can't write in his language. I can, but my grammar would make the reports quite painful to read. In any case, everyone in the Mitsubishi corporate labs is supposed to be able to read English because they come from famous or semi-famous universities; anyone who can't is told to burn the midnight oil, pass the company English test and get up to par as quickly as possible. Shinsetsu-GR wants to know about the computer programs I wrote in the university. Do they have any possible practical use?

He means are my programs just the usual academic toys that students amuse themselves and their professors with in order to get their degree. I think my programs are not toys, that they are practical and useful. I just have to decide what they're useful for. That is my task for the first few weeks. After that, I will do some real work and produce some exciting new software for the elevator factory so that Mitsubishi elevators can remain the fastest and the smoothest in the world. And if I don't I'm sure the elevators will still be the best and Mitsubishi won't fire me. Mitsubishi are a gentle bunch, according to Riko-T, not tough like Sony and Hitachi where they work even longer hours than us – though he is not sure about that. Aren't we lucky we're such a gentle bunch in Mitsubishi?

In mid-afternoon people relax. They stare over the grey partitions at the company wall posters or they go to the refresh-room for a cup of tea or coffee. There is a low-technology machine dispensing free Japanese green tea, Chinese Oolong tea and plain coffee; next to it is a high-technology machine covered in buttons and flashing lights dispensing drinks that are not free: American coffee, which is weak, Jive coffee, which has a baseball player on the cup, and God coffee, which is not weak and has three varieties, black, Brazil and mocha.

If you don't want coffee, you can buy garden lemon tea, royal milk tea or one of a dozen juices and colas. A panel of buttons allows you to choose whether you want your drink ice cold (with or without ice cubes) or hot. A notice on the machine says, *Hot News! These paper cups are specially designed so that you can hold them without burning your hand!* The design is realised by making the cups bigger than usual so that they are only two-thirds full: you hold them at the top and don't burn your hand.

Other drinks are in small cartons which have a straw attached. An explanation on the side of the carton claims that this is an *etiquette straw,* which, although it looks like any other straw, is specially designed to minimise noise as you suck. There is a yoghurt-flavoured aloe-and-white-grape drink if you want something healthy, and a cigarette machine nearby, if you want something unhealthy. The cigarette machine has the standard government warning that must be printed on every cigarette packet: *There is a danger that smoking may damage your health, so let's be careful about smoking too much.* This gentle warning is the result of a compromise between Japan Tobacco Inc., backed and partially owned by the powerful Ministry of Finance, and the much less powerful Ministry of Health. Next to the cigarette machine is the smoking room, which has the best view in the building, looking out over the Shinto shrine and the trees near the entrance. The bosses like to smoke.

When I see Shinsetsu-GR in the refresh-room I ask him what I should do about my noisy home life.

He sits back, sips his coffee and says such problems are common in this country but people usually put up with it.

– Or else they move. That is why concrete apartments are becoming more popular. Maybe you should move to a concrete apartment, even if it is much trouble for you. Let us talk about it at your welcome *konpa* tonight.

The *konpa* is an important part of the salaryman life – the after-work party, the time to let off steam over a beer or two, the time for straight talk when criticism and, on some rare occasions, even praise are allowed, things that would be out of place during the day. You can say almost anything at a *konpa* because all will be forgotten next morning when the noisy night-time salarymen become silent and hardworking again. Although I made up my mind that I would never go to a *konpa* just to keep my colleagues happy, I can compromise now and then – otherwise I wouldn't have become a salaryman in the first place. I'll join the welcome party. It will be a one-night chance to forget my noisy home life and see how the group – the fundamental unit upon which our organisation is built – functions off time.

All ten of us go to the local *izakaya*, the pub, which owes its existence to the pockets of the 950 Mitsubishi men and the few women next door. With all of us salarymen and OLs nearby there's bound to be a *konpa* every night of the year for some group or department.

We leave our shoes at the entrance and squat at the low tables. I make sure I sit next to Shinsetsu-GR and Riko-T because I know they'll talk to me. They are the internationalists of our group, irrespective of what language we speak. I don't like sitting next to people who don't talk back because it's like sitting next to my computer.

The little speeches begin. A *konpa* would not be a *konpa* without a few speeches.

– Welcome to Mitsubishi, Muruta-T, Shinsetsu-GR says. Welcome to the Machine Intelligence Group. Some day we will let the machines do the thinking and we can all relax, enjoying the easy life. But for now, we have to work. Still it's not a bad life, is it?

The others have recovered from their late-afternoon fatigue and the answers to Shinsetsu-GR's question come quickly – yes it's not a bad life, no it is a bad life, yes for the bonuses we get when business is good, no the boss is too tough, yes for the *sake* and the beer on warm September nights like this when work is done and we can drink till we've no more money or till the last train is ready to leave and let's cut the speeches, can we?

– No, we cannot, says Shinsetsu-GR. This is Muruta-T's *konpa*, isn't it? Muruta-T is not just another foreign visitor or trainee. He is a colleague and will stay with us, we hope, for a long time. Muruta-T, I'm sure you can learn many things in our company. If you have any problems, any questions, please ask Riko-T. He will be your trainer.

Stay with the company a long time? But I'm just here for a year or two. And what does he mean by trainer? A trainer makes me think of discipline and hardship, which I can do without, thank you for offering, Shinsetsu-GR. But I will keep quiet about those things tonight because people can say anything at a *konpa* and all will be forgotten next day. When I think about it, a trainer might be useful, someone who might solve my noisy apartment problems and tell me how to house-train my neighbour upstairs.

Each member of the group gives a little speech: name, rank, current work, and if that is not enough and you really want to talk more, tell us about your hobbies. Work is what you are doing now and what you want to do next, a chance to give the boss a hint. Your hobby is something outside of work that you do at least once a year. If you do nothing except watch TV and sleep, your hobby is what you did, at least once, when you were a student. If you did nothing as a student except hit the bright lights of Shibuya and study a little in between, your hobby is what you might have done if you had had the time. Shinsetsu-GR's hobby is sailing and he used to go every summer to the marina south of Yokohama where the company sailing club has a few dinghies. But since he became a manager two years ago he no longer has time to go, even in the summer.

– Have you ever sailed? he asks me.

– Oh, a little bit.

– Really? says Riko-T. Hey, listen everyone. Muruta-T has the same hobby as the boss! He used to sail in his home country. Please tell us more about your hobby. Did you sail a lot?

– Well, I only sailed, eh, once. With some people I met. It was a bit of an extended sail – but only once.

– Only once? Is that all? Looks like you are not in the same league as the boss, says Riko-T.

– No, I'm not in the boss's league. Never did any proper training course.

– That sounds risky to me, Shinsetsu-GR says. I'll give you some advice, just in case you ever sail again. You should learn all the rules before you get into a boat, even for a little trip. I myself did a training course before I stepped into a dinghy. If you don't know the rules, you might do something dangerous, like forget to wear a lifejacket or tell people on shore what time to expect you back.

– Yes, of course, Shinsetsu-GR. I should learn the rules.

I've said enough about that. I'd like to keep the quiet salaryman image for now. I'm only in my second week.

Reisei-C is sitting across from me. He is a C, which means he is more senior than Riko-T, Majime-T and me. His hobby is golf. I don't mind talking to him about golf because I've never broken any golf rules because I've never even played golf. Reisei-C can't afford to be a golf club member so he practises at the driving range near the company. He shoots a bucket or two of golf balls every Saturday morning or sometimes after work, after overtime, at ten, eleven or even midnight because the golf driving range is good late at night with only a few people hitting balls and it's not hot or crowded as it is earlier.

– But your real hobby is not golf, is it? says Riko-T. It's programmable controllers, right? Rumour has it that you take the circuit board home in your bag at night.

– Only when I have a problem to fix, Reisei-C says. I get good ideas while sleeping. It's handy to have the circuit board close by to look at. I recommend you do the same.

Sleep on a controller circuit board? It sounds worse than a noisy neighbour.

Ando-C introduces his work – a national project with researchers from half a dozen big companies who meet to share ideas every month. Reisei-C and Shinsetsu-GR want to hear the latest news.

– You know Yamazaki Corp who make the machine tools, don't you? Ando-C says. They want to change the research topic. Automated production lines – that's all they want, and it's not what we want.

– Why did they change? says Shinsetsu-GR.

– Because Toyota changed their plans, that's why. The Toyota manager and the Yamazaki guy were students together in Osaka years ago. They're old friends. That's the reason Toyota joined in the first place. I don't know what we should do now.

– Let's talk to our department manager, says Shinsetsu-GR. I'm sure he can fix things. He too has some old friends in Toyota. Let us leave off the work talk till tomorrow. Tell Muruta-T about your hobbies.

– Hobbies? says Ando-C. I've no hobbies.

– Come on, you must have had a hobby or done some sport sometime or other. Didn't you run around the company block during recruit training when you joined?

– We had a choice the year I joined. We could either run or stay inside and write an essay. I did the essay. Will I tell you about my essay?

– No, please don't, says Riko-T. Let's move on to Muruta-T.

I don't have a lot of new things to say because I said everything I want to say about myself in my introductory speech the first day. It's question time. Any questions? I'm still an outsider and the questions are tactful and restrained, at least at the beginning.

Why did I come to Japan?

– Because it's far away. I like faraway places.

Why did I choose a Japanese company rather than a Western one?

– I know Western companies already. I don't know Japanese ones. And Japanese companies are more flexible.

– Really? says Riko-T. Where did you hear that?

– About starting dates, at least. I didn't have to start in April.

– I suppose that's true.

Then the questions begin to get personal.

– What is your *type*? says Shinsetsu-GR.

He means female *type*. I have to answer carefully because if I say I'm open to offers, I know I'll get suggestions about all the eligible OLs on our floor and any other available *types* in the building. I have the impression that Shinsetsu-GR is one of those caring managers who would like to see eligible members of his staff married off – to an OL, if there's one available – and settled down in the company housing block so that the contented staff member would work happily every after. I'd prefer not to marry the company and work happily ever after. I'd prefer to keep work and play separate, especially in this cosy organisation where everyone knows what the others are doing and sometimes what they're thinking. Relations are complicated enough without adding romance. Do I want my colleagues' assistance in finding my *type*? No, thanks. I need to put them off.

– I prefer international *types* with international minds who know how foreigners think.

That's a tough order because how could anyone know how an inscrutable foreigner thinks? There are no helpful suggestions. The question session ends and I'm free to relax for the rest of the evening.

I ask Riko-T for advice, if he has any, about how I should tackle the noisy-neighbour problem.

– So you have a noisy apartment, have you? Never lived in one, myself, but I know about them. There was a guy with a noisy neighbour – where was it? Nagoya, I think. He decided to shut the noisy neighbour up – with a handgun. Didn't shoot him or anything. Just shut him up. A few shots in the ceiling, that's all. It was enough. And there was a woman in Sapporo. She didn't have a gun but what did she do? She cut the electricity wires to the neighbours who were impolite to her and this was in the middle of the snowy winter of the far north. Mind you, I'm not recommending you do the same. You might get fired. But isn't it amazing what can happen when people live so close to one another and someone is not considerate, not respectful. Just amazing.

– Yes, it's amazing.

But it doesn't help me much.

I head home after the *konpa*, hoping I won't have to do anything amazing to my inconsiderate neighbour. I think about moving out, but I postpone any decision because the next few nights are mysteriously quiet: no thuds in the middle of the night, just the relatively soft pitter-patter of normal feet on the floor above and not a sound after midnight. The heavy sleepwalker is out of town. Please don't come back, I tell the ceiling. Nights in the Yokohama suburbs as they should be for a tired worker laying his weary head down.

But soon my noisy neighbour is back. Now it is time for drastic action, as drastic as a Mitsubishi employee can make it, short of doing something amazing like Riko-T described. I will start by consulting Anshin-T again. I'll tell him it is a matter of life and death because if the situation does not improve I will think of doing something amazing to my inconsiderate neighbour.

But next day, before I can call him, he calls me. He doesn't ask if the problem is still there, but can I come for a chat? Good, I think. Perhaps he has a solution and all will be well in no time.

– The landlord has telephoned me this morning, he says.

Ah, someone else has probably informed the landlord about the problem and he has called to apologise. I can accept an apology, as long as the noise stops and doesn't start again. Ever.

Anshin-T hesitates, then continues.

– There has been a complaint made about the noise coming from … your apartment.

– What? My apartment? You mean the one above me? Remember I told you all about the awful noise?

– Yes, I remember. But it seems the complaint is about your apartment. The television or radio, it seems. Noisy. You will have to do something about it. You can't go around disturbing the neighbours.

– But it must be a mistake. Someone must have thought the noise from the apartment above was from mine.

– Well, all I know is what the landlord told me. It doesn't seem to be a mistake. Please remember you are not just another foreigner. You are an employee of Mitsubishi. You must remember that the honour of the company depends on its employees, so please avoid any friction with your neighbours.

– Yes, okay. I will investigate this evening.

But who could have complained? Is the complaint really about *my* apartment? What noise could I have made? I did move my television the previous evening up close to the wall of the neighbouring apartment but the volume wasn't high. At least I think it wasn't. I moved it into the kitchen where the floor is hard, not *tatami*. With only thin partition walls between the apartments, it might have disturbed highly sensitive people. But if they are so sensitive, surely they would have heard the thunder from the apartment above?

I pay a visit to my neighbour next door.

– Yes, who is it? a voice shouts out. People in this country don't open doors before finding out who is there. Though the chances of the caller being a mugger are very remote, people seem to have some ingrained fear of uninvited salesmen selling kitchen air filters or new religions.

I tell him I'm from the next apartment. The door opens and a man in T-shirt and jeans appears.

– The landlord has passed on a complaint about noise. I was wondering if it was you who made the complaint? I ask, skipping the usual polite introductions because I'm not in a polite mood.

– Yes, we heard some noise.

– But wasn't the noise from the apartment above?

– No. We only heard noise from your apartment. Last night.

– Well, I'm sorry you were disturbed, but couldn't you have told me about it? You didn't have to tell my company.

– We didn't contact your company. We only informed the landlord.

– But the landlord telephoned my company. I would have preferred if you had just told me directly, I say, forgetting that people don't do things directly in this country. Can you tell me what was noisy – was it the television?

– Yeah.

– I'll move it to the other room. You can come and see, if you like.

– No. It's okay.

I leave him with a small apology and go back to my apartment, ready to laugh, ready to cry. Here I am thinking about moving out or doing something drastic to escape the noise above, only to have a complaint by my neighbour forwarded to the landlord and to my company about me being noisy. Why didn't my sensitive neighbour just tell me? If he had to tell the landlord about it, why didn't the landlord contact me directly?

I decide to pay him a visit.

– Did you contact the company about noise from my apartment?

– Well, yes. I passed on the message I got from the tenant next door to you.

He seems taken aback, as though he realises he has made a mistake.

– Could you not have contacted me directly? It would have been much better than telling my company.

– Well, I thought it might be easier ...

– Do you know the apartment above me is very noisy? I was surprised that someone else could complain about me.

– No one has complained about the apartment above you.

– It's very noisy some nights. It's hard to sleep.

– We all have to live together … in harmony, he says, trying to sound philosophical but not really succeeding.

He looks uncomfortable. I tell him I will see to it that no more noise comes from my apartment.

– Please talk to me directly if there are any problems. There's no need to inform my company.

As I walk back to my apartment, I imagine him saying to himself, Just as I thought, foreigners are hard to deal with, even if they come with Mitsubishi pedigree and are supposedly well behaved and house-trained. This may be an international age, but I think I'll have to avoid foreign tenants next time.

And me? I'm thinking what an unsociable neighbour, what an awkward landlord, what a lousy house design and why didn't Anshin-T tell me about these timber-framed houses in the first place. I shift my television set to a corner of the *tatami* room farthest from the neighbours and hope Keiryo-*san* upstairs will stay quiet because I haven't heard any noise for a few nights now. Perhaps the landlord told him the tenant below has to sleep at night. But a couple of nights later the thunder above begins again. I resolve to act, nothing drastic but well considered and strategic. I won't ask the landlord to tell Keiryo-*san* to keep quiet. I will do it myself, directly and politely. Next evening, I go up the outside stairs and knock on the door.

– Yes, who is it?

– I'm from the apartment downstairs.

The door opens and a smiling woman in her thirties appears, a young child tugging at her apron.

– Sorry for disturbing you.

– No problem. Was it the water? Did it leak? I'm very sorry. Just last night we noticed.

– No, there's no water leak.

– Oh, I'm so relieved. I was worried that it would go through the floor. It is such a problem trying to watch after all these things.

– Actually, it's the floor. It seems to be very thin.

– Yes, these timber-framed houses are like that.

– And in my apartment, sometimes it's a bit … *noisy*.

– Oh, I'm sorry. Little Rie is so noisy when she plays.

– No, the noise was late at night, so perhaps it was your husband walking around.

– Yes, the apartment only has partition walls. And goodness knows what the floors are made of. But I'll tell him when he comes home.

– Thank you for your understanding.

– No, no. I'm glad you told me. I hope we don't disturb you anymore. And the water company will fix the leak soon.

– No problem with the leak. Just the noise. Goodnight.

That was well done, I tell myself. I've made my complaint at the right level, no friction, no cultural problems. But with all the talk of the water leak, I'm wondering if I got my message across.

A few days later, the noise is back. I'm sure she didn't understand. I must have overdone the indirectness. It's hard to get things right, isn't it? I go up the stairs again, time for some straight talking.

– Who is it? says the voice from inside.

– I'm from the apartment below.

The door opens.

– Oh, is it the water leak?

– No, there isn't any leak.

– Oh yes. The thin floor. I'm sorry that it is noisy.

– Unfortunately I still find it hard to sleep.

– Don't worry. I will make sure it's quiet. Sorry to have disturbed you.

– Thank you. I would be happy if you could do so.

– Thank you for telling me about it. This type of building is not so good for living in. What with the leaking tap and ... By the way, we'll be moving soon.

That's great, I think to myself, the best news I've heard since I moved here.

– Oh, I see. That's ... a pity.

– Well, thank you for coming.

– No problem. Goodnight.

It's quiet for a few nights, then a little noisier as the effect of my visit wears off. I can tolerate it because soon it will end, and so it does, when the apartment becomes vacant. New tenants move in, but there is no heavy neighbour pacing the rooms above and the nights are peaceful. I sleep soundly, content at not having to look for a new apartment and realising that it is indeed possible to live normally in these timber-framed homes in the boondocks of Yokohama and that neighbours lacking in house-training can be tackled without doing anything amazing.

4

急がば回れ

Isogaba maware
If in a hurry, go the long way round

At 8.20 every morning the ceiling loudspeakers jump to life and the exercise music begins. The drill sergeant shouts out his wake-up call to arms, his musical pep talk to make us feel healthy, active and ready to meet the day, ready to hit the software, ready to think of new ideas for the high-tech gadgets that will be on the market next year or the year after, in Japan, America and everywhere. At first I'm worried that someone might tell me to obey the commands of the exercise sergeant because I'm not in healthy exercising mood so early in the morning and I don't remember anything about company exercises, healthy or otherwise, in my job contract. But I need not worry; most of my colleagues in the research division are not morning people either and there are only a few of us in the office this early. Leave the exercises to the healthy factory workers. We will stick to tapping away at our keyboards and looking nerdy.

– Good morning, everyone, the drill sergeant shouts over the one-fingered staccato piano tune. Let us freshen up as the morning sun climbs high in the wide sky above us. Now we stretch. Sway to the left and to the right, slowly, like the willows in the green forest bending in the breeze. Now we move our arms up and down, flowing like the streams tumbling down from the snowy mountains, a little faster, a little faster. Now we bend backward and forward, easy and slow, like the waves of the big blue sea.

Indeed, it is a good thing to remember the green forest, the snowy mountains and the big blue sea at the start of the working day here in the concrete wilderness with only a few over-worked bushes and cherry trees to remind us of the non-concrete world far away. The voice and the music blare from speakers on the ceiling of every office, locker room, toilet, refresh-room and stairway in the building, from the nearby factories and from speakers attached to walls or poles at strategic locations throughout the complex. The sounds carry across the company road to the tiny car park reserved for important visitors, the bicycle park and the little Shinto shrine, as far as the streets and houses where the local residents no doubt appreciate the morning call to arms from the company. Those who don't must have moved a long time ago or else bought soundproofed windows.

The factory workers do the exercises from start to finish, no exceptions. They stand in front of the factory doors in blue overalls, yellow safety helmets and black boots. They limber up with the music and the drill sergeant, swinging, squatting and stretching, like willows in the forest, streams in the mountains and waves in the sea. They hop from side to side, bop up and down and swing their arms, like aerobics in overalls and boots. The music finishes and the factory workers give a cute little curtsy, almost like ballet dancers.

– Please remember to look tidy at all times, the drill sergeant says. It is said that clothes are the window to the heart. Have a good day, everyone.

In mid-afternoon he's back but he seems gentler than in the morning. Instead of the one-fingered staccato piano tune, he calls out the movements to the orchestral sounds of 'Love is Blue'. Reisei-C, Shinjin-T and a few of the others go to the passageway to limber up because if they start swinging and hopping at their desks they'll hit something or someone. But most of us just keep working away. I think most of us don't even hear the music and the exercise sergeant. The research division is a little different from the factories, a little less conformist. I ask Kawaii-T if they do the exercises in Personnel.

– Well, if our manager is at his desk and if he stands up to do the exercises, then we all do so. But otherwise, we don't. I suppose we are too busy. We have much work to do.

Soon the exercising routine begins to feel normal and I no longer smile at the workers in boots and helmets and the less heavily armed software engineers in my group bopping up and down, back and forth, right and left, because this exercising is really a good idea, giving people a chance to loosen up, take a break from the routine, a chance to stop pushing buttons or stop staring at flickering screens, bent over grey steel desks, which they've been doing for hours on end. I'd even join Reisei-C and Shinjin-T and bop to the strains of 'Love is Blue' in the afternoon except that I wouldn't feel comfortable moving to the commands of the drill sergeant, who sounds too army-like for me. But who knows? If I stay another year or two, some day I might start bopping, swinging my arms, bending forward and stretching backward, like willows in the forest, streams in the mountains and waves in the sea.

Besides the exercise music, there are the bells and chimes, telling us when to start work, when to take lunch and when to finish. I try to ignore them because I don't like being controlled by bells and chimes, but it's not easy. They sound everywhere, even in the elevator and the small library. You can run, you can hide, but you can't escape the bells. The first one sounds at 8.30 in the morning and ding-dongs for ten seconds to signal the start of the workday; at noon another bell ding-dongs the time for lunch, and forty-five minutes later, the time to get back to work if you haven't already begun. During lunch there are other bells, a couple of quick dings and one dong. They might be telling us when to start eating and when to clean up and get ready for the afternoon, I don't know. I ask Riko-T what they mean but he doesn't know either and I think he doesn't even hear the dings and dongs, just as he doesn't hear any phone ringing except his own.

There is no official break time for coffee or tea. You can go to the refresh-room to get a drink whenever you want. At five, the bells ring for the end of normal working hours and a lady's voice comes over the public address system thanking us all for working hard today, please tidy up your desk and get home safely, though no one ever tidies up and goes home at five, not even the OLs. When I hear the bell dinging at five I remember my first job, a few months in an office in Dublin where no bell ever ding-donged but still the technicians and some of the secretaries would be getting ready at 4.55, getting set at 4.57, then go go go at five. But that was half a planet away.

At 5.15 another bell dings to announce the start of official overtime and again at seven to remind us to take a break. I believe there is a final bell at 9.00 p.m. for another quick break, although I never stayed that late.

At 4.30 on a Friday afternoon the bells announce cleaning time. Each of us takes his waste paper basket and waste plastic basket and puts the contents into the appropriate semi-transparent plastic bags, whose size, colour and transparency are regulated by the city authorities. Two people from each department take the rubbish to giant bins behind the building. The younger staff take turns at vacuum-cleaning the carpet floor; the rest of us brush off any dust that might have collected on our desks. Contract cleaning staff look after the toilets, but no one except ourselves cleans the office.

We have flexible working hours in the research division, which means we can come a little late if we wish and leave a little early, though not too early, please, because it's just not done. Riko-T goes home very early sometimes, six or even 5.30. I know he is very efficient and no doubt has finished his work, but still he sneaks out without saying anything to anyone, like he knows he's doing something bad. I don't want to be like that. If I leave early, I say *osaki-ni – I'm off* – to Majime-T and Shinsetsu-GR. If they have a problem with that, then that's tough. But no one has a problem and I think I can still make the three-month deadline Shinsetsu-GR gave me for my report.

Many of my colleagues don't like the early mornings and don't appear till the last few minutes of the flexible zone at 10.00 a.m. but they make up for it by staying till all hours of the night. The last man out has to switch the lights off, lock the doors and sign out on the chart on each stairway landing. He has to write down the time, which is sometimes 23.45 or 25.30, or 27.00, meaning 3.00 a.m. After a 27-hour day he comes in a little late next morning, 9.45 or ten. The ultra-overtimers form a small but select group. They are proud of their overtime feats and it does them no harm in the promotion stakes and the annual evaluation. I know it did the manager of the group next to ours no harm. He is often the last to leave because his name is on the sign-out chart, but the guys in his group don't appreciate his management. They tell me his name goes on all their reports and patents, though he doesn't understand what they are about. But he is good at pleasing the department manager and he shows he has a good attitude by staying late, whether there is work to do or not.

The medium-overtimers do a few hours, and for the minor-overtimers, like me, Riko-T and sometimes my boss, Shinsetsu-GR, an hour or two is enough. We think having results to show for our work is more important than time spent in the office and we want a life away from the company. We don't want to be like the ultra-overtimers who only get home to eat dinner at ten or eleven every night and who sleep through the weekend. They are the salarymen who might end up as *karoshi* cases – death due to overwork – that we read about in the newspapers. There are a few potential *karoshi* cases in Administration and a lot of them in the factories, where they don't have flexible working hours and they all start early and finish late.

Officially there is no clear distinction between white-collar and blue-collar workers. We are all Mitsubishi salarymen, wearing a suit in Head Office, a Mitsubishi jacket in the labs and overalls in the factories, although behind the apparent equality is a strong hierarchy that shows itself in the way we address one another using company titles and take seats at a meeting. Reisei-C used to work in the Nagano factory before he was moved to the lab in Yokohama. He says the factory salarymen work longer and harder than we do in the labs. They don't write down the actual hours they work and they only claim expenses for half their overtime because it's just not done to go claiming payment for every single hour if you're a good, conscientious employee.

Reisei-C says, Aren't we lucky to be in the research labs, not in Administration and not in the factories where they work so hard?

Riko-T says, Aren't we lucky to be in Mitsubishi, not Sony or Hitachi where they put in even longer hours than us – though he's not sure about that?

I guess we're lucky.

When the lunchtime bell ding-dongs no one moves for five or six minutes. Then we file out, down the stairs and across to the canteen building that we share with the factory workers. Everyone takes a *bento*

lunch box, a pair of chopsticks and a cup of green tea from the counter near the door and we sit at the tables. The first time I look at the long parallel rows of seated workers, everyone wearing the blue company jacket or overalls, everyone eating the same rice, fish and vegetables from the same brown-coloured boxes, it looks like soup time for the chain gang, and my appetite fades. What have I signed myself up for? But I force myself to eat because there's a long afternoon ahead. After a week or two the chain gang feeling fades. It's more like a boarding school cafeteria and my appetite improves, though I can only eat half the rice because there's always too much. Another month passes and I forget the chain gang and the boarding school. The food might not taste great, but it is healthy and almost free and we cannot complain about that. I just wish they would go easier on the rice because I'm never going to eat it all and it's a waste to leave a big pile behind. One day I tell the lady at the counter there's too much. Please, can I have less rice? She gives me a funny look and smiles as if to say, Never before has a salaryman wanted *less* rice. I don't ask for special treatment after that.

After lunch there's the *hiru-rei* – the afternoon call to arms. Everyone stands to attention facing the boss – not in a line, because it's not the army – but at our desks. No one minds that I prefer to slouch. Shinsetsu-GR makes an announcement that we will have a meeting tomorrow, that we should get our work reports in early this week or that we should not forget the quota of one patent per person per year. If there is nothing official to say, he might announce that it's springtime, let's enjoy the blossoms, that it's summertime, let's not be defeated by the heat, that it's autumn, let's enjoy the beautiful red leaves if there are maple trees near where we live, or that it's wintertime, let's not catch a cold. Sometimes he announces that there are no announcements. If he is away Reisei-C substitutes, and if they are both away, someone else, though it never gets as low as one of the Ts.

There used to be a *cho-rei* – a morning call to arms – but since flexible working hours began and people started arriving at nine or even ten, the *cho-rei* was made a *hiru-rei*. In other companies I hear that everyone in turn has to make a little speech at the *cho-rei* or *hiru-rei*. We're lucky not to have that because I wouldn't want to listen to silly speeches every day.

I get used to the quiet working style in the lab, where even the telephones ring softly and people don't chat unless they have to. But it's not all quietness. When he is in the mood, Reisei-C taps his keyboard so hard I think it might break. Majime-T hums quietly to himself when things are going well and talks to himself when they're not. The bells are noisy when they ring out a half-dozen times a day and the public address system is noisy too. It's a strange mixture of quietness and noise.

I get used to the shortage of office space. I'm careful not to let my books or papers extend over the desk line onto Riko-T's desk to my left and not to push out my chair too far because I might bump into a colleague sitting behind me. I don't know why space is so tight. It's a cultural thing.

The salaryman train commute is harder to get used to. The trains, of course, are clean, punctual and cost about the same as London, although they are more efficient. On the Tokaido line linking Tokyo and Yokohama the morning trains arrive at three- and sometimes two-minute intervals. Each train has fifteen long carriages and each carriage carries 150–250 passengers. (I did a rough head count.) If there is a delay of more than a few minutes an apology is made over the public address system. Once there was a major delay – someone jumped under a train at some faraway station, I heard later – and the trains stopped running for almost twenty minutes. When I finally reached my destination, the train officials at the exit were bowing and apologising to everyone. I was handed a piece of paper which I read as I walked to work:

> *Proof of Train Delay*
> *This certificate is to indicate that the train you boarded was delayed by the time [in minutes] indicated by the punch marks on the right, at the time and date stamped above. Japan Railways humbly and unreservedly apologises for this delay.*
>
> *JR Station Manager*

The paper was for submitting to a boss to prove that it was not the employee's fault for being late, but since we have flexible working hours in the Mitsubishi labs I don't need to submit it. I keep it for myself, a souvenir of JR customer care.

I have to change trains once on my commute. The station where I board is not too crowded, particularly towards the front and rear carriages, and on the Odakyu line they even take measures to neutralise unpleasant smells during the hot, sweaty summer by installing air conditioners with cartridges containing natural vegetable oil extract. According to a notice posted near the train doors, the oil extract, which is taken from several dozen different types of plant, removes unpleasant odours and provides a relaxing and refreshing environment for the two million passengers who ride the Odakyu trains each day. Just in case some passengers do not want to breathe in any minute quantities of vegetable oil extract, the cartridges are only installed in every second carriage.

Other lines closer to Tokyo are much more crowded and at some stations the famous white-gloved railwaymen stand at the train doors ready to push any part of any commuter that protrudes from the door. Often a couple of pushes are necessary before the doors close properly, which is why the trains lose a few seconds at each station and eventually end up a minute or more late.

Although there are no white-gloved men where I change train, it is uncomfortably crowded at peak time. Inside the train, there is no natural vegetable oil extract to neutralise odours. In the summer it's hot because the air conditioning is in energy-saving mode; in winter the windows are often closed because there is always someone with a cold near the window who won't open it even a little and is wearing a white anti-germ surgical mask as proof.

I've been on crowded trains before – third class in Peru, hard seat in China, dirty floor in Burma. I shouldn't complain about a few crowded minutes on the Tokaido line in the morning. Compared to Peruvian, Chinese and Burmese trains, my commute is not so bad, is it? Yes, it's bad because this is not an adventure anymore. This is everyday life and I want some sort of life. I decide to avoid the rush hour.

I come to work earlier – eight, still crowded, 7.30, not much better, seven, where do these commuters come from? Any earlier and I may as well stay overnight in the office, like Matsuno in the university. It might not be a bad idea and my colleagues would be impressed. They would think it was dedication to work rather than aversion to the trains. But there would be procedures involved. Permission would have to be obtained and I haven't seen any sign of a foldaway bed. Matsuno's solution won't work so easily here. There must be another way.

I decide to ride my bicycle the few miles to work. It's lucky I don't live an hour's train ride away. I ask Riko-T about it.

– You must apply for permission.

– Permission to come to work by bicycle?

– Yes. If you wish to park your bicycle in the company grounds you need a permit to pass the gate. And since the company has already paid for your train pass, the bicycle permit will probably not be given.

– What if I cancel the train pass?

– You may still be refused. There are rules about how employees should travel to work. If you want to use a bicycle, you must live between one and four kilometres away. The personnel department wants you to come to work the safest way. If there's an accident on the way to work, the company will have to pay compensation, so they worry about how you travel.

Nice of them to worry about me, but I can worry about myself by myself.

The trains are getting stuffier in the cold weather. I've had enough. I decide to cycle. I don't apply for permission because it would take days or weeks to get an answer and the answer might be negative. I leave my bicycle outside the company grounds in a nearby street that doesn't have bicycle-parking restrictions. No one need know or care.

On the second day commuting by bicycle the telephone call comes through from Personnel.

– This is Kawaii. The security section has just contacted us. Did you come by bicycle today? And did you park it outside on the street?

I'm speechless. How could the security section possibly know? I left it far from the main gate in a place that few people pass. There was no one around when I parked it and yet somehow it was seen or I was seen. Could there be a security camera with a telephoto lens pointing down the side street? Or could one of the guards have noticed that I approached the gate from a different direction, then gone to investigate and noticed the solitary bicycle down the side street? I don't know, but the company knows I've come to work by bicycle and the company knows I don't have permission.

– Yes, Kawaii-T. I left my bicycle outside, but it is in a place that won't interfere with anyone.

– It is against the rules to leave a bicycle on the streets near the company. What would happen if everyone did the same? It would surely inconvenience the local people.

Well, if all 950 of us park bicycles in the same street, it would indeed make things crowded. But nearly everyone comes by train, don't they? And the local people are already inconvenienced by loudspeaker announcements, exercise music every morning and afternoon, trucks and vans going to and from the factory and those big ugly advertising boards telling everyone what a great company we are.

– Then can I get permission to park it inside the company grounds?

– You can apply, although I do not know if permission will be granted. In any case you must not leave the bicycle outside. Please park your bicycle in the official bicycle park at the train station until the result of your application is known.

The next few days I leave my bicycle in the multi-storey bicycle park near the station, paying the equivalent of a train ticket for the all-day parking permit.

A week later, an envelope arrives with news of the permit application. Riko-T was too pessimistic. I am formally given permission to commute by bicycle and to park it on company premises. Maybe they made an exception for me because I'm a foreigner, I don't know. Inside the envelope is a sheet of rules and a parking sticker to attach to the handlebars so that the security men can check that I'm an officially sanctioned bicycle commuter. I read the bicycle rules:

1. *Always stop at the gate when entering or exiting the company grounds.*
2. *Leave your bicycle in the bicycle park, in space number 23.*
3. *Do not use your bicycle during work hours for any reason.*
4. *Ensure that your bicycle has a front light, rear reflector, bell and stand, and that the front and rear brakes are functioning.*
5. *You should check the above items and submit a report to your manager at the end of each year.*

6. *Bicycles may be inspected by the administration department to ensure compliance with these rules.*
7. *Instead of the usual subsidy for commuting by train or bus, the company will pay 3,000 yen per month for bicycle maintenance.*
8. *Failure to obey the rules may result in cancellation of the bicycle-commuting permit.*

It's nice to get 3,000 yen (about $25) a month to keep my bicycle in shape. I obey all the rules, except for submitting the report. No one seems to mind.

No matter how talented or ambitious you are, no matter how hard you work, if you are not fit and healthy you cannot achieve good results, the *Guidebook for New Employees* says. All employees must take the yearly health check.

First there is the questionnaire, ten pages long, with questions about every disease known to the company doctors. It's good to be thorough. You never know what disease some employee might have picked up or inherited because there are over 100,000 of us in our organisation, coming from here, there and everywhere, Hokkaido in the far north, Kyushu in the south and – who knows? – there might even be a few employees from faraway places like the islands south of Kyushu or even Okinawa, though I've never heard of anyone coming from *that* far away.

Filling out the questionnaire is a strenuous task that makes me think what I am supposed to answer, what the consequences will be if I don't answer and what the consequences will be if I do answer. First come the easy questions:

Are you allergic to sawdust, fish, alcohol, eggs? Do you have any of the following thirty deformities? Have you ever suffered from any of the following sixty-two diseases?

I don't know because I've never heard of half of them in any language. I assume the strange diseases don't apply to me.

How long does it take you to get ready to go out in the morning? How long do you spend in the bath every night? How many bowls of rice, types of vegetable, quantities of meat, fish and eggs do you eat for breakfast, lunch and dinner? Do you eat bread, rice or both at breakfast-time? Do you drink green tea, red tea or coffee? List all illnesses you have had in the past including dates and recovery, if you recovered, and if not, why not? List all diseases contracted by your brother, sister, parents or grandparents, and state whether they have recovered. Do you have symptoms of any disease? Do you see rainbow colours in the light? Do you have buzzing in the ears, a rough coating in the mouth? Do you have bad breath, in other people's opinion?

I've never asked my colleagues for their opinions about whether I have bad breath and I don't want to start now. I will assume I have good breath, in other people's opinion.

The questions get more awkward, more personal, and I wonder if I should tell the truth or not. I write my answer in pencil, just in case I change my mind.

Are personal relations in your office good? Yes – except for the quiet people who don't talk to one another and the shy types who feel uncomfortable with foreigners.

Do you try to see the good in others rather than the bad? Yes. If I didn't I'd be long gone.

How many hours' overtime do you work? As few as possible. No one seems to mind.

Do you take vacations? Yes. I plan to take at least fifteen of my permitted twenty-five days' annual leave, as well as the national and the Mitsubishi holidays.

Do you make frequent errors in your work? My computer programs are full of errors but I'm fixing them.

Do you feel it is too much trouble to do any work? Not too much.

Do you dislike your own personality? Only when I put my Mitsubishi jacket on.

There is no mention that the information will be treated confidentially or that it will not be disclosed, no assurance that my boss will not be told. I wonder if employees with bad breath, in other people's opinion, will be disqualified from promotion because the bosses with good breath wouldn't like it. Or what about those who feel it is too much trouble to do any work? They will probably never make it to the Board of Directors. That's if someone finds out. But no one will find out. The company is only worried about our health and I trust the company. More or less.

But just in case something might be leaked, I change a few of those answers, even if they were the truth. I write proper answers that the Mitsubishi medical staff would expect a good employee to write.

As I fill in the last answer to the last impertinent question, I stop and think for a moment. Perhaps the questionnaire is not meant to be taken so seriously. Perhaps its role is to make us think about being healthy, to smile before we take the physical. If I worked for an American or European company I would never see questionnaires like this, never have to answer questions like whether I have bad breath, in other people's opinion, and life would be dull. At times like this, it's almost fun to be a salaryman. It depends on how I look at things.

One day I ask Riko-T about the questionnaire. Does he really take it seriously?

– Yes. We must answer the questions, even if they are very detailed.

– But why does the company want to know all these details? Are you honestly telling me they are so worried about all of us that we have to answer ten pages of surprising questions?

– No, no. The company is not worried about us individually. Annual health checks are a government requirement. All companies above a certain size have to do them. And if we become ill it will cost the company more to look after us and pay for medical treatment.

I knew there was a reason. It's economics. It's cheaper to keep us healthy.

After the questionnaire with the surprising questions, there is a more serious check-up in the company clinic. I drink an awful white liquid and have a dozen X-rays, right side, left side, up side, down side and everything in between. I have an eye test, ear test, give them a little cup of my own liquid and that's all, thank you, see you next year – unless there's something not right.

When the results come through, there's a note to say that something is not right. They have found an irregularity during my eye examination. I should go to the hospital for further tests. I haven't noticed anything unusual with my eyes, but when I think about it, yes, there could be something wrong. What with staring at a computer screen all day and studying the Chinese characters – the *kanji* – year in, year out, anything is possible: eye stress, eye fatigue, eye burnout.

I recall seeing a television programme which claimed that eyesight in this country is worse than almost anywhere else. A panel of experts discussed how such a situation could have come about. The first expert said people here are short-sighted because of the size of the houses and apartments.

– Living in small rooms where you cannot see farther than a metre in any direction and your TV is much too close, your eyes cannot be expected to be normal. In foreign countries, living rooms are so big that the TV can be positioned several paces away from the viewers. That is why people in other countries have better eyesight.

The second expert said, no, no, it's nothing to do with the houses. It's the food.

– The reason for our short-sightedness is that we eat less meat than other nationalities. In fact, until the US occupation, we ate almost no meat. Even now, the older generation does not eat much meat. This, I believe, is why our eyesight is inferior. By eating less meat, you see, the jaw muscles and those around the eyes get less exercise. They get soft and weak and don't do their job properly. Result: short-sightedness.

The third expert said, no, no, it's nothing to do with the houses or the food. It's the writing. The *kanji.*

– Eye strain is caused by reading all those *kanji,* focusing on the complicated strokes of the characters from the age of six or even younger, memorising two or three thousand of the damn things before reaching the age of eighteen. It makes the eyes work too hard for too long. By the time we reach adulthood we can hardly expect to have normal eyes.

I think about my sight irregularity. I've lived for years in tiny dormitory rooms and apartments with the TV stuck wherever I could put it. I don't eat much meat. My budget doesn't allow for it. My jaw muscles must be out of condition, weak. And how about all those *kanji* characters I've studied, some with two strokes, some ten, some twenty, with lines and squiggles that go this way and that? They're bad news for my eyes without even thinking about the flickering computer screen at work. It all adds up and I must be in the high-risk category for a sight disorder. I will go to the hospital right away and take the detailed examination.

A few minutes' train ride from the company stands South Central Yokohama Hospital, a six-storey concrete building with rows of small square windows and signs outside about all the diseases they cure. They give me a card and tell me to proceed to the eye doctor by following the yellow line painted in the centre of the corridor floor – not the red line or the blue one, which would bring me to the internal medicine or orthopaedic department – just the yellow one. The yellow line leads upstairs, along a couple of passageways, splits from the blue line, and I see a row of people sitting outside the eye surgery. I sit down and stare at the wall opposite, covered with posters showing what happens if you don't lead a healthy life.

I take a cue from the other patients and shut my eyes. I should rest them as much as I can. When I open them the scene has changed a little: one or two of the patients have gone from the queue and a couple of new arrivals are settling in. Another twenty minutes pass and the nurse calls out my name. The doctor takes a look, doesn't say anything, writes something in a file and tells me to look into the big machine and keep looking till a green light flashes. The light flashes and the nurse says, That is all for today, please come back next week for the result.

I return a week later, a little worried, but hoping my sight irregularity is curable. When I enter the doctor's office, he is studying the photographs and charts laid out on his desk.

– Please sit down, he says with a smile. Take a look here. See the photo scan of your eyes? It's different from the normal one. That's why the original test said there was an irregularity.

I look at the photo but don't notice anything unusual.

– The tests we did here have shown what the irregularity is. As you know, in this country all eyes are dark brown or black in colour, but there are no blue eyes, like yours. I'm afraid the checking system doesn't consider the possibility of blue eyes.

He stops for a moment and smiles.

– There are no problems with your sight. The irregularity found was, well, just the colour of your eyes. You have nothing to worry about.

– That's all?

– That's all. The machines and the technicians will know better next time.

I smile, thank him and go outside to wait for my bill.

Real salarymen don't have blue eyes.

5

裏には、裏がある

Ura ni wa ura ga aru
Behind the façade is another façade

Six months have now passed since I became a Mitsubishi man and somehow I've handled the salaryman life so far. It has taken a bit of compromising, a bit of getting used to, but I've handled different lifestyles before. This is just another one. I can ignore or sidestep most of the heavy rules, the things that make me think, I'll be out of here soon enough and it'll be nice to look back on it all, like a tough year in a strict school or like military service. But there are some things I can't ignore or look forward to telling people about some day and I meet one of them one stressful lunchtime. Tanki is his name and even among the salarymen of Mitsubishi, where we keep our opinions to ourselves, especially if they are not polite opinions, he has a nickname – Terrible Tanki – because that's what he is, terrible to behold and terrible to listen to. He spent a few years in the new factory in China, where he achieved some impressive results. I'm sure he gave the local staff a hard time but he increased productivity by 20 per cent and this was noted back in Head Office. He was rewarded by having his tour of duty shortened and he returned in triumph to the homeland, where he was crowned manager of external planning in Head Office. He might have been made general manager if he had been a little older, but he was still in his thirties, too young for such a position.

Everyone in my group is invited to a compulsory working lunch in Head Office near Tokyo Station. There will be no chain gang canteen today. Instead, we will discuss the work being done and strategy to be adopted in the coming months in order to set our group back on the right track because it seems we have derailed from the plans the Important People like Tanki-GR have drawn up. Reisei-C tells me to expect a tough meeting because he knows about Tanki-GR.

We take our seats in the meeting room but don't touch our lunch boxes or chopsticks till the planning managers arrive and introduce themselves – Tanki-GR and his assistant, Nakada-KS. The usual chatter is replaced by an air of respect or even fear, and the lunches are finished in silence. It's the strangest meal I've had since I came to this country. I feel I'm back in school again, having lunch with the principal and vice-principal, except that the pupils here are more obedient and quieter than they ever were when I was at school and the principal is trying his hardest to look mean.

– I think we have finished eating now, says Nakada-KS, which means we should stop eating whether we have finished or not.

– We would like to hear about the work you are doing. But first Tanki-GR will say a few words. Over to you, Tanki-GR.

When Tanki speaks, everyone sits up and his thunderous voice echoes like the morning exercise drill sergeant throwing a tantrum without the background music. No one looks directly at him, but I steal a glance at his sharp, angry eyes. Where has the civilised salaryman-world gone? Tanki is not civilised, even if he is a salaryman and a Mitsubishi man like the rest of us.

– Okay, you bunch of laggards. I've heard about the reputation of this group – wasting resources on useless plans and software for the birds. Just because you can't get fired doesn't mean Head Office is going to keep throwing money at you forever. Now, let me hear what you've been doing.

Each member of our group speaks in turn. Nakada-KS stays quiet but Tanki says what he thinks. He doesn't think much of the senior staff and I feel sorry for them. They are working so hard but they get no thanks for it, at least not from Tanki. I know they won't try to argue with him. They'll just put up with it and try to please him as much as they can.

Tanki says he wants to hear from some of the junior staff and it's the turn of Shinjin-T, who only joined the company last spring. He says he's writing a scheduling program for the engine production line in the Shizuoka factory.

– Why are you supporting Shizuoka? says Tanki. Don't they have enough people to do the work? Isn't it a waste of resources to be supporting them? Will they provide enough funding?

Shinjin-T cannot answer any of these questions – he's just a new recruit, for God's sake, just doing what he was told, but Tanki tries to put him on the spot, make him feel small and make his bosses even smaller. Shinjin-T doesn't answer. He sits there in silence. I'm not sure who his boss is – perhaps it is Shinsetsu-GR, perhaps Reisei-C – but no one says anything. No one owns up.

Tanki shouts, Next, and the spotlight is on me. I don't have any impressive results to talk about. The programs I wrote in the university were just academic toys after all and won't be of much use for those world-class Mitsubishi elevators. My plans to write a bunch of new programs are still at the thinking stage. Shinsetsu-GR told me not to worry, just keep working away, because Shinsetsu-GR is a gentle type of boss, but I don't want to tell Terrible Tanki I've got nowhere.

– I'm writing new programs for the elevator factory.

Tanki doesn't say anything to me. He asks Shinsetsu-GR how long I've been in the company, nods and shouts, Next. He's treating me differently from the others. I'm sure he has never shouted at anyone with blue eyes and brown hair before and doesn't know quite how it should be done. Maybe he is afraid I might switch languages, shout back at him in English and cause an international argument that he might not win because he's not able to get angry in English, which would make him look foolish in front of all the people he's just shouted at.

When the reports are finished, Tanki-GR continues his tongue-lashing.

– The way things are going, we'll have to start learning from the Chinese. The Chinese don't work till they're pushed but when they work, by heaven, they get results. Maybe you would learn something if you all moved to the Chinese plant for a year.

Move to the Chinese plant? He doesn't mean it, does he? But what if he does? Mitsubishi people do get transferred all over the country and even abroad without being asked for their preferences. My colleagues wouldn't want to move anywhere, especially abroad and more especially China, which would be like banishment to the edge of the world. They would do anything to avoid it, even work twice as hard. But I wouldn't mind it at all. In fact I'd love a chance to go back to China. The place must have changed a bit since 1983. That time seems like a different life, looking back at it now – ferry boat up the Pearl River from Guanzhou and all across the warm south through Guilin to Yunnan province and up to Sichuan as the autumn chill came down from the mountains. There were hardly any outsiders in China then and no Mitsubishi factories. It would be nice to go back – in style this time – and stay in a clean hotel and go to the places I'd been before, walk along the riverfront in Shanghai in the early morning and watch the slow-motion *tai chi* in the park as the sun rises over the river. I'd like to go back to Sichuan and climb Emei-Shan again, stay in that monastery at the summit, untouched by the Cultural Revolution, and look out over the plains below and west towards the snowy peaks where Tibet begins.

But that is enough daydreaming. A transfer to the Chinese factory might mean hotels and taxis but it wouldn't mean weeks or months wandering through Yunnan and Sichuan. It wouldn't mean taking boats down the big river from Chongqing to the sea or watching the slow-motion *tai chi* on the riverfront in Shanghai as the sun rises across the water. It would just mean the company, work and probably a tough boss. But I'm sure Tanki only said it as a threat. He doesn't have the power to banish anyone to China.

As we head back to our lab in Yokohama after that heavy lunchtime, Shinsetsu-GR approaches me.

– We only have meetings like this very rarely.

He's trying to say, Don't worry too much about Tanki-GR. He's not on the lunch menu very often – which is just as well because he makes the chain gang canteen feel like a party.

– Was he upset for some reason?

– Not really. Perhaps Tanki-GR developed his style in China. Perhaps he is not a typical manager in Mitsubishi. Tanki-GR is always ...

He searches for an appropriate word and I think, Good, I'll learn a new swear word today.

– Tanki is always very *genki* – lively.

Sometimes this Mitsubishi politeness goes too far.

With people like Tanki around I'll have to watch my stress level because I don't feel relaxed when people shout, especially in the normally polite salaryman world. I'm not the only one, it seems. The Mitsubishi labour union has taken notice of the stress levels among employees, not just because of angry managers but also because of the stresses of company life in general. Membership of the company-run union is compulsory for all of us, with the exception of management, and we pay subscription dues of roughly 1.8 per cent of our monthly salary. Later I find out more about union power in organising industrial action and improving our lot in the company, but during my first year all I know is that, in return for paying our dues, the union does its best to look after our psychological well being. It provides a members' room in an annex to our building, stocked with magazines, videos, video-cameras, travel goods and camping equipment for borrowing. It offers discounts on tickets for the cinema, art exhibitions, concerts and even Tokyo Disneyland. It tries to make it easier for us to take our annual leave by setting targets: last year the average number of leave days – which includes sick leave – taken by lab employees was 17.3; this year's target is 18 days. It also thinks up excuses to make taking annual leave easier, like the rule that you can take a day off on your birthday, during the week of your birthday or, if that is difficult, during the six months following your birthday.

The union organises talks to help us in our work and life, usually on a Wednesday, which is the officially sanctioned no-overtime day when we are all supposed to finish by five or at least by 5.30 p.m. Just to remind us, the public address loudspeakers inside and outside the buildings jump to life after 5.30, a lady's voice tells us that it is Wednesday, no-overtime day, and the sounds of the 'Tennessee Waltz', sax version, echo loudly through the building, meaning hurry up and go. If we don't go, 'Auld Lang Syne', also sax version, also very loud, starts a few minutes later, meaning it's really time for home, although if you really, really want to work late no one will complain and you certainly won't get fired for disobeying the no-overtime recommendation. You just have to ignore the lady's voice, the 'Tennessee Waltz' and 'Auld Lang Syne' as you work away.

One Wednesday there's a talk by a famous stress expert, a lady who has been on TV and has given lectures all over Tokyo because she can predict when someone is under stress simply by looking at his or her face. After introducing her new book, she tells us to look at the slides she will show us.

– Look at the faces. Look at the position of the ears relative to the forehead. The ears should not be too high. Look at the mouths, the eyes. All the stress information is there. You just need to have the knowledge and you can see it.

The few dozen of us attending the lecture look at the faces she shows but we don't have the knowledge and we don't see any of the stress information. She shows us a photo of the former emperor, Hirohito.

– Notice the eyes. There is white below the pupils, which means they are not touching the bottom, a sure sign that someone has had a stressful life. Now look at the foreign musician, Freddie Mercury. The same – especially when he is gripping the microphone stand and singing, Mama, I've just killed a man.

I don't see the similarity between Freddie and Hiro, but then I'm not a stress expert. I don't have the knowledge and I probably won't get it during this lecture.

The stress expert shows us a face we see every day – the president of our company, who looks down on us from all those posters.

– The position of the ears isn't perfect, she says, but it's not the worst. He will overcome the obstacles he meets.

She is being diplomatic.

We sit there looking at the faces of famous people as the expert on stressed-out faces tells us what's wrong with this face and that. I expect her to finish by giving us the contact details of a good face-lifting plastic surgeon who, if we feel we need it and can afford it, will put the bits and pieces of our faces in the right place for a happy stress-free life. But instead she finishes by telling us all to smile, have happy faces and buy her book if we need to know more. I'm wondering what good will smiling and having a happy face do if the vertical level of our ears or the whites of our eyes are wrong.

I talk with colleagues after the lecture and we agree we didn't learn much about stress control. Some of us feel even more stressed, seeing the way the union is squandering our hard-earned subscription money with talks like this. There must be better ways of managing the stresses of life in a big corporation.

I join the company sports club. I fill in the forms and the man at reception shows me the machine room and the gym. He tells me where outdoor shoes can be worn, where indoor shoes must be worn and where no shoes are allowed. He shows me the pool and says I shouldn't swim at the deep end unless I'm confident in deep water. I tell him I'm confident because I swam in 3,000-metre deep water a while back. He tells me I mean millimetres and if I'm bad at figures there's a walkometer and a stepometer to do the counting, as well as massage machines and weight machines.

I hit the pool first. There are a few fast swimmers who zoom down, back and down again, and a few out-of-form swimmers like me, who struggle down the pool, back and down again, but even if I'm an out-of-form swimmer it's nice to pass the really bad swimmers in the neighbouring lane, who are so slow they seem to be going backwards. It's even nicer one Saturday when I look through my goggles and recognise Terrible Tanki there in the next lane. I've caught up with him and I'm about to overtake, slowly but surely, and that will put him in his place. We turn at the end of a length and suddenly he is looking straight at me through his dark goggles. I'm sure he notices me because even with dark goggles an Irish suntan is hard to mistake and he speeds up just a little. He's not bad for a manager. He must have been good when he was younger and now he wants to show he's better than me, but I'm going to make it hard for him and I kick a little harder, stretch forward a little more. We're swimming down and back together, neck and neck, straining to go faster, he knows it and I know it, and no matter how out of form I am or how many lengths he swims, I'm not going to be beaten by Tanki after all his shouting that lunchtime. I get ahead of him for a length of the pool or maybe two, then he catches up with me. I can't shake him but I'm sure I can outlast him if I hang on for a few more lengths and I'm right because ten minutes later he stops, probably out of breath from too much shouting at too many people, and I continue, clenched fist forward but he doesn't notice because I'm still swimming. Nice one. That put him in his place. He may be a good shouter but I've shown him he's a lousy swimmer. Anyone who can't beat me must be a lousy swimmer.

We avoid each other in the gym and sauna but the following week I have to visit Head Office and when I step into the elevator who is standing there but Terrible Tanki with the angry eyes. There's no one else so I can't pretend I don't notice him and he can't pretend he doesn't notice me. I do the minimum that politeness requires, give him a nod and say good morning. He glances at me but doesn't answer. Maybe he's peeved he couldn't outswim me in the pool.

Later I talk to Reisei-C about him.

– Does Tanki ignore people when he doesn't feel like shouting at them?

– It is because you are a foreigner. Tanki-GR doesn't know how to react to foreigners, except maybe Chinese. You should forget about Tanki. He doesn't come to our lab so you won't see him often.

I wonder if I'll have to race against him in the pool again, but I don't.

There are other managers who are more friendly. They always say hello when they see me – how's life, the language, the commuting, the work. I say I'm struggling away, thank you, doing my best, which is the proper answer. It would not be good to start complaining about the ding-dong bells, the chain gang canteen, Terrible Tanki or the quiet colleagues who don't talk to foreigners and hardly talk to anyone else either.

One day I'm a little late for lunch after being held up at a meeting and I'm eating alone. A new manager from a department on our floor notices me and joins me, telling me his name. Yamada, he says, not bothering with the formal company title, but I know he's a B because he is a department manager. Yamada-B asks how long I've been working in Mitsubishi, have I made friends, do I have any communication problems and can I manage the life here.

– I'm struggling away, thanks for asking. Everything is as good as can be expected.

– I spent three years in the US myself, he says. It's tough settling into a new company in a strange country with a strange language. It's tough getting used to everything new.

– I've been in this country a while, so I know my way around, thanks again, although some of the company rules and customs are hard to get used to.

– Yes, the company has its own style. Do your best. But if you have any particular problems, please let me know. I'll try to help.

– Thanks, Yamada-B. I will.

It's nice to know that for every Terrible Tanki there's a friendly Yamada out there, somewhere.

We don't invite one another to our homes much, us salarymen. It's not that we are anti-social. There are other reasons. Many of us live in small apartments, cluttered with new gadgets and old laundry, new books and old newspapers that should have been thrown out weeks ago but we have to wait till the newspaper-recycling day comes. A few of the younger salarymen among us live in the dormitories, but who would want to go on a social visit to a dormitory? The older salarymen have houses in the suburbs but the houses are often tiny and cluttered, and even if they're not tiny, there never seems to be enough free time for social visits, what with the long weekdays working and commuting, and the short weekends spent catching up on lost sleep. Aren't homes for wives and kids, and *izakaya* pubs for hardworking company men? Yes, that's all true, but there are exceptions. One day, out of the blue, Yamada-B asks me if I can come to visit his home, his family, have a drink and eat dinner, talk about work, life in Yokohama, anything. His wife would also like to meet me.

– Nice of you to invite me. I'll be free this coming Saturday or Sunday. What would be convenient?

– I would suggest a bit later. Let me see. Perhaps the last Saturday in

April, ten weeks from now. Would you be free then? You could come around five in the afternoon.

Forward planning is an acquired taste – just like spontaneity. I tell him I would be honoured to visit his home at around five in the afternoon on the last Saturday in April, ten weeks from now.

– Good. I will prepare a map to show you where my house is and which train to get. I will also make a schedule and give it to you next week. Besides my family, I would like to introduce someone to you.

– Sounds good.

– We will look forward to seeing you in April. By the way, you are single, aren't you?

I confirm that I am and begin to wonder about Yamada-B's forward planning.

A week later he gives me two pages with detailed plans for the visit: a map showing where to change trains, where to get off, which exit to use, and a schedule that leaves nothing to chance, even the weather.

Schedule for Muruta-san's visit to my house.
Date: 25 April
Time: 5.00 p.m.
Meeting Place: Okurayama Station. Please wait at the central exit.
If it is fine, we will walk for ten minutes to my house.
If it is raining, I will pick you up in my car.
Visiting time: 5.10 to 8.50.
Return to station by 9.00.
Catch 9.04 train.

On the last Saturday in April I arrive at the station. Yamada-*san* – I don't call him Yamada-B outside the company – is already there because it's polite to come early. The weather is fine and we walk for ten minutes to his home, according to schedule. His house is a narrow three-storey concrete building squeezed between a block of apartments and Kato's clinic, which is hidden behind a large sign listing Dr Kato's specialities: digestive diseases, stomach problems, wind.

– I would have preferred a wider but lower house, he says as we take off our shoes and put on the slippers carefully set out for us at the door. But the block of land was narrow and so we built our house high.

We climb the stairs to the living room, where his wife is waiting and bowing. She apologises for the narrowness of the house and the awkwardness of having the dining room upstairs. She hopes I like the food she has prepared.

– Don't worry, Yamada-*san* says. Muruta-*san* can eat the company lunch, so he can eat any food, right? But first, I will introduce my wife's friend. This is Miss Kekko. Muruta-*san*, do you have your card?

Of course. I wouldn't feel dressed without it. I offer my card. Miss Kekko looks at it carefully before putting it on the table.

The wife takes over.

– I should mention that Miss Kekko is single. And you are single too.

– Well, I can't afford to be anything else now. But maybe if I get a salary increase this year …

– One never knows, the wife says.

She introduces me to the other member of her household, a rabbit called Peeta.

– In the warm weather we put his cage outside on the balcony. In winter he stays inside. And he eats carrots and lettuce all day.

At dinner, her husband is quiet. Miss Kekko is quiet. The wife is not.

– The only problem with Peeta is when we go abroad. We have to put him in the animal hotel near the station. It is quite expensive, just for a little rabbit. But he is one of the family and we have to make sure he is looked after. Now, I would like to show you some of our travel photos.

She digs out an old box from a cupboard.

– As you can see, when I go abroad I like to go native.

– Same as me in Japan, I say.

– A little different. Look, I have a German overcoat when I visit Berlin, just like the natives. And in Italy I made friends with this man many years ago. Oops, my husband should not see this one.

But her husband is smiling. He has seen everything before.

– Back then I was – what is the word for it? Passionate, that's it! I was passionate.

She says the word in English because a word in a foreign language can be very flexible and can mean whatever you want it to mean.

– But I got scared of these Italians, she continues. They were too romantic for me. They asked which hotel I was in and once a man asked me for my room number. That is why I came back quickly to Japan and married a Japanese. Japanese men are not passionate. But they work hard and are good husbands.

Her husband smiles. Miss Kekko listens.

– Now, Miss Kekko, please tell us about your hobbies.

Miss Kekko's hobbies are shopping for Italian designer handbags and appreciation of foreign films, which means watching movies. The wife thinks her interest in Italian handbags sounds cosmopolitan. I think it sounds expensive. Yamada-*san* thinks the film appreciation suggests an artistic sense. I think it depends on the film. Peeta just stares out from his cage.

Yamada suddenly says that Muruta-*san* may become a permanent employee, trying to drum up some interest in Miss Kekko. I want to tell him not to bother trying. I'm not interested in Italian handbags and movie appreciation.

– To be honest I only planned to stay a short time in Mitsubishi. I don't know about lifetime employment. It sounds like a big commitment.

– It is not such a commitment. None of us thinks about staying in the company for a lifetime, at least not when we join. It just means the company will not get rid of you. It gives a feeling of security. Think about it.

– Okay, I'll think about it.

– And I am sure the company will gradually become more international, the wife says. Which will be a good thing, don't you think? In the future there will be many more foreigners.

Her husband thinks it will be a good thing.

– Mind you, I don't like the foreigners in Tokyo, the wife says. They are too … what is the word? Dry. That's it. They are too dry. I mean they act as if they are bored and don't want to talk.

Then, glancing at me, she adds, But you are not like the foreigners in Tokyo. You are like a Japanese. That is why I am glad you could come and visit.

But I don't feel *that* localised. I'll have to watch myself. I must be blending in too well, giving wrong impressions to people. Yamada-*san* thinks I should be a permanent employee. He thinks I'm quiet, hardworking, a perfect salaryman. It makes me feel uneasy because it's not the whole story, is it? I'll have to find a way to give a more balanced impression.

– But, to be honest, I think I'm a bit different. Kawaii-*san* in Personnel knows that I even broke the company rules.

– Really? What did you do?

– Well, I came to work on my bicycle without permission.

– Oh, that's nothing. I did the same once or twice, says Yamada-*san*. I mean when the trains weren't running, due to some technical problem, he adds, just in case I might think he's not a good manager.

I'm not getting very far in giving that balanced impression of myself. I'll have to think of something worse that I've done. What else can I confess? Something to let them know the real me.

– Well, I broke other rules. I was once almost arrested, and deported, sort of.

Surprise. Shock. Yamada-*san*'s mouth drops. His wife almost spills her tea. Good, that's done the trick. They will never consider me a plain old salaryman again. Or have I gone too far?

– Where? When? How?

– Not in Japan. It was Colombia. Before I started working in Mitsubishi. I arrived there without a visa and the immigration police threw me out of the country and they weren't very nice about it either.

Yamada-*san* looks a little relieved.

– Well, I suppose a visa mistake is not a terrible crime. Was it not the mistake of your tour guide or your travel agent?

– I didn't have a guide or a travel agent.

– Amazing. But what were you intending to do in Colombia?

I could say I was on my way to Tierra del Fuego by bus, but they might think I was exaggerating.

– I was on my way to … Brazil.

Yamada-*san* is beginning to look worried again. What sort of a salaryman is this Muruta-T, wandering about these faraway, dangerous places? I look at his face and decide I'd better back-peddle a little.

– I wished to visit a friend in São Paolo who was a research colleague when I was in Tokodai, I say, which was true, even if only a secondary purpose. But it has the right effect and Yamada-*san* looks more at ease.

– You need to be careful travelling around those places.

– Yes, of course. But this was before I entered Mitsubishi.

– Well, please do not go to Colombia again. You know that a Japanese company man was kidnapped there last year?

– I think I heard something about it. But the immigration police in Colombia are probably scarier than the guerrillas and the militias.

– In any case, please be careful when you go abroad. It is not just your own affair if something happens to you, you know. The company is also responsible.

– It seems you are a little different from the average salaryman, says the wife.

She is probably thinking that all foreigners have strange tales to tell, even those who live a quiet life in Yokohama and those who aren't *dry* like the foreigners she met in Tokyo.

I've probably scared off Miss Kekko. But I have the feeling she has been pushed into this meeting. She is not really interested in dating a foreigner. That's fine. I don't want to spend my Saturday nights discussing Italian handbags and foreign movies.

– Well, please take care of yourself in Japan, says Yamada-*san* when it is 8.45 and almost time to leave, according to the schedule prepared and agreed to ten weeks before and printed on the sheet folded in my pocket.

– Yes. I'll take care of myself.

I thank my hosts for the evening, walk back to the station and catch the 9.04 train home, as scheduled.

I'm glad that Yamada-*san* and his wife have now got a balanced view of Muruta-T. I'm also glad that things didn't get complicated with Miss Kekko – because I've someone else to meet.

It takes me some time to settle down after my pre-salaryman trip, to get used to staying put. Gradually I stop asking myself what I'm doing here, because this job gives the stability I sometimes wanted those times I was free, and it gives me a way to make a living, which was always a minor objective I had in the back of my mind. Even if I don't appreciate the finer things in the Mitsubishi culture, at least it's not a conventional job in a conventional company. I don't know how long this salaryman stint will last, but I may as well make the best of it while I'm here. I start digging out previous friendships, people I knew when I was in Tokodai. I'm just in time to catch Li because he is about to quit his job in Kawasaki. His company wasn't run like a primary school, he tells me, not like his lab in Tokodai. But because he was Chinese, his bosses only gave him boring tasks and didn't pay him much, even though he had a PhD. He finally decided to return to China. He has a good job waiting for him – assistant professor in Beijing University. We were both outsiders back in Tokodai, but in the company I think I'm getting a better deal than him. I tell him I will try to wangle a work trip to China and maybe we can meet again.

I contact Miyuki. I think she's surprised I didn't disappear without trace in Amazonia or Patagonia, never to show up in the Eastern world again. It was a possibility, I admit, but it didn't happen. She is impressed that I've found my way back to Tokyo and that I have a normal job at last, even if it is in a staid, traditional organisation.

Her part-time work is in the Japan International Cooperation Agency, a governmental organisation for supporting developing countries. She takes foreign trainees to research and education institutes in Tokyo, shows them around, makes sure they don't get lost. Some of them are hard to handle – they don't eat the local food, can't study on Fridays, want to know if their visa will allow them to do a bit of work on the side. I'm easier to handle. It's probably the salaryman training I'm getting from Mitsubishi.

– Next time you go on a trip, I'll come too, she says. As long as it is not Tierra del Fuego by bus.

It's not. It's only across the mountains to the Sea of Japan by train. At the New Year holidays we travel to the snowy coast of Ishikawa and walk along the winter beach, talking of families, parents and obligations because this is still an old-fashioned country. Her father is a traditional salaryman, her mother a traditional salaryman's wife and she grew up in a company apartment in the suburbs. But she is not much into traditional working styles and prefers the part-time job to work as an OL in some big corporation. I'm not a traditional salaryman, even if I am part of what is probably the largest and most traditional corporate group in Asia. I think she understands my strange logic – which is often more than I myself do.

At New Year she stays over in my apartment. I'm glad I am not living in the Mitsubishi dormitory because I would be breaking rules. I'm not sure about traditional family rules and parents, though. One day she'll introduce me to her traditional parents, she says. One day soon.

6

生兵法は大怪我のもと

Nama byoho wa okega no moto

Military tactics not carefully planned result in major casualties

I hear it first on the evening news. Our company has been found out, caught red-handed, exposed. Mitsubishi has been caught doing some deals with the *sokaiya*. The *sokaiya* are the racketeers who buy company stocks but don't wait for price rises or dividends to earn some profit. Instead, they attend the shareholders' annual general meeting and inform the company beforehand – some of the Important People in Head Office – that they plan to attend and that they have some difficult questions to ask, embarrassing things the Important People would rather not have to answer in front of all the big shareholders who might pull out their investments or might start asking awkward questions themselves. The *sokaiya* would, of course, be open to a little persuasion to keep their mouths shut – that is if the Important People think it worth their while to have a quiet, short, smoothly executed AGM. An Important Person in Head Office decided some years earlier it would be worth his while to do a little persuading and the *sokaiya* were so thankful that not only did they keep their mouths shut, they also marked the AGM date in their diaries and made meeting attendance and collection of that little bit of persuasion an annual event not to be missed no matter how busy they were.

We are not the only ones. Hitachi and Toshiba have also been caught out recently, but now the spotlight is on us. Our company president and the director of public relations appear on TV at a hastily convened press conference, apologising and bowing low, fifty-degree bows or even sixty, there's no excuse for it. They say that all necessary measures will be taken to ensure it never happens again and they bow again. The director of public prosecutions also believes there's no excuse for it. He investigates which laws have been broken and who will be prosecuted. An official corporate ethics committee decides on what punishment should be handed down because they have to make an example when a blue-chip, world-famous corporation is caught in the act. A few weeks after the news hits the headlines, the punishment is announced. Our company will be suspended from carrying out normal business for a period of one week. During that week, manufacturing, research and development, movement of personnel and other internal work may be carried out as normal, but no financial deals must be done, no business with clients, no sales meetings with customers. Head Office announces that the company will strictly observe the penalties imposed.

Shortly before the no-business week is due to begin, we receive details of how we should carry out no business during the week. There should be no discussions concerning prices and costs with anyone outside the company, no procurement of materials, no supplying of products of any type. The company intends to go even further: no meetings of any kind with outside parties are to take place during the week. We must not only accept the penalties, we must show how contrite we are and be seen to be humbly respecting the authorities. No emails are to be sent to anyone outside the company. No company name cards are to be given to anyone. No business-related phone calls are to be accepted.

– But what happens if we receive an urgent email from that company we've been in contact with about the new displays? Reisei-C asks. Do we just ignore it?

– The other companies read the newspapers, don't they? says Shinsetsu-GR. They should know the situation. If you get an email, send a brief reply stating that due to a legal requirement we cannot answer till the following week. That's all. Don't send any detailed reply. We don't want any emails going back and forth about the penalties and how they are being implemented.

Shinjin-T is thinking hard.

– What happens if someone loses his wallet with his business cards inside? The finder will have the cards and when he gives the wallet to the police they will also see the cards.

– Perhaps it would be best not to carry any cards at all during the week, says Shinsetsu-GR. Then you can be sure of not giving out a card by mistake.

It will be a relaxing week, I'm thinking, something different, and a change is as good as a holiday. It will be nice to postpone urgent business and not feel guilty, to purposely forget to keep a few extra business cards in my wallet, to be able to ignore emails, if they come.

But when the no-business week begins, it's not much different from normal in the research labs. At lunch I ask Reisei-C if that display company has been in touch. He says no, not yet, and they probably won't be, because they know about these things – weren't they themselves caught doing something naughty a year or two ago? They were part of a *dango* – a small group of like-minded companies who get together, become good friends and agree on reasonable prices in order to keep profits steady, none of this cut-throat competition that might be the ruin of them all. When the *dango* friends were caught out, the company presidents, who were also good friends, appeared on TV, apologised profusely and gave fifty-degree bows, there was no excuse for it. They humbly accepted the penalties handed down – fines and temporary suspension of business – and promised they would stop being good friends and start being rivals again. Riko-T says that with so many good friends among the companies this sort of thing is hard to stop and has been going on a long time.

During the no-business week I don't get telephone calls about important business or urgent emails to ignore, and besides the lack of commercials for our products on TV it is an anti-climax. The real non-action is taking place in the sales divisions, where some huge contracts are being postponed or even lost and our company is getting its knuckles rapped. No doubt we will feel the sting when the bi-annual bonuses are announced. But the earnest and penitent way our company is reacting to the punishment will send out the right signals to the public and maybe even gain some positive publicity – hey, people, anyone can go wrong once, can't they? Look how apologetic we are, fifty-degree bows by the top brass on national TV, no business for a whole week. Aren't we really a fine organisation after all? Yes, we are. We just went a little bit wrong and we are doing our best and more to get back onto the straight and narrow once again.

To make doubly certain we will never again go off the straight and narrow, the *Corporate Ethics Guidelines* booklet is distributed to everyone. The problem is that issuing ethics guidelines and actually implementing them are two different things. The *Guidelines* say that in April 1990 our company took the initiative and was a pioneer in introducing an ethics policy well ahead of other companies. In Chapter 4, Section 1, it says that *no gift may be offered without receiving the permission of the company.* If permission is granted, *it should be only a small gift appropriate to the season or occasion, the equivalent of a greeting. Deciding what is or is not an appropriate gift may be a difficult matter, since these things change with time; if the situation is not clear always consult your superior and obtain his permission.* I wonder if the Important Person in Head Office who gave those gifts to the *sokaiya* read the *Corporate Ethics Guidelines.* Perhaps he did; perhaps he even asked someone in Head Office for permission, but the someone was probably himself.

Chapter 3, Section 3 states that measures are being taken to prevent monopolistic cartels – *although, to our shame, our company recently violated this law with regard to bidding for a sewage disposal electrical equipment contract.*

Over the following months emails regularly come through from senior management telling us how to avoid unethical corporate behaviour and I'd like to hit the reply key and say, Give us a break, will you? Why should Head Office be lecturing us ordinary employees, lowly Ts and just a little less lowly Cs, telling us how to behave ourselves, when it is the Important People who were caught offering the corporate cookie jar to the *sokaiya*? It is us, lowly Ts and Cs, who should be lecturing the Important People, telling them to behave themselves and stop being such hypocrites. I don't hit the reply key because it's no use flaming the messenger.

The *Corporate Ethics Guidelines* and the emails will ensure that we will all be squeaky good from now on. And are we not already good corporate citizens? We donate to local charities, sponsor the summer fireworks festival and even help clean up our local river, don't we? Every year when the autumn comes and the typhoon rains are over, the Mitsubishi people join in the clean-up, collecting the plastic bags, rubber ducks and soccer balls that have fallen in over the previous year. The city council is pleased and gives Mitsubishi an honourable mention in the report on socially responsible companies. The local people who read the report or who pass by the river during the clean-up must think, What a fine company, a credit to our city and our country; they must be a fine bunch of salarymen working in those factories and offices. Our public relations department is pleased because they've got their money's worth already. But, to be honest, I should admit it is only the factory workers who are a fine bunch of salarymen – mainly a few senior employees who enjoy cleaning rivers and the young workers who are told by their bosses to do their duty as good citizens. We in the research labs are not asked to join in the clean-up – perhaps because the managers think we are too nerdy to get our hands muddied.

In the court case the following year, the errant manager from Head Office and the racketeer are found guilty and receive sentences of four months in prison but the sentences are suspended so they do not have to serve jail time. In Chapter 4, Section 1, the *Corporate Ethics Guidelines* state that according to Clause 78 of the Statutes of Employment anyone guilty of violating the rules concerning the giving and receiving of gifts will be dismissed. But since the errant manager was clearly a loyal Mitsubishi man in this case and had the interests of the company at heart, my colleagues say that demotion was more likely than dismissal.

The fuss over the *sokaiya* scandal passes quickly and it's back to the usual quiet days, writing software, testing it with data from the factories, going on the odd trip. I go to Nagoya once to see the world's only glass-walled elevator that looks out on rice paddies. No one tests the smoothness of the ride by putting a ten-yen coin on the floor as we glide upwards. The view of the rice fields is what counts. Next to the elevator is the world's most advanced spiral escalator. It sweeps upwards in a huge curve like a palatial stairway to heaven with silver steps that move. It is impressive, although it's not really spiral. But if we're looking for new customers with fat chequebooks and we are the only company in the world that makes escalators like this, then I suppose we can call it spiral rather than curved or twisted. Who would want to buy a twisted escalator even if the technology is the most advanced in the world?

Once a week we have our group meeting, sometimes to discuss our work, sometimes to hear what management are planning or whether the bonuses will be up or down. Shinsetsu-GR usually reserves a meeting room in advance because there are only three small rooms for the whole department of sixty people and there is always someone wanting to have a meeting. One week the competition for the rooms is stiffer than usual. All the rooms are occupied. Shinsetsu-GR says we can still have our meeting; the small rooms can be divided into even smaller meeting areas.

– We will share with the Numerical Control Group, he says. We will have the window side. The Numericals will have the door side.

He enters and tells the Numericals to shove over, politely, because we will be sharing the compartment. The Numericals separate the two tables, manoeuvre the whiteboard into the gap between the tables and we have two mini-compartments. It's a squeeze to get past the Numericals to the window side but we are used to squeezing into small spaces.

We sit down – anywhere will do for a group meeting, although the senior members have their preferred places. Shinsetsu-GR begins to talk, quietly, so as not to disturb the Numericals on the other side of the white-board, but the Numericals are not talking quietly. He has to raise his voice to be heard and it becomes a noisy little compartment.

– We will start with safety this week, he says. One or two of you use bicycles, so please pay attention. Someone from the power systems department was cycling last week with his umbrella up in the rain and ran into an elderly lady, who sprained her wrist. He has to bear her medical costs because he has no insurance. Personnel have decided that from now on everyone who commutes by bicycle must have insurance. It is not expensive, so please get insurance by the end of this month if you cycle. Furthermore, the gate guards have been instructed to report anyone seen cycling while holding an umbrella in one hand. Yes, I know everyone does it, but from now on Mitsubishi employees will get a warning if caught cycling with an umbrella up and their bicycle-parking permit may be revoked if they are caught twice. Any questions? None? Good. Next, I think we will skip the individual work reports this week because we have another pressing matter to discuss. The general manager has announced the lab income balance for the last year. As you know, we are expected to get two-thirds of our funds from the factories who want quick results they can apply to current products. The remainder comes from Head Office, who want glamorous ideas, the breakthroughs for products a few years down the line. The problem is that funding from factory commissions is now below 50 per cent. We have to increase our factory-commissioned work, appeal to the factories, and also decrease our breakthrough work.

Breakthroughs? I'm wondering what breakthroughs our group has achieved in the last year. Perhaps it was helping to make the elevators so smooth a coin standing on its edge would not fall over after zooming seventy floors up to the top of Landmark Tower at world record speed, although I think the elevator factory was responsible for that. In any case it doesn't sound like much of a breakthrough to me. Breakthroughs are probably in the eyes of the beholder. Or of Head Office.

The Numericals are still talking loudly on the other side of the whiteboard. I'm sure Shinsetsu-GR wishes they wouldn't talk so loudly and wonders why they can't be quiet like they are at their desks. But he doesn't ask them to pipe down. Nobody says anything. Everybody puts up with it. I'd like to ask why, with all the funds we have, we cannot afford an extra meeting room or two; why it is necessary to share a small compartment between two groups and have two people babbling away about different things at the same time; and why we seem to have almost limitless budgets for buying computers and software but have almost nothing for buying space. That is what I'd like to ask. But those would be dumb questions because everyone knows space is a priceless commodity.

Shinsetsu-GR continues, his voice a little louder so as to be heard above the Numericals.

– The general manager believes the shortage of factory-based commissions is due to an information deficit. Information about the lab is not getting through to the plants and factories. They are not aware of our expertise. To remedy this situation, each department and each group in the lab is required to define its identity. We must list up our areas of expertise and submit them to the general manager within two weeks. With clearly defined expertise and identity, we can attract factory commissions. Today I would like to prepare our list.

The Numericals on the other side of the whiteboard finish their noisy meeting and the room is peaceful with no half-disguised contests to see who can talk loudest. Shinsetsu-GR writes *Machine Intelligence Group Identity: Summary of Expertise* on the whiteboard and we start thinking about our expertise. What have we got?

I have no suggestions. Nobody else has any suggestions either. Everyone is quiet, too modest to shout out his expertise. It's often like this at meetings. We don't talk till we have to.

– Come on now, everyone, Shinsetsu-GR says. Have we no expertise at all? Just tell me some areas you work in and we'll see if we can make them into a list of topics. Majime-T, your expertise is?

– Network communications.

– Good, at least we have something to start with. But I think network communications may be difficult to grasp. We need something clear and descriptive that even the factory people can understand. How about *interactive network control protocol specification definition languages*? Yes, that will do for starters. Something everyone can grasp. Now, anything else?

– Intelligent elevators, says Riko-T.

– That's good, but let us make it more descriptive. Let us say *programmable in-house mover signal technologies.* That should do the trick. It should let the factories know what we can do. Now, Muruta-T, can you give us a simple description of your expertise? It should be something that reflects your abilities, including the dissertation you wrote in Tokodai and the paper that was published in the US and it should not sound too complicated, nor too easy.

– *Configuration-oriented automated reasoning algorithms using forward and backward propagation heuristics.*

– Sounds good. That should impress the general manager. I will add that to our list. And Shinjin-T? Have you anything to add?

– *Realtime operating system kernel architecture.*

– That will do fine. Not too simple, not too complex.

Shinsetsu-GR adds a few more examples of our expertise in easy-to-grasp techno-babble. Soon our Machine Intelligence Group has got an identity that anyone can understand and if anyone can't understand it then at least our group manager, Shinsetsu-GR, can and he is the one that counts. He is pleased with the afternoon's work.

– That's good. I believe we have an identity now, distinct from the other groups in the department and different from the factory development centres. I will pass our list of expertise to the department manager. With a few more commissions from the factories we can proceed to achieve breakthroughs in our domains of expertise.

The meeting drags on and by the time we get back to our desks the bells are ding-donging for the end of the official workday. I say *osaki-ni* early because it is Wednesday, no-overtime day, and I don't want to wait around for the 'Tennessee Waltz' and 'Auld Lang Syne' to remind me to go home early. I head home thinking of techno-babble and breakthroughs. I'm also thinking of expertise because I need some – not about techno-babble but about something more important – expertise on how to manage delicate relations with traditional Japanese parents because Miyuki will introduce me soon. I have an American friend who has expertise in this area; he has even achieved a breakthrough and he doesn't talk techno-babble. I'll consult with him.

Dave has burnt and built romantic bridges across the ocean several times. He learned the hard way when some of his romantic bridges fell down. The last fell badly when he mismanaged his girlfriends' telephone numbers. Someone-old found out about someone-new and came to visit while someone-new was moving into his apartment. Dishes and plates flew and cool Californian Dave lost his cool and threatened to call the police, which further annoyed someone-old who pulled the phone wires out of the wall before bidding Dave and someone-new goodnight. But he learned his lesson and not only is he careful about managing his telephone numbers now, he is about to make his new bridge permanent by marrying Kyoko next spring. There will never be plates and dishes flying in his apartment again.

We sit down over a beer and he tells me how he bridged the Pacific and tackled the traditional-parents problem. Kyoko had been afraid hers might not approve of an international liaison. Dave believed that Kyoko was old enough to make up her own mind about such things and parents shouldn't matter that much, but Kyoko said she had to maintain good family relations in all cases and it was best she keep things quiet. She did so until one day they walked out of the station and who did they run into but her parents. Introductions followed, mixed with frowns, mixed with smiles. That evening Kyoko knew she had some explaining to do. If only Dave had had his name cards with him. If only he had not been wearing a T-shirt and shorts. If only he had been wearing long trousers and a shirt. A necktie would have been good. And perhaps even a jacket. It may have been summer but, as our Mitsubishi exercise drill sergeant shouts to the world every morning, clothes are the window to the heart.

Her father did not approve of his daughter walking around the city with a foreigner with naked knees, a flimsy T-shirt, without a name card and maybe he didn't even own a suit. Still, times were changing and he would think over the matter. In order to think it over he would need to see Dave's curriculum vitae or at least a short résumé. Kyoko asked Dave for his résumé, a summary of his background, family and work history.

– Résumé? I'm not looking for a job. And what has my family got to do with it?

Kyoko said that her father was old-fashioned and the résumé was to help him come to a decision. Her father said, *uma no hone* – a horse's bones: if you don't know anything about the horse's bones you have to assume the worst – that the horse has doubtful origins.

Dave said he didn't feel like a horse and his bones were fine, but after some female persuasion he provided a short résumé, which Kyoko submitted to her father. It must have been a good résumé because a week later she was given permission to continue the relationship, provided Dave learned to dress better. The horse's bones were satisfactory.

– So, be prepared to be asked about your background, he tells me. Otherwise they will assume the worst about the horse's bones. Dress up rather than down and don't say too many negative things about anything, especially your company.

◆◆◆

The telephone call comes through from Miyuki. Would I be able to meet her parents next Saturday afternoon? The west exit to Shinjuku Station? For an hour or two?

I think about clothes being the window to the heart but it would be false to dress up too much. I wear my usual weekend gear – a T-shirt and jeans – but no naked knees. That will do.

When we meet, Miyuki's father is wearing a suit, white shirt and tie. They bow, I bow and Miyuki announces that we will go to a hotel restaurant for coffee. This is the international age and a *tatami*-floored teahouse with green tea and tradition will have to wait for another day.

– Does your father always dress up like that? I quietly ask Miyuki.

– Usually he does. He has been a salaryman his entire career. He would not feel dressed without a suit.

I walk with her father but he is not used to making small talk with a foreigner. It's probably the first time in his life to even talk to a foreigner. I quit the small talk and try work talk.

– Miyuki tells me you are a department manager in the news section of NHK. It sounds very important.

– Yes, it is an important job, I suppose. We have high standards to maintain. We have to be better than the commercial TV and radio. I do my best.

– I listen to the NHK news often to hear what perfect Japanese is like.

– It is not always perfect. NHK is not what it was a couple of decades ago. I'm afraid the young employees nowadays do not have a mastery of the language any more. I often have to correct their errors.

We sit down in the restaurant. Miyuki's mother says, Please teach Miyuki good English. I say, Of course I will, even though she doesn't need any teaching because she already speaks it fluently. But at least her mother is not dropping hints that I keep my big foreign hands off her innocent daughter, even if they are not so big. That is as positive a sign as I can expect.

I tell them where I am from and what I work at. I skip the parts of my career that might be difficult to explain, like those extended periods when I found better things to do with my time than go off to work everyday.

I tell them I was a hardworking graduate student in Tokodai. Her father says, yes, it is a famous university and having a degree from Tokodai is a good thing, a very good thing. He himself went to Sophia, a famous private university in Tokyo, and he knows that the Mitsubishi employees all went to famous universities, Kyoto and Osaka and even Tokyo University – Todai itself, and I'm wondering if there is anyone in this whole damn country who didn't go to a famous university and if there are any non-famous universities at all out there. I ask Miyuki about it afterwards. Yes, she says, there are non-famous universities. She went to one of them.

Really? A real, run-of-the-mill, non-famous university?

Yes. And she even graduated from that non-famous university.

I'm impressed. It's the first time I've found a real non-famous university graduate and that's something.

Her mother is talking to me.

– Miyuki tells me you visited many faraway countries but you found Japan to be the best.

– Did I? Oh, yes. Of course, Japan is the best in some ways. I mean most ways – except it is a little crowded sometimes.

– Faraway countries may be interesting, says her mother, but all sorts of strange things happen in faraway countries. You never know what will happen if you go far away. I think home is best.

– Yes, I agree that strange things can happen in faraway places, but it depends where home is.

– And you would like to live in Japan?

I reflect for a moment. To be honest, I wouldn't. I'd much prefer to live in a little oasis in the desert of northern Chile, in a village called San Pedro de Atacama, in a little adobe house near the plaza or at the edge of town with a view out over the empty landscape towards the Valley of the Moon and the endless salt flats to the south, or towards the snow-capped peaks of the Andes to the east where wisps of white smoke rise from the Licancabur and Lascar volcanoes into the bluest sky in the world, and if San Pedro isn't enough, I could take a bus ride down to the Pacific at Antofagasta or over the mountains to Argentina or Bolivia like before and breathe some of that clear Andean air, drink that Chilean red and life would be easy. But I need more than clear desert air and views of snow-capped volcanoes to live. I have to eat. Japan will do.

– Yes, I say, I'd like to live in Japan. And work for Mitsubishi. For a while.

Her father says Mitsubishi is an important company and they surely need foreigners who speak the language and can work like all the other Mitsubishi salarymen. By the way, can I work like the other Mitsubishi salarymen?

– Sometimes it's difficult. It took me a while to get used to the lunches. The long rows in the canteen with everyone in the same uniform, quietly eating the same lunches from the same boxes remind me of –

– It is probably like our canteen in NHK, says her father. What do they remind you of?

Oops. The chain gang canteen might not be the best comparison. Neither would the boarding school cafeteria. But the brave salaryman asking, *Please can I have less rice?* might be okay.

– It reminds me of … of big helpings of rice. I once asked them for a smaller portion but they didn't understand how any salaryman could want less rice.

– Well, if that is all that bothers you, I'm sure you will fit in very well, says her mother. And if you come to visit our apartment, we won't give you too much rice. Next time, please come and eat at our home. It's just a small apartment but it only takes forty minutes by train from Shinjuku.

– I will look forward to that. Thank you for the invitation.

As we walk back to the train station, Miyuki says her parents are really quite modern, after all. They understand that a foreigner has to overcome some obstacles in a big company like Mitsubishi and that not everyone likes large bowls of rice. More importantly, they don't require me to submit papers about the horse's bones, *uma no hone.* Just as well, because there are a few cultural skeletons hidden in my *uma-no-hone* closet. I'd like to keep them there.

7

袖摺り合うも他生の縁

Sode suriau mo tasho no en

Even a chance meeting is decreed by destiny

We decide to skip the wedding ceremony entirely. Who needs a wedding ceremony? Love and enthusiasm are enough for us. We don't want to mortgage our future with a no-expenses-spared wedding spectacular designed to impress relatives, friends and colleagues who don't really want to be impressed.

But throwing out all the traditions and ceremonies suddenly seems to be overdoing it. We compromise and organise a small luncheon party. It will be low-key and relaxed, with just a few friends. We send out the invitations, then some more. Soon we have over a dozen and it's not as low-key as we would have liked. At least we'll skip the complicated present giving and taking. But Miyuki says her friends want to give us something – it wouldn't do to deny them the chance. We end up with a pile of standard congratulatory envelopes with the standard 5,000- or 10,000-yen notes inside, and in return we give them the mandatory reverse-presents we have prepared. At least there will be no long-winded, formal speeches. But one of my colleagues feels he has to say something, then everyone feels they too have to say something and we end up with a bundle of speeches. It's hard to be non-conformist.

Miyuki's mother doesn't have many requests. All she asks is that we don't marry on a *butsu-metsu* day because it's the unluckiest day in the Buddhist cycle and it wouldn't do any good at all to start out on such a day. We carefully avoid *butsu-metsu* but don't avoid the torrid heat of late

July. We go out into the scorching sunlight to be photographed. I stand wiping the sweat from my forehead, trying to smile for the camera but squinting in the glare. We retreat to a cool studio where the real photographs are taken. They give me a *hakama* and *haori*, the samurai suit for formal occasions. I struggle into it and it feels more comfortable than it looks. Miyuki goes off to a special dressing room and takes almost an hour to change into a brightly coloured kimono. Her face is powdered white as snow and an ornate wig covers her already thick black hair. My cherry-blossom-in-kimono has arrived. We're ready for a stage version of *Shogun*. It pleases her parents to have some tradition and probably makes up for the shortage of ceremonies. I wonder if it makes up for the shock of their daughter marrying a foreigner.

The company give us the official marriage present of 20,000 yen, enough for one night in a good hotel, but it's the thought that counts. I get the official honeymoon leave of three days, which can be added to the normal leave, as long as I don't take more than a couple of weeks in total. We take a train west to the Seto Inland Sea, island-hopping to Shikoku – not so exotic but some non-exotic travel will do this time. We watch the waves of the Pacific roll up on the beaches of Kochi, hallowed ground for a Mitsubishi man because this is where Yataro Iwasaki was born and where the three-diamond Mitsubishi symbol originated. I forget about Iwasaki-*san* and Mitsubishi because I've better things to think about now.

We take slow trains through the mountains, along the tumbling river in Oboke gorge, staying in mountain villages so different from the concrete city we have come from. We stop off at friends who take us to the local summer festival, where there's music in the warm night air; people walk by in *yukata* gowns, fireworks crackle and sparkle and the *obon* dance begins. Old-fashioned music blares from speakers dangling from trees and street lights and everyone joins in, young and old, because it doesn't matter if you've never tried the *obon* dance before, hands to the left, one step forward, hands to the right, one step forward, follow the old man in front even if he's only walking because it doesn't matter on a hot summer festival night when you've just married the woman you love and life is good. Who cares about the Mitsubishi world on a night like this as we all go round in the circle and the music plays over and over and the air is heavy with summer.

◆◆◆

I return to the company wondering what changes will come with marriage. The personnel department add Miyuki's name to the company insurance policy using the standard Japanese name order: Muruta Miyuki, but they insist on keeping my name in the foreign order, even when it is written according to the Japanese pronunciation: *Niaru Muruta.*

Riko-T tells me they will put a note on the department noticeboard.

– It is a company tradition to put up a small announcement when employees marry so that colleagues can offer their congratulations.

– Sure, I'm used to company traditions by now.

He'll write a little background information in the notice – nothing personal or private, just where and when the happy couple met, where we dated, where the sparks ignited, who proposed, when and how it was done, who gets up first in the morning, as much detail as possible – nothing personal or private, of course.

I tell him I'll consult with Miyuki to find out what we'd like reported. She will know what to say.

– Just tell them we met coming out of the *kabuki* theatre on a rainy night in Ginza, nothing more, she says.

– But didn't we meet at that Russian restaurant in Shibuya?

– Ginza sounds better. More high class. The Mitsubishi people will admire a colleague who goes to watch *kabuki* in Ginza more than one who goes eating borscht in Shibuya.

– Okay. I just hope they don't ask me about the *kabuki.*

When the notice goes up, it gives the official line about the rainy night in Ginza, about love blossoming under the cherry trees of Yoyogi Park and about the international age we're in, with knots being tied across continental and cultural divides. The notice has the Mitsubishi logo on top and is stamped and approved by the personnel department and my department manager. It states that anyone feeling so inclined is invited to sign on the attached sheet to express his or her congratulations to the newly wedded couple and to join in making a small contribution for a gift. There is no problem with the notice except that it is just across from the poster about a company-sponsored introduction agency that helps shy or workaholic employees to graduate from the singles dormitory. If you only glance at the noticeboards as you walk by, as most people do, you would think they make a set – *before* and *after* posters.

Riko-T brings me the gift a few weeks later. It's a company envelope with a neat bundle of 1,000-yen notes and a list of all the people who wish to congratulate us. We buy telephone cards with our names printed on them, the standard return present, put each card in a neat little envelope and send them off. Finally the gift-giving business is complete and I can relax.

But not just yet.

Riko-T approaches me and asks me what night would be suitable for the *storm*. Storm? Does he mean typhoon? How do you choose a night for a storm or typhoon?

– It is a tradition, he says.

Oh no, not another tradition. What will this one involve?

– After someone marries, his colleagues celebrate by storming his home some night when he is not expecting it. I'm afraid there will be much noise during the *storm*, something the newlyweds will never forget. But it is exciting.

I bet it is, especially if the storm happens when the newlyweds are in bed, contemplating the birds and the bees.

– Normally, he says, no warning is given before the storm but I am telling you because you may not know about the tradition.

He is giving me advance notice and is even asking permission. Nice of him. I tell him I will let him know in a day or so.

Miyuki says it's not a Japanese tradition. It is a Mitsubishi one and it sounds unpleasant.

– Tell them we would really prefer to skip the storm.

I don't think Riko-T wants the storm either, but he wouldn't like me to feel left out or to feel I'm missing any of those old-time Mitsubishi customs, good or bad.

– We are not sure about the storm just now, I tell him, and my neighbour is a bit sensitive about noise. Once he complained to the landlord, so we have to be very careful. Why don't we cancel the storm and have a small party instead one Sunday afternoon? No noise, no attack, no storm. Just some rice crackers and beer that won't scare my neighbour or my landlord.

We won't mind skipping the storm, honest, even if it is a time-honoured company tradition. We'll survive without it, somehow or other.

– Fine. We'll cancel the storm. No problem.

Anshin-T comes to my desk one day. We occasionally pass each other on the way to the canteen but otherwise we have hardly spoken in a year – which is a good thing because it means my apartment is quiet, the landlord is behaving himself and so am I. He tells me now that I'm married I am entitled to apply for a company family apartment like the other married employees. The family apartments are not like the dormitories. They don't have managers checking that nobody is oversleeping, that sheets have been changed, that the air conditioner is set below the official temperature or that there's nothing strange hidden in the closet. Nor are they timber-framed, noise-generating, neighbour-baiting rabbit hutches that require the company to act as guarantor before they rent to a foreigner. Anshin-T shows me lists of available apartments and I choose one a reasonable distance from the company, bigger and newer than the place I've lived in up to now. It is a concrete building so it won't be noisy no matter who is living upstairs, and the walls are solid so neighbours next door won't be disturbed. We move in, get used to the area and I begin to enjoy the new turn my life has taken. I've realised the Japanese Dream: a pretty wife, a job in a big corporation and a small but cosy company apartment in the concrete suburbs. Who needs an over-sized Western house with a flashy car in the driveway when Mitsubishi housing and a bicycle to get to the station will do just fine?

A man from Head Office with a heavy briefcase and a senior face arrives one day in our department, has a brief word with Shinsetsu-GR, and my life in Mitsubishi is never quite the same again. Watanabe-B is department manager class, which means senior management. He is not an actual department manager but he acts as though he is, so I call him Wanabe-B. It is unusual among the non-assertive managers of Mitsubishi to meet someone who actually behaves like a leader and that may have worked against him so that he hasn't risen higher yet. But whatever else, he has style. Over the next couple of years I learn more about *salaryman style* from Wanabe-B than all the salarymen I've met in Mitsubishi up to now put together. When he sits down to give me the news that day, I know he means business.

– An international research programme on next-generation products is being planned by the Ministry of International Trade and Industry, he says. Our participation in this NGP programme has been approved by the honourable Komon-H, Director of Research and Development. Our academic adviser is a professor from the University of Tokyo. We would earnestly request your cooperation in putting an international consortium together.

I understand this to be a polite way of giving an order. But I wouldn't mind a change, especially to a project important enough to be organised by the Ministry and to have a professor from Todai as adviser.

I had read that the Ministry of International Trade and Industry (MITI) was the key player in guiding the national economy from its rebirth in the 1950s to its status as the world's second-largest economy. In reality MITI acted more as facilitator than leader, encouraging industries and companies that were capable of growth, ensuring healthy competition and overseeing change in declining industries. Over the years MITI has provided funding for selected national projects, such as this NGP programme that I am about to work in, and it continues to do so under its new title, the Ministry of Economy, Trade and Industry (METI), which it adopted in 2001. Participation in national projects is optional but companies that have strong ties with the ministries, particularly those who depend on government contracts for much of their income, would not reject a Ministry invitation without good reason. Mitsubishi has always had good relations with the government, dating back to 1874 when Iwasaki offered his ships to the military, so our Director of R&D is an enthusiastic supporter of this project.

– If you agree, you will be acting as my assistant, Wanabe-B says, not waiting for me to agree. First, we need to prepare a project plan and contact potential partners in Europe and the US. Then we will visit several companies overseas. As an English-speaker, your assistance would be appreciated. I will send you background material tomorrow and you can prepare the necessary documents. I expect to depart for Europe and the US within two weeks.

Big corporations move quickly when the Important People decide to move. Shinsetsu-GR is informed of the change. He will not be my boss any longer but he doesn't object because Wanabe-B is department manager class from Head Office and he is used to sudden changes by now.

– Do your best, he says.

I do my best for Wanabe-B. He is from Hokkaido in the north, snow country. He has been in the company almost thirty years and is proud of it. He knows everything worth knowing about Mitsubishi but don't ask him about computers and all the new technologies that weren't even dreamt of when he joined. Those things are for me to know about. He will look after the rest.

I write up a research plan based on drafts from the Todai professor and our partner companies in Japan – Nissan, Fuji Xerox and the two largest construction companies in the country, Shimizu and Kajima. Our project will investigate next-generation home electronics, cars and buildings, which will be safe, intelligent, easy to use and easy to dispose of when no longer useful. This will all be achieved by gathering the knowledge lying around in people's heads, particularly the Mitsubishi heads in the factories and the Todai heads in Tokyo University. After we collect all the knowledge, we will put it in neat computer programs and knowledge bases, ready to use when needed, and companies like us who get started before the others will have a bright future. It's all a little too good to be true, but research proposals are supposed to promise the earth and sky to impress everyone, at least at the beginning.

Two weeks after that meeting with Wanabe-B, we take off on the first of many trips, introducing our project and our company to managers from Paris to Detroit and Helsinki to Sydney. We start by visiting the Eurocrats in Brussels. We stay in the Hotel Metropole, marvelling at the antiquated elevator cages and the old furniture.

– Mitsubishi should sell more to the Belgians, says Wanabe-B. They are still using nineteenth-century technology. I'll have to report this to Head Office.

The Eurocrats hold seminars about their own research programme, which will include, for the first time, joint projects with Japan and North America. They announce the funding they have available and the requirements for getting it. We hear this information second-hand. We are not allowed to attend any of the seminars because we are outsiders, non-Europeans, organisationally speaking. We don't complain. We wait in the lounge till the seminars are over and talk to anyone who wants to talk to us. Any takers for our project? No qualifications necessary – just a big-name company required, the bigger the better.

We find a few takers – a scientist from Siemens, a research manager from Philips and a few Finnish engineers. Siemens and Philips look good, and Wanabe-B wouldn't mind having the Finns on board since they come from the north, snow country, like his home in Japan. The problem is that the Finns only work for small fry – a little company we never heard of, called Nokia. Originally it was in the tree-chopping business, they say, used to make paper and rubber boots, now is into televisions and communications.

– Sorry, never heard of you, we tell them. But we'll keep your name cards anyway.

They would all like to join our project but they cannot make promises till Brussels decides who will get funding.

– We understand, we tell them. Do your best and we might meet again, in Tokyo, at the Brussels Metropole with the antiquated elevator cages, or who knows where.

I talk with Wanabe-B afterwards as we flick through the business cards we have collected. He thinks we will get a few partners, maybe a few big companies with lots of potential, certainly more potential than that little Finnish outfit with the funny name – what was it called?

– Nokia.

We reflect on how hard it seems to be for the Europeans to get funding. Where we come from, it is easy, once your company is big. The Ministry in Tokyo trusts the big-name companies like Mitsubishi because big is beautiful, in corporate Japan at least. I wonder if the Ministry trusts us too much. But we don't complain. We are happy to have funding to fly here and there, business class all the way, good hotels and conference rooms to impress the important people who might want to talk to us. I'm happy with the change of scene. After the first year or two in Mitsubishi, I was beginning to feel I had become a nobody, beginning to think about moving on to somewhere else, but now I've suddenly taken a step up in the world, even if I am only Wanabe-B's sidekick.

We fly across the Atlantic, where it is harder to drum up interest. MITI tries to help by announcing they will fund American companies who wish to join any of their projects, because the Ministry is still rolling in yen from the affluent eighties. The Americans are suspicious. The *Wall Street Journal* calls these next-generation products a Japanese Trojan horse. Watch those Japanese industrialists, they say, they're after our technology once again, our bright ideas, because all bright ideas come from America, don't they? The Americans have a simple solution to the Japanese Trojan horse. Watch out for Japanese bearing gifts, accept funding from no one, don't give US government financial support to anyone and don't encourage anyone to join those MITI-supported projects. If an American company wants to join, fine, let them join, but they will be on their own. And there will be no gifts, no Trojan horses.

Wanabe-B tackles the Trojan horse image problem by getting his boss's boss, the honourable Komon-H, to sign letters, written by me. We send them off to Komon-H's important friends, who are US company directors or university professors. Our letter is full of buzzwords like synergy, trans-national collaboration and return on investment. A few of the big guns are willing to talk to us. We visit United Technologies in Connecticut, a General Motors subsidiary in Michigan, then Berkeley and Stanford on the west coast. They are polite and interested in our work and not under the thumbs of the bureaucrats in Washington. I off-load some of the stack of brochures and papers I have been dragging around, glad to lighten my load, and they take us out to lunch.

– Keep us informed, they say. Let us know what's going on, but things are tight. No promises about joining. But let's keep in touch. Drop by next time you're in the States.

– Yes, we'll drop by next time. We'll keep in touch.

They give me a pile of brochures and my load ends up heavier than before. Wanabe-B agrees to share some of the burden – the thin brochures with colour pictures and few words.

He changes his style when we are with foreigners, real foreigners who live in foreign countries and work for foreign companies. He suddenly becomes quiet and hesitant like a normal salaryman overseas. I like him when we're with foreigners, real foreigners. After brief introductions in English, he talks to me in his own language, gives long-winded statements I can't make sense of, then taps my arm.

– Translate.

– Yes, Watanabe-B. Here goes.

I talk away. I talk about what I think he said, what he might have said or what he should have said. That's the beauty of being an interpreter for Wanabe-B. Though he knows basic English, he doesn't care how I interpret his carefully considered, strategic ramblings. I can say almost anything I want. I can even leave Wanabe-B out of the discussions for a while and he doesn't mind. He likes a break so that he can think of new things to say. He likes having a sidekick interpreter whose arm he can tap and say, Translate, because it makes him feel like an important international dignitary, not just a salaryman trying to flog a project. And I like playing interpreter. I feel important because I'm the only one present who understands, more or less, what is being said by both sides. It's a change from communicating with computers all day back in the office. The only thing I don't like is his arm-tap that doesn't do my ego much good because it seems to say, Do your party piece, boy!

But he doesn't kick.

For the average salaryman sent out into the big wide world, far away from company and country, the world is a very foreign place. No one speaks his language, few places stock the food he likes, and the foreign natives often misunderstand, but politeness requires that he refrain from telling them they have misunderstood. Wanabe-B is trying to break out of this mould, bravely going where the project requires him to go, armed only with a video camera and a sidekick interpreter who will help him out in difficult situations. But he is traditional enough to pay homage to expatriates holding the flag for company and country in far-off climes.

Chuzai-*san* from the London office takes us to dinner and tells us where the London Japan Centre is located, in case we are feeling homesick for *yakisoba* noodles or want to read the *Asahi Shimbun*. Wanabe-B says he's doing fine without *yakisoba* and the *Asahi*.

Chuzai-*san* asks how things are back in the home country. Wanabe-B gives him the news.

– The good old days are gone. It seems only a few short years ago that the economy was growing and growing, and my job of looking after clients seemed set to continue another decade. It was hard work then but at night we would adjourn to some high-class club in Ginza. Hard work, hard play, that's the way it was. Ah, those Ginza nights …

– Ah, yes, the old days, says Chuzai-*san*. Hard work in Head Office, golf weekends in Chiba, and he has that faraway look in his eyes, remembering his old desk in Head Office and golfing buddies in Chiba.

– And the trains always arrived on time, he says. Not like London. Life was good back then. The old times just a few short years ago.

I'd like to join in and reminisce about my old times a few short years ago, but my reminiscences would be out of place. They wouldn't be about my desk in Head Office, golf in Chiba or nights in Ginza. They'd surely think me an odd sort of salaryman if I started talking about watching the moonrise over the Andes from a café in San Pedro de Atacama, sipping Chilean wine in the cool desert evening.

Chuzai-*san* drops us at the airport next day. Wanabe-B sees a receptionist stepping over a rope partition, low enough for it to be almost touching the floor. He frowns and shakes his head.

– A British Airways receptionist! A Japan Airlines employee would never do that. She would always go around the end of the partition.

– Sounds like a waste of effort, I say.

– What is the rope for, if not to go around?

– Just to separate the two areas. Japan is too formal.

– But Westerners have formalities too.

– Like what?

– Like … for example, don't Europeans say it is bad manners to make noise when you eat noodles?

– Well, I don't mind people slurping their noodles. We say it's bad manners because we think humans shouldn't make noise like animals do when they're eating.

– Animals don't make noise eating.

– Yes, they do. Pigs make lots of noise eating.

– Pigs are good animals.

– They're dirty.

– You get lots of vitamins from pork, you know. It's good for you, he says, and I remember how he often orders pork for dinner.

We're at the check-in counter and we stop discussing pigs.

Next day at lunch Wanabe-B notices I haven't touched the meat on my plate.

– Muruta-T, don't you like good meat? I thought all Westerners were meat-eaters.

– I don't like the fatty parts. Anyway the fat is no good for you.

– Nonsense! Who ever said that? The best meat always has about 10 per cent fat. That's why Kobe beef is so famous. Ten per cent. That's why they feed the cattle on beer. You know they feed the cattle beer, don't you?

– Yes I do. It's one of the first things we learned in language school: Kobe cattle drink beer.

– A little fat makes the meat taste better. Ten per cent. But, you know, meat-eating can be a dangerous thing. Until the mid-nineteenth century, when the Americans forced our country to open its ports for trade, no meat was eaten in Japan and we had no trouble with foreign countries.

– How about the *eta* in Tokyo? They were meat-eaters, weren't they?

– They were just the bottom of society. No samurai ate meat. But after the Americans came and meat became more common, we began military expansion. The meat-eating culture makes people hunters, you see. We used to be a non-meat-eating society. We were farmers. Farmers don't need to chase and conquer. Hunters do. I believe that …

He bites into a chunk of pork.

– I believe that most of the world's conflicts are due to meat-eaters. Hunters. Now if only we remained as farmers, like we were before the foreigners came and made us eat meat.

– What about all the wars before the foreigners came?

– They were only about who was ruling who. Not really about conquering territory.

Soon we have a group of foreign companies and universities who want to join our project – IBM France, Cambridge University, the Fraunhofer Institute in Stuttgart, and some Finnish, Swiss and North American companies. We didn't get Siemens and Philips after all, and we just didn't click with that Finnish outfit, Nokia, who think they'll succeed in the communications business. Fat chance they'll have against the big boys like us in Mitsubishi.

We have our consortium. Now we need a name.

– Our work is about organising knowledge. We should call it *knowledge systematisation*, says our academic mentor from Todai.

– Sounds too complicated, says Wanabe-B. Can't we shorten it?

– How about *know-sys?*

We consult with our European partners, some of whom are classical scholars as well as manufacturing specialists. Why don't we spell it *Gnosis*, they say, which is Greek for knowledge inspired from above? We will be inspired with knowledge from the manufacturing god. There has to be a manufacturing god if we believe in manufacturing. We believe, and Gnosis is born. With newfound faith, we get to work.

Wanabe-B stays late in the office every night, making preparations for meetings and overseas trips, and shifting all the foreign reports and letters to my desk.

– Could you please find out what is in the reports, write it all down in plain, simple Japanese and have it on my desk by lunchtime?

He has bought me dinner often enough on the trips, so I don't complain. Still, there's no need to rush.

– Sure, Watanabe-B. I'll have it done by … let me see. How about the day after tomorrow?

Wanabe-B knows that foreigners move to a different rhythm. The day after tomorrow will do.

He is a non-conformist at heart and I admire him for it. I try to imitate him, though I don't have his style. When the accounting department give us instructions on how to fill out the time sheets for each working hour of each working day of the year – this is a project sponsored by the Ministry, remember – I wish I could tell them what to do with their silly, time-wasting time sheets, but I don't say anything. Wanabe-B, however, decides out loud he will tell them what to do with the time-wasting time sheets. He summons Kanryo-C of the accounting department.

– Why do I have to write my time sheets for the whole year? I've already submitted the totals for each month!

– Sorry, but that is the way it has been decided. It has always been that way for national projects. In order to get funding, we need reports for every month and we also need details for each day spent working on the project.

– Who ever said it was necessary to fill out all the hours for each day?

– That's the rule. It was decided by the Ministry.

– It's a silly rule.

– We have to obey the rules.

– Look, Kanryo-C, you won't get fired over it, so just refuse to do it! That will make those Ministry guys change their minds.

I feel like applauding him, *banzai, Wanabe-B,* but this is not the time for a lowly T to join the fray.

– Please, Watanabe-B, we have already got time sheets from employees on other Ministry projects. We just need yours.

– Okay, okay. But can I at least do it on my computer?

– No. I am afraid you must handwrite everything. Using a ballpoint pen. No pencils allowed. In black ink only. I am afraid the ones you did before in blue ink must be redone. And no corrections of any type are allowed. If there is any error you must rewrite the full sheet. You must sign each sheet to indicate that you have carried out to the best of your ability all the stated work during the stated hours.

This is too much for me.

– But, Kanryo-C, how can I honestly say I've worked all the stated hours? It was your department that decided in advance how many hours each of us worked. I haven't worked the hours stated in the sheets!

– The figures are based on our estimates. Just sign, please.

He is giving me short shrift. I don't have the power of Wanabe-B. I'm only a lowly T. Okay. Even if it's all fiction. I'll sign.

Wanabe-B thinks it's worse than fiction.

– Bureaucracy gone mad, he says. Just to satisfy those mandarins in the Ministry of International Trade and Industry. Maybe I'll call up the Ministry and tell them what I think of their stupid rules.

– No, please don't do that, says Kanryo-C, looking quite worried. That would make things very difficult. All administrative correspondence with the Ministry should go through my department. It's a rule.

– Okay, okay. I give up. I'll do it.

– Your cooperation is highly appreciated, says Kanryo-C, and he looks relieved as he heads back to his desk.

– Or maybe I'll get someone else to do it, Wanabe-B mumbles, when Kanryo-C is out of sight.

Well, you'd better not ask me, I think to myself, because if you do, I'll tell you what you can do with your time sheets. Writing my own and signing my name to all those hours I haven't worked is plenty for me.

– I'll bring the time sheets home with me tonight, Wanabe-B says. The wife will fill them in for me. She has nothing else to do.

The months fly by. Wanabe-B works hard, delegating the administration tasks to the accounting department, the time sheets to his wife, the international and technical matters to me, and the research to Riko-T, who has been drafted in to help run the project. Ueda-KS, recently transferred from Osaka, joins us and we now have an official group, known as the NGP Group, managed by Wanabe-B. Overall, he is a good manager, his strong points being building strategic relationships, going on foreign trips and delegating things he doesn't understand to others. He refrains from giving his opinions on the time sheet rules to the Ministry people and builds some ministerial relationships. One day he announces he will be attending an important conference in California.

– The Ministry have requested me to, eh, lead the national delegation to the Next-Generation Products Conference, he says, holding back any inclination to be modest. I'm just a little concerned about whether I will be able to understand the speeches. It's so hard trying to follow rambling lectures spoken at high speed in a foreign language. Muruta-T, perhaps you have some idea about how to solve the problem.

I think about it for a moment. I wouldn't mind a trip to California.

– How about bringing me along as official interpreter, like before?

– Ah, yes, that would be a good idea, but unfortunately, the Ministry have already decided on the Japanese delegation members. I wonder if there might be a technological solution to the problem.

The technological solution would be to send someone who can understand English, like myself, but that might be hard for Wanabe-B to explain to the Ministry.

– You could get written versions of the speeches, scan them into your computer and run translation software on them. How about that?

– I may not be able to get written copies of everything. But that gives me another idea. I have just bought a new video camera. It might be useful at the lectures.

Two weeks later when he returns from the conference, he comes to my desk with a friendly smile and a bag full of videotapes.

– It was as I thought. The foreigners all spoke too fast. But, Muruta-T, you can help me out. Can you review these tapes and write down the content? Oh, you can skip the ones marked *golf.* Just do the others. You don't have to do it in great detail. Just the main ideas in simple Japanese.

I take the bag from the Ministry-appointed leader of the national delegation and put on the headphones. I listen to the start of the first two tapes, look through the accompanying text and write a few details about each speech – a little of what the speaker said and a lot of what I think he or she should have said. The delegation leader is happy.

It is December and preparations are underway for the Gnosis *bonenkai,* the forget-the-year party. Eizo-*san* from one of our partner companies is appointed party manager. He sends out the invitations by email:

Gnosis Project, Japan Division
Concerning: Bonenkai

Dear Fellow Gnostics,

This year our international research project kicked off in February amid the continuing economic slump in our country. We got a new prime minister, once again, but no change in government, once again. We saw the start of the professional soccer league and the conclusion of the Uruguay Round of trade talks. Indeed it has been an historical year.

But the end of this memorable year is fast approaching, and though it is a busy time for all and the location may be inconvenient for some of you, I hope you can come to our forget-the-year party.

Normally, it would seem appropriate to have our bonenkai *in a lively city tavern where we could forget the troubles of the year amid the bright lights and crowds. But with the type of eventful year that has passed, I thought it would be good to hold our party in a peaceful spot where we can hear the sound of the wind rustling the bamboo leaves and the chirping of the birds in the nearby woods. So I have organised our party in Tsurumaki Onsen, with its hot springs, old-fashioned houses and sense of history. I propose that we call our party the Tsurumaki Round. We do not know what will happen in the New Year. We do not know how Gnosis will fare, or even when we will have the next meeting. So I urge you all to come to Tsurumaki on 18 December.*

The party will take place in Jinya, an elegant restaurant dating back to the times of the samurai. It is located in a garden of more than a hectare – a big place indeed, big enough to get lost in. I will explain how to find our meeting room. After you pass the outer bamboo gate, go straight ahead till you reach the Wealthy-Moon Pond, then turn right along a gravel pathway through the bamboo thicket. Outside the second pavilion you will see a sign for our meeting, indicating the room we will be in.

If, perchance, there are any cancellations, or if additional members wish to partake in our final event of the year, I would request you to contact me by the end of this week.

I look forward to seeing you all in Tsurumaki.

Saburo Eizo

Gnostic Party Manager

Since our forget-the-year party will be an official Gnosis event, it would not be right to simply while away the hours eating and drinking without doing any work. A seminar is hastily arranged for the late afternoon. The party will be all the more enjoyable after working up a thirst with a few hours of discussions.

A speaker from each company makes a short presentation, one or two questions are asked and it is time for free discussion. There isn't a lot to discuss, but Wanabe-B is chairman and he finds something to talk about.

– Remember we are part of a groundbreaking international programme, the first time Japan, Europe and North America are collaborating in a research project. Even the *Wall Street Journal* wrote about it and they wrote about it in classical terms. It is our Trojan horse.

He is so proud of our Trojan horse and the project getting a mention in the *Wall Street Journal* that he forgets the article was not exactly positive about the whole thing. By the time he has finished talking we are all tired and more than ready to adjourn to the dining room. Eizo-*san* declares the business proceedings complete and we move to the *tatami* room with sliding paper screens and long low tables. Toasts are made to the success of the project and to the coming year, and the serious business of the day begins as the food is tackled. The conversation gets livelier till Eizo-*san* announces it is time for karaoke. Some objections are raised on the grounds that singing will interfere with the *sake*-drinking and talk, but they are quickly overruled. The karaoke machine is switched into action and Wanabe-B lilts and groans his way though old-fashioned *enka* songs about unrequited love and last farewells, about leaving home and family behind, back in the hills of Nagano or Hokkaido, and setting off into the big, bad world, to Osaka or Tokyo, so far from home. He surprises everyone by having a good voice. Then I remember what he told me about the Ginza nights. He is a professional.

– Watanabe-*san*, you're a good *enka*-singer but you are too long-winded in your speeches, says Eizo because it's that time of the night when people can say what they think and no one will take offence.

– My talks are long because they are important. You don't even understand my speeches, do you? Remember, you are talking to the leader of the Japanese delegation to the Next-Generation Products Conference in California.

– I heard that conference wasn't up to much, says Eizo. Did you learn anything new there?

– Of course, I got a lot of new ideas. Valuable information. So valuable that I recorded everything on tape. I even got the main ideas translated into Japanese. Isn't that right, Muruta?

– Yes, Watanabe-B. Lots of ideas. Well, some ideas. But I'm not sure how valuable they are.

The banter continues till Eizo-*san* stands up and announces that we must leave because the kitchen staff have to clean up. We stand for the traditional clap: at the signal everyone claps once, all together, and the party is over. Or, at least the first session is over. Eizo says we should move on for a second session at his favourite watering hole. Two younger salarymen from his company say, Yeah, yeah, let's go. Eizo looks pleased to have such loyal staff.

– Don't you have a home to go to? I ask him, as we search for our shoes at the entrance.

– I can't go home at this hour. It's only nine! If I go home at this time, the wife will make fun of me. She'll start asking if I've been fired.

Riko-T says he is on for another session, but wait! Has someone taken his shoes?

– Black ones? Size 26? Anyone? These shoes don't feel right.

He tries on the only pair left. They are the same style as the ones he came in but they're too tight.

– Anyone whose shoes feel too big? Anyone got the wrong shoes?

The others are already walking down the path. Who cares about shoes when there are important topics to be joked about and work worries to be forgotten?

– Riko, you probably just drank too much, says Wanabe-B. The beer and the whiskey have caused your feet to swell. Those shoes look fine to me. They will probably fit perfectly tomorrow when the effects of the party are gone.

Riko-T didn't really drink that much, certainly not enough to make his feet swell, but he doesn't argue with his boss. He is expecting to be promoted to C next spring and is on his best behaviour.

– I guess I will have to make do with these, he says, and he walks unsteadily away.

A few of us call it a night, the diehards head off to the second watering hole and the Tsurumaki Round is concluded.

Two days later a parcel arrives at our office. The sender is Eizo-*san*. Inside it are Riko's shoes and a little note requesting him to return the ones he wore home that night. It wasn't Eizo-*san* himself who made the mistake, of course. It was one of his staff.

Up to now I have been a contract employee in Mitsubishi, which is normal for foreigners working in large Japanese companies. I have a contract that states the conditions of employment, much the same as would be done in a Western company. I receive a monthly salary in addition to two lump sums paid in June and December – often called *bonuses*, though they are really part of the salary. Employee benefits such as basic health insurance and company payment of commuting expenses are the same for contract and permanent employees. Foreign employees hired in their home countries may receive subsidised apartments in Japan and flights home every year or two. Unfortunately I was not one of those.

For permanent employees the biannual bonuses are flexible, the amount varying according to the company's financial situation and employee performance. In Mitsubishi each lump sum is usually between 2.3 and 2.6 times the monthly salary. The total salary for a 25-year-old is around 3.5 million yen (approximately $30,000); this rises to over 9 million for a non-management salaryman in his early fifties, and decreases between fifty-five and retirement age, which is sixty. Compensation is more egalitarian than in the West: the salary of the president of a large corporation, such as one of the Mitsubishi companies, is less than ten times that of one of the lowest-paid new recruits. An American CEO might earn 100 times more.

One of the few advantages of being a contract employee is that you have the right to refuse a transfer to a different company location. Permanent employees have to accept transfers wherever and whenever the company decides. In the unlikely event of a permanent employee refusing, he would be reprimanded and possibly demoted, although in my time in Mitsubishi I never heard of anyone turning down a transfer for any reason. One colleague had just bought a house when he received an order to transfer to a distant part of the country. He did as he was told, in spite of having to sell the house at a significant loss. Another was given a transfer to Germany even though he knew no German, only a little English, and his wife was ill. But he went, alone.

The company rules state that an employee must be given at least two weeks' notice before being transferred to another city or prefecture within Japan, but in practice most people find out about their transfer a month or more in advance. Later, when I got an unexpected order to transfer, I was given a couple of months' notice, although the manner in which it was done was not to my liking.

If a contract employee and the company agree, the contract may be renewed each year for several years, but if there is an economic downturn or if budgets are cut, it will not be renewed no matter how good he is; a permanent employee, however, will never be directly fired, under normal circumstances.

A permanent employee does not have a contract. He just has to obey the company rules. Normally he would join the company directly after university or school. Even in the 1990s a new recruit would be expected to stay with the company for his entire career, although this is slowly changing, at least in the high-technology companies.

I sometimes asked colleagues why they chose to spend their lives in Mitsubishi. The official reasons, which are listed in Mitsubishi surveys of new recruits, are an interest in the company business areas, the Mitsubishi reputation for looking after its employees and the high-quality products it makes. My colleagues give different reasons – reasons which might not be appropriate for the official company surveys: the father of one of them was a Mitsubishi man and helped find an opening for his son; another chose the company because it has large facilities near his home. Others ended up in Mitsubishi because it was decided by their university. Shinjin-T told me Mitsubishi was his third preference after Toshiba and NEC.

– I wanted to work in computers. Toshiba and NEC are stronger than Mitsubishi.

– So how did you end up here?

– The professor in the university decided. The year I gradu were several students who had Toshiba and NEC as first choices either got good results in the exams or the professor liked their work. My professor told me to join Mitsubishi because the university has to spread the graduates evenly among the big companies and maintain relationships. So here I am.

– And Mitsubishi automatically accepts the students the university decides?

– Usually, but not always. The company can turn someone down if they want to. For example, if you announce at the interview that you are not in favour of nuclear power, Mitsubishi will not hire you. You have to be pro-nuclear in Mitsubishi, or else keep quiet about it.

Another colleague told me Mitsubishi was his first choice because he wanted to work on train control systems, particularly for the most famous and oldest high-speed train in the world – the *shinkansen*. But after the initial company training course he was assigned to factory automation and never went near the train development unit in his entire career.

After joining, new employees must take a three-year company training course, which includes writing a graduation thesis and being moved around among several different locations so that they can learn how the organisation functions. The friendships they make during this period will usually last till retirement. After the course, they are assigned to particular locations: Head Office, the factories or the research labs. The brightest recruits are not always sent to Head Office or the research labs – although most people in the labs have some sort of postgraduate degree. Later, when I worked with people from the refrigerator factory, I asked one of the younger guys, who was wearing the standard factory overalls, where he had studied. The answer was not a trade school nor an ordinary university, but Todai, the pinnacle of Japanese academia. Although there was no outward difference between him and the other workers, he was on track to be manager, while the trade school graduates could most probably only aim at supervisor level.

◆◆◆

In January Wanabe-B tells me I should become a permanent employee. He knows I don't work late every night and that I take two weeks off in the summer, or longer when I combine it with the mid-August company holidays. I even have the odd argument with him. On one trip to Europe when I skipped off from my hotel room to visit friends without telling him, he left a message for me to telephone him urgently. When I returned to my room and phoned, he began reading me the riot act in a voice that made the phone and myself jump, so I let the receiver slip back into place and terminated the call. But we made up and let bygones be bygones. In spite of everything, he appreciates me. He likes having someone to write reports and papers and put his name as joint author. He likes having a trusty sidekick whose arm he can tap and say, Translate, when he wants to announce his thoughts to the world.

But this talk of becoming permanent has come out of the blue. At first I say no, no thanks, not me, not permanent. Somehow I cannot imagine myself as a lifetime employee in Mitsubishi. I may be a reasonably hard-working salaryman most of the time, but something doesn't gel with all that went before, my free and easy lifestyle, nothing fixed, not even what country I would live in. Me, a lifer in Mitsubishi? It's too weird. I can stay as I am – a contract employee. It means my contract has to be renewed every year, after evaluation, but I feel freer this way.

Then I think a little more about it. What would happen if I have a bigger argument with Wanabe-B and don't get a good evaluation? What would happen if my contract is not renewed and I'm not ready to look for another job? I cannot just switch companies because in this country you have to do things slowly, making connections and gaining trust. If I quit Mitsubishi, I want to do it on my own schedule. I don't want to leave this country yet either. I turned down a few job offers I got through people I met on my work trips – Siemens in Munich, the Commonwealth Scientific and Industrial Research Organisation in Australia and a university in the UK – because working in Mitsubishi is still a buzz, even if it is frustrating and weird at the same time. Sure, it doesn't compare with life on the road, but Mitsubishi is more fun than a normal Western company, once I force myself to switch into bi-cultural mode. Yet becoming permanent in Mitsubishi is something else.

I talk to Riko-T about it. He says it is better to be permanent. Lifetime employment does not necessarily mean I'm a lifer. It just means that unless I do something awful like assassinate the company president or sell trade secrets to Hitachi, I cannot get fired. Miyuki thinks I'd be better off permanent too. No need to ask what her parents think.

Finally, I decide that being permanent does not really mean I'm a lifer. It's weird enough that I'm a salaryman in the first place. Going a little further will not make things any weirder.

I apply for permanent status. Wanabe-B says it is a good decision. I might even get promoted at the same time. He tells me to go to Personnel and do the paperwork. I go to talk to Tetsuzuki-KS.

– Can I change to permanent employee status?

He gives me a funny look.

– Well, I don't know about that. It might be very difficult. Such a request would have to be made through official channels, filling out many papers, submitting reasons for the application, in triplicate, three months before the current contract ends. There would be no guarantee of a favourable decision.

I go back to Wanabe-B.

– The man in Personnel says it's not as simple as it seems, becoming permanent.

– Who is that little bureaucrat in Personnel?

– Tetsuzuki-KS.

Wanabe-B picks up the phone, talks to Tetsuzuki-KS in a loud voice for about thirty seconds, puts down the phone and tells me everything is on schedule. The application forms are on my desk an hour later. They don't have to be submitted three months in advance – a day or two will do.

The following week I am invited to an interview with Personnel. Tetsuzuki-KS is there, trying to look very serious to show the solemnity of the occasion because it's not every day or year that a foreigner is considered for lifer status. It is surely the first and maybe the last time in his entire career that he will officiate at a ceremony where a foreigner gets life.

– Today's meeting concerns your application to become a permanent employee of Mitsubishi, he starts off. While it is not normal for foreign contract employees to be made permanent, yours is an exceptional case.

It has been noted that you speak the language and are sufficiently literate to handle the necessary documents. It has also been noted that you have married a national and have the possibility to live here permanently. Furthermore, your annual evaluations have been satisfactory and Watanabe-B has supported your application. Therefore, I can now announce that the personnel department, after deliberation and due consideration, have found in your favour. Your contract status will be changed to permanent on the first of next month.

On hearing this, I feel uncomfortable. I suddenly remember the advantages of being a contract employee: when something annoying happened, I would tell myself that this job and place would pass and I would be on my way soon enough. Now I can no longer tell myself I am just passing through. Now I am really one of the boys in blue, with the three-diamond logo on my lapel. Before, I had the small worry that my contract might be terminated for some reason at an inconvenient time. Now, I'm worried that I might be here a long time and maybe I am a lifer. It gives me a strange feeling. I console myself that at least I'm not in a normal company opting for a normal career. I think about the conventional jobs I might have ended up in but didn't. I'm glad about that. But when I think about those adventurous years, bumming across continents, travelling light and easy and rough, I get the feeling I've come down in the world, compromised too much. Still, life is a compromise. And I've found my Japanese Dream, haven't I? A pretty wife, a company apartment and a bicycle to get to the station. It looks like Mitsubishi is part of that dream.

Tetsuzuki-KS is still talking.

– We have reviewed your performance and considered your position in the company. In view of your experience, it has been decided to assign you to the level of *shuji*. Effectively you will be assistant manager. You will be given a small increase in salary. The exact amount will be determined by the accounting department, in accordance with your age and performance. From now on, you will be Muruta-C. Please consult with Personnel if you need clarification. Any questions?

– No, I say, as I take it all in.

I get promoted, just as Wanabe-B said. For free. I'm no longer a lowly

T. I'm a C, a *shuji.* This is almost enough to make up for the uneasy feeling about becoming a lifer.

– You will be given new name cards next week to reflect your new position, Tetsuzuki-KS says. We congratulate you on becoming a permanent employee of Mitsubishi. That concludes the meeting.

I thank Tetsuzuki-KS, bow and head back to work. Wanabe-B is pleased that all is settled. I'll be staying around a while and he will be able to delegate more of the project to me. I'm a lifer now. I get used to it and no longer feel uncomfortable. Lifers do get out on parole, don't they? For good behaviour? Life doesn't really mean life, does it?

8

能ある鷹は爪を隠す

No aru taka wa tsume o kakusu

The hawk with talent hides its talons

A copy of the *Economist* magazine arrives on my desk. A friend in London sent it to me so that I can see how the outside world looks upon my company. I turn to the article on Mitsubishi to read about our president, Mr Shacho, and I think, Oh no, not him again! He's everywhere. His half-smiling, half-frowning mug shot not only looks down on us as we work and as we eat in the chain gang canteen, his face is in most of the company newsletters and he is quoted in company propaganda all over the place, telling us what to do, how to pull our socks up, how to work better, and we're all supposed to think, Yes sir, Mister President, right away, it will be done today if not sooner.

I have always had a problem with boss veneration, unless it is deserved, which is rarely or never, but what got me about Mr Shacho was a headline in the company magazine a few months earlier. It said, in big, bold characters:

I'M DISAPPOINTED WITH YOU GUYS

And next to the headline was Mr Shacho's frowning face.

That was when profits were down, when the company was getting its first taste of recession in a decade. I thought it was a dumb thing to say because everyone was working as hard as ever, and the reason profits were down was because of bad management, bad policies at the top, not at the bottom. But the top guy blames everyone except himself.

I may not be a big fan of Mr Shacho but I still want to read what an international magazine like the *Economist* has to say about him and my company. It says that Mitsubishi is a high-tech firm, yet is not known for its inventions. It has operations in over thirty countries, but its chief of International Personnel does not speak English. It prides itself on quality, but its future probably depends on mass production for Asia's growing markets. Still, all is not lost – Mr Shacho is going to turn around the fortunes of his organisation.

But first I hope he stops blaming us for the mess he has got us into.

Mr Shacho is a man of the nineties, the article says. He jogs each day, talks straight and laughs a lot, unlike his stiff predecessor. He has told white-collar employees to write down their aims for the coming year. Rewards include a certificate signed by Mr Shacho himself, as well as cash prizes. Mr Shacho stands for change – like Clinton or Yeltsin, one manager is quoted as saying, intending to sound optimistic.

Clinton, maybe, but surely not Yeltsin? I wonder who that manager was. Who does the talking when the *Economist* comes calling? An important somebody in Head Office, I suppose, ready to rattle off prepared slogans for the press without understanding what he is saying. And what about Mr Shacho's stiff predecessor? He passed away, didn't he? Worked too much. Gave it all for the company. But for a good company president, that's the way to go.

Mr Shacho doesn't have to tell us to write down our aims for the coming year. We have to do it anyway. It is a rule. Its purpose is to fix the budget for each group, decide who needs new hardware, which is easy to get, or work space, which is almost impossible to get, and put pressure on us to achieve the things we say we will achieve, to make sure we are not writing fiction in our yearly plans, things that look good on paper at the beginning of the year and are then quietly forgotten. I remember Shinsetsu-GR telling us that Mitsubishi was not in the science fiction business. He hadn't read our Gnosis project proposal, which had quite a bit of science fiction in the guise of state-of-the-art research requiring inspired knowledge. But we had to do that to impress the management of our partner companies. The Mitsubishi managers don't want science fiction, and perspiration is preferred to inspiration.

What about those rewards for writing down our aims and plans? The only rewards we get are the red stamps of the group manager, the department manager and some other bosses in Administration. That is plenty for me and my colleagues. We don't want our aims and plans autographed by any more Important People and certainly not by the president of the company, who might as easily be disappointed as pleased. Getting those autographs would put us under more pressure to achieve each and every aim before the year is over and make us feel really bad if our plans turned out to be fiction after all.

The *Economist* was right when it said Mr Shacho stands for change. But the changes I've seen are not what the *Economist* was talking about. They're not about management strategy and policy, but are more down to earth, and the next one is announced by email:

On 31 January the NGP Group will move to Building 2. Please prepare for the move before 7 p.m. on 30 January. Please commence moving at 9 a.m. on 31 January. Please complete moving before 5 p.m. Detailed instructions will be given by your group manager.

This is my sixth move in two and a half years. I wonder why we are always moving. There must be a reason for this move, perhaps an important strategic reason, but nobody asks about it. Except me.

– Watanabe-B, every time we move we have to swap telephone numbers with some other group and have to transfer their calls for weeks or months. It's so inefficient. Do you know why we are moving this time?

– Yes. It was decided at the department meeting last month.

He has that busy look on his face, which says he doesn't want to answer why-questions. Why-questions are for kids, not company men, who should be seen and not heard. I don't ask any more why-questions. Maybe I will understand the reason for the move later.

We work away at our project, programs, patents, plans, papers. Wanabe-B tells me the laboratory general manager, Nishi-M, thinks we are no longer controlling the direction our project is heading in, that we have too much faith in Gnosis, in the inspired manufacturing knowledge from above. But no one tries to change direction to focus on more practical ideas because it would go against our project's technical adviser and effective spiritual leader, who is a professor in Todai. No salaryman would openly question the wisdom of a Tokyo University professor. All our consortium members, Mitsubishi, Nissan, Fuji Xerox and the others, and even the Ministry itself bow to Todai, which is understandable, since most of the Ministry mandarins and many of the top brass in the companies graduated from Todai, and nearly everyone else wishes they did.

There are no changes in work content but there is another change in location. Our group is shifted upwards, to the twelfth floor. This time we are assisted by professional movers – factory workers who do the morning and afternoon exercises every day without fail and who look forward to shifting desks to release pent-up energy. We put everything into boxes and stick sheets with our names and departments onto each box before heading home one Friday evening. When we arrive on Monday morning the boxes are at our new desks, the computers already set up and ready for action. This is a good move because we now have an office with a view. When Wanabe-B and the others are away at some meeting, or in the late afternoon when people are relaxed, I can stand at the window and look out over the company walls to the blue-, grey- or brown-tiled roofs of the houses, crowded into clumps between little car parks. In the distance I can see the steep, wooded hills of Kanagawa as they change from tawny brown to green and then soft white, and it's cherry blossom time again.

This is the time of year when the company complex looks pretty. The tree-lined entrance is transformed into a white canopy in the daytime and the floodlights at night make it like a stage set for a musical. I'd like to see the factory workers in their boots and helmets doing their aerobics under the floodlit cherry trees as the early April evening closes in, or singing the company songs. They don't do any exercises, but one evening they sing.

I leave the office early that evening with Wanabe-B and Riko-C, who has recently been promoted to *shuji*. We head out towards the floodlit trees where the office and factory workers are gathering and we find a place to sit on the rugs. Crates of beer are set down and soon everyone is talking, drinking and wishing every night could be like this. Aren't the cherry blossoms early this year? I hope they last another week. A few of the factory workers have a karaoke machine and they sing songs about cherry blossoms, *sakura, sakura, oh sakura,* but they don't sing the employees' song. Corporate anthems going *oh-oh techno-life* would not go with the blossoms, the beer and the night that's in it.

Riko-C lies back on the rug and stares up at the blossoms.

– Nice, isn't it. Makes you wonder what we're doing sitting at our desks like robots all day. You know, some fine day I might quit the company and work for myself.

– Well don't dream of quitting till our project is finished, says Wanabe-B.

– Only joking, says Riko-C.

But Wanabe-B is not amused. You shouldn't joke about things like that, especially after being promoted.

None of us gets drunk or noisy because that would disturb the people in the houses nearby and would probably disturb Kawaii-T and her bosses in Personnel. It's not at all like the blossom parties in the park I pass on my way home, where everyone can get drunk and noisy if they want to, can sing any old song till any hour of the night and who cares if someone doesn't like it because this is the only time of the year that a hardworking salaryman can sing in the park under the cherry blossoms like there's no tomorrow, and can get drunk with beer, with song or with talk, and forget work and worries because those blossoms only last a short, short while and then they're gone forever, with the wind and the spring. They won't be the same next year. They'll look the same but they're never the same because a year is a year.

Wanabe-B comes to me one day and says I should apply for a further promotion. But was I not made assistant manager and given the title of C less than a year ago? I ask him what the catch is because there has to be a catch. I'm worried about getting myself too tangled up in the company. Theoretically, I'm still just passing through, remember, just seeing what it is like, although it is becoming a bit of a long see. Wanabe-B says there are no catches that he knows of, except for the responsibility that goes with being a *shukan*, which means manager class, with the grandiose title – in Mitsubishi at least – of KS.

– There will be more decision-making if you are promoted. You will have to manage projects and make proposals. But I think you can deal with it. You should not let the chance slip.

Wanabe-B is right. I shouldn't let the chance slip. I'm already tangled up with the company and obligations. A little more tangling and a few more obligations won't do me any harm. Wanabe-B also mentions that there should be a salary increase. I can handle that too.

I fill out the application forms and answer the questions.

How long have you been in the company? Four years. It's a bit short compared to the others who went in straight from university and didn't spend years bumming around the world with occasional interruptions for graduate school. I know that promotion is related to length of service in the company. I'm not looking good here.

How many patents do you hold or have pending? Six. It's not a great total, not compared to colleagues who have twenty or thirty to their name. Perhaps they will take into account that I have only been here a few years.

How many research papers have you written? I'm okay here. I've written plenty of research papers, some in English, a few in Japanese and lots in techno-babble.

Has your work contributed to company profits? I haven't contributed to profits although I may have contributed to losses. I got shifted from the elevator work before my computer program could do anything to improve those world-record-breaking elevators. What about our Gnosis project and the NGP programme that is so important the *Wall Street Journal* saw fit to criticise it? That will sound good. I write about the Gnosis mission and the research plan that I wrote for the entire consortium – with plenty of input from the Todai professor – and the tens of millions of yen we now get in funding from the Ministry.

Next comes the difficult part. I have to write a short essay describing future directions for my work, using one side of an A3-sized sheet, divided into three columns, with a border 1.5 centimetres wide, and with diagrams and graphs in black and white. It's a struggle, but I get it done. Wanabe-B checks the grammar and I send it off.

A week later I get an email from the personnel department. They don't shoot down my application. They request me to attend an interview with the laboratory general manager, Nishi-M. I know Nishi-M. He's a friendly type, always says hello when we meet in the corridor. I hope he stays friendly at the interview.

He is sitting at a big table with my application set out in front of him.

– Please sit down, Muruta-C. How do you feel about being the international face of our division?

– I'm working too hard to think about it.

He smiles.

– Of course. You know that this is the first time a foreign employee has attempted the examination? Did you write the essay all by yourself?

I feel I'm back in school about to be praised for being a good pupil. I can tolerate the praise if he promotes me and increases my salary.

– Yes, I wrote it, but Watanabe-B kindly checked the grammar.

– I see. Very good. Now, how is your work? That Ministry-sponsored project, isn't it?

– Yes. Everything is going well. We have a few big Japanese, European and North American companies in the consortium and some universities too, like ETH in Zurich, Cambridge in the UK and even Todai itself. Mitsubishi is the coordinating partner and Watanabe-B is making sure our company has a strong influence on the research being carried out.

– My advice to you and your boss is not to focus too much on your project. Personally I don't think the Ministry has a clue how to organise a research programme. They just like grandiose schemes involving all the big companies to make themselves feel important. You remember the Fifth Generation Computer Systems Project in the 1980s? I and many of your older colleagues remember it very well. The Ministry told – or perhaps I should say *advised* – all the big companies to join and we did as we were advised, spent much time and money, and what did we end up with? A pile of reports, some artificial intelligence languages and a heap of parallel inference machines that take up valuable space in our warehouse. I do not put much faith in anything the Ministry comes up with.

I hadn't expected Nishi-M to be so negative. His opinions are not typical of Mitsubishi top management, who have always held the Ministry in high regard. In our company it is important not to forget old relationships, which is probably why Mitsubishi participated in the Fifth Generation Project and why we are now in this NGP programme. But Nishi-M is not a typical Mitsubishi man. He knows the Ministry sometimes get it wrong. When they do, companies like us have to clean up the financial mess they leave.

– So … so, should we continue?

– Yes, you should continue. Mitsubishi cannot quit just like that. But make sure you do some useful research, not just write big reports every year for the Ministry mandarins. And do not let the academics take over, even if they are from Todai itself. The professors have their own agenda, you know, and it is not the same as ours. I plan to let your bosses know my ideas soon.

He looks through the rest of my application and tells me what he likes about it – the bits about doing something useful. He doesn't care much for academic papers, which are for attention-seeking professors. He's more interested in my patent applications. Are they of any use? What are they about?

– One of them helps robots control a production line using a vision system and a database. It may be useful in the new plant in Ibaraki.

– Have the Ibaraki people decided to use your ideas?

– Well, eh, no, they haven't.

– I see. What else?

– I have a couple of software patents. One of them was designated as Important Intellectual Property by the patent department. It will be very important if Nagoya decide to design their programmable controllers over the Internet.

– Have they decided to do so?

– No, not yet. They are, eh, very cautious about moving into new business areas. They prefer the conventional ways.

– I see. So is there anyone at all who is using your ideas?

– Yes, yes there is. The Hiroshima plant have contacted the lab about my patent for automatically diagnosing faults in electrical appliances. It will be possible to determine if there is a problem or to predict when one may occur in refrigerators, air conditioners or other appliances by automatically checking the way electricity is being consumed. The Hiroshima plant said they are very interested in commercialising the idea.

– Good. At least you have done something that might be useful. In my opinion we have too many defensive patents, just for trading with Hitachi, Toshiba and the others, or to stop others using the technology for free even though we do not use it ourselves. You know that our company submits over 8,000 patent applications a year, don't you? Each Japanese application costs our lab a small fortune, without considering costs for overseas applications and patent attorneys. The US patent attorneys charge us up to $500 an hour and sometimes all they do is write letters and forward documents to the US agencies. It's not cheap, this patent game. But that's the way it is. Now, anything else? Tell me, are you able to work well with your colleagues? Any problems?

– Some people are not used to working with foreigners but I can manage.

– They have to learn. We need to make our labs more international. We need to have an atmosphere where foreigners can feel comfortable. You are comfortable here, aren't you?

– Reasonably.

– You're coping. That's the main thing. It's not meant to be easy. You are the only permanent Westerner we have. I hope you can be the first of many.

– I hope so too.

– Well, that will do for now. Can you tell the next candidate to come in?

A week later word comes through about the promotion. Of the five candidates, four are promoted to manager class, including myself. Not bad. In a little over a year I've gone from being a mere T to a respectable C and beyond it to a high-class KS. Nishi-M told me that I was the first Westerner ever to take the KS test. That must have made up for not contributing to company profits.

But there is a catch with the promotion. I have to attend a lecture and do some homework as part of the deal. I go to the lecture room and sit with the fifteen others who have been promoted – three new KSs and twelve Cs. We listen to Nishi-M as he gives us his thoughts on research and management strategy. He is not a bad lecturer. He tells us he wants to imitate Jack Welch of General Electric, the greatest CEO in America. He reads books about Jack and he is waiting for Jack's memoirs to be published, *Straight from the Gut,* where, among other things, Jack writes about how his Irish mother inspired him to become the CEO of General Electric. Maybe I could write a memoir about how my Irish mother inspired me to become a salaryman in Mitsubishi. Naw, it doesn't sound right. And I shouldn't try to blame my mother for my career decisions.

Nishi-M talks about Jack's visionary management and how we in Mitsubishi might learn from him. He talks straight, probably like Jack, straight from the gut. But he skips the details about how Jack's gut made him fire workers, close plants, sell off unprofitable units and look after shareholders more than employees, as a good American CEO should. That would never do in Mitsubishi, where old-time traditions still hold and we still treat employees like people – at least I think we do. In our company it's all right to be a Jack fan but it's not all right to have Jack's gut.

Nishi-M tells us his ideas for making the research labs more useful in the future. We must balance the traditional Eastern values with Western ones, he says, and I begin to understand why he promoted me.

– If you have a task to do, how do you set about carrying it out? Muruta here is our Western representative. Let us assume, for a moment, that he works for General Electric. Muruta will probably think about what results he wants; he will want to know the big picture. Sano, Nakamura and all of you others, you will probably not think about the results as much as the process, the way to carry out your task. You will be specialists more than generalists. You will enjoy the details and not worry about the big picture. Muruta will prefer definite things, facts and figures. You others will accept rough, fuzzy ideas.

He continues for well past an hour, telling us how to combine the traditional Mitsubishi style with the Western style. I'm wondering if I really think about the big picture, not the details, and if my colleagues really prefer rough, fuzzy ideas. At least Nishi-M's lecture is a change from the usual slide shows we get about java programming and neural networks. We pay attention to what he says and write a few notes because we're all diligent employees. Finally he says he will conclude by giving us our homework. We are split into groups. I am with the senior bunch who have been promoted to *shukan*. Over the next few weeks we should meet at least four times and prepare a presentation. Our topic will be: how to turn Mitsubishi into a high-growth corporation.

– The last few years, we have been contracting more than growing, Nishi-M says. I want you to plan how we can regain our former position at the top of the domestic league. Each group will submit a report about twenty pages long and present the results in this lecture room in six weeks' time.

Sano, Nagai and Nakamura are in my group. At our first meeting we introduce ourselves, our departments and what work we are doing, then set about organising and planning. I don't want to be leader but neither do the others and it becomes a very democratic group, each of us voicing opinions, no one dominating. We set up a schedule: we will each write a short report on the ideas we produce during our meetings, read some papers in the company library and add our opinions, then meet again to put everything together and practise for the final presentation.

We talk about how to improve the company.

– The problem we have in this country, says Nakamura, is that we're not allowed to fail. The managers all say we should not be afraid to try new ideas but really they want us to take the safe option.

– That is the problem in Mitsubishi, says Nagai. If there is a choice between spending six months on some new idea that no one understands, and spending a year on a conventional idea that everyone understands and approves of, I know which I will choose. No one will say anything if the conventional idea produces no results, but if the new idea fails, you have big problems to explain away.

We talk about Mitsubishi's patent policy. If a new invention or idea is in any way connected to current products or business fields, it will be immediately patented in Japan, America and probably several of the larger

European and Asian countries, even if it is relatively trivial. But if the idea is not directly related to current business fields, it probably won't go far: the patent application will be made in Japan only and it will be left *pending* for as long as possible. Ultimately it will be abandoned if there is no push from top management to use it. I saw several good ideas being cast aside in this way. Top management is always hesitant about moving into new fields, and lower management doesn't dare try anything new unless they are sure they have approval from above.

– We should consider how we would run things if we had free reign, setting up our own company, says Nakamura. How would you manage a start-up?

– I would firstly employ a few experienced people with business, marketing and technical backgrounds.

– I think having some alliances with other businesses is the most important.

– You have to be prepared in case your first plan does not work – what to do if it fails.

– Do you think our experience here is useful for a start-up? I mean, can we use our work here as a springboard to working independently?

As I listen to the opinions I'm thinking what a surprising meeting this is. Four of us diligent company men, about to be made managers or at least manager class, preparing our report for the general manager to evaluate, and here we are talking about how we might set up a little company of our own, away from the safety and security of Mitsubishi. We're not quite as loyal as we seem, are we?

We write down the ideas that come to us – only those ideas that would be suitable reading for Nishi-M. I'm sure he would not be pleased if he knew we were discussing how we might work independently if conditions were right.

When I head back to my desk I ask myself if my KS colleagues would take a big risk in this country where it is no good to fail – not like America where you can bounce back as many times as your credit rating allows, once you've got a gut like Jack Welch. Would they really leave the security and protection of a big company and start out on their own? They just might. And cherry trees might blossom in December.

At the second meeting there is no talk about start-ups and working independently. We were pushing our imagination that first meeting, although it was good to hear what the others were thinking and to realise our ideas are not so different. But now we have to concentrate on the task at hand and prepare our report.

On the day of the presentation we each talk for a few minutes to an audience of Nishi-M, two people from the planning department and the others who have been promoted to KS and C. Our presentation avoids any controversial topics or suggestions that we are anything but loyal Mitsubishi men. Then Nishi-M talks. He says our homework was satisfactory, although he would like to have heard a few more radical ideas. He tells us what Mitsubishi expects of us now that we are manager class.

– You have new responsibilities. You must not only look after the younger staff, you must also give direction to your bosses and when the time comes you should be ready to become leaders yourselves. As managers you must guide the research to fruition. So many ideas perish in the Valley of Death between the research labs and the factories and never become products at all. Getting through the Valley of Death is your mission. Our company depends on the ideas of all senior staff, not just the top, not just the CEO and the board of directors. To be frank with you, I feel we have become a second-rate company, compared to Toyota or General Electric. We need more than just hard work. We need to change, and change should come from you.

No it shouldn't, I'd like to say. It's no use if we try to change something because the company culture is one of respecting elders. If there is to be change, then it will have to start at the top. If we KSs, Cs and middle managers say anything that our bosses don't like, we will not get far. But if we tell them what they want to hear, then life will be easier for us all.

After being elevated to manager class I begin to feel more important. I still write the odd fax or letter for Wanabe-B, but when I sign my name at the bottom he no longer goes to his desk to quietly blank out my name with correction liquid and add his own before sending it off. He lets me chair some of the meetings – the international ones – and treats me less as an assistant and more as an associate. I've reached new heights in Mitsubishi.

One day Kawaii-T, who is now in Administration, comes to me with a request. A company seminar is being held in the local conference centre. As the only non-Asian permanent employee, would I accept an invitation to participate in a panel discussion about the internationalisation of Mitsubishi?

– I'd be honoured.

And I would like to see what our local conference centre looks like. There are lots of shiny new conference centres and public buildings in this country that hardly anyone knows about except the local city councillors and their good friends in the local construction industry. Our conference centre is one of those. A few of the councillors and one or two of their good friends will attend our seminar. They're happy to see that someone actually uses the building. The guest of honour will be Komon-H, a very important person from Head Office – the same Komon-H who signed those letters to important people in the US when we were trying to flog our project. It is an honour to have him join the discussion. The international part of the seminar will be made up of myself, Marume-C, who has just returned after several years working in one of the US factories, and Oseji-T, who studied in Canada.

Oseji-T works in the department next to ours and is very diligent. When he hears that the honourable Komon-H will be participating, he makes a list of Komon-H's recent achievements. He writes notes in a little notebook, which he is reading when Komon-H appears at the conference centre. Oseji-T puts the notebook away and introduces himself to Komon-H. He says what a great honour it is to meet him, how impressive his recent research paper was, what a great influence his previous work has had, not only on the company but also the industry in general, and the country itself should be proud of Komon-H's achievements. I feel like telling Oseji-T to just shut up. But the honourable Komon-H is enjoying the flattery and chats away with zealous Oseji-T, who has probably now moved onto the fast track for promotion to C-class. Oseji-T finally shuts up.

We go into the hall and take our seats facing the small audience. Kawaii-T and two other Ts from Administration sit at a table to the side and the honourable Komon-H sits at a special desk with the laboratory director and Wanabe-B, who is acting as chairman. Kawaii-T starts the meeting by thanking Komon-H for taking the time and trouble to come. Komon-H is such an important person she uses a respectful title for him even in front of outsiders, ignoring the company rule about titles.

– We realise how busy you are, Dr Komon, and what an important job you do, providing direction for the corporation worldwide. We are honoured by your presence and we thank you for finding the time to attend.

She does not mention the time the rest of us are spending at the seminar.

The honourable Komon-H begins to talk. I glance over at Kawaii-T and the Ts from Administration to see them writing down every word he says, not missing a syllable. In triplicate.

– As you probably know, the research environment has changed much since I entered the company. That was quite a few years ago. You can guess how many by looking at my head!

Everyone smiles politely. Komon-H is quite thin on top.

– I remember my first visit overseas. It was to a conference in New York. In those days we had no direct flights and the planes were not big. Our propeller aircraft hopped across the Pacific, from Tokyo to Midway, then Hawaii, California and Saint Louis, and I could see that Japan was just a little country in the big, big world. I was the youngest member of our group, so I had to help my seniors with their bags. The US was a very expensive place for us. We didn't have much money and we had to share a hotel room, but I did not mind because it was an adventure to go overseas. It was also an honour to represent our company. Nowadays, you can fly directly almost anywhere and I guess the experiences of the other panellists here on their first big trip abroad were not as rough as mine.

As he talks Kawaii-T and the other two scribes keep writing furiously. Then he says he would like to hear the impressions of the other panellists. The three scribes stop writing and sit back as Marume-C begins to talk.

– I only arrived back in Japan a few weeks ago and my opinions are based on what I felt while working in a foreign country. Mitsubishi is already a leader in quality and in many forms of product innovation but is trailing in flexibility and could learn from the way they work in the US. They are not afraid to quickly introduce new technologies or to shift production depending on economic conditions.

He talks about what Mitsubishi should do and how we should follow the example of the US. Most of what he says makes sense from a US perspective but not from a Mitsubishi one. I don't think anyone is going to take his opinions too seriously, especially Komon-H.

Komon-H thanks him for his comments and says, Yes, we must learn from the Americans.

The scribes grab their pens and write furiously as Komon-H speaks. When he finishes, they sit back again, look out the window, fiddle with their pens, and it is my turn to say something. I could say what a great guy Komon-H is to have roughed it like he did to New York, taking a slow plane, sharing a hotel room and even carrying some extra bags, which must be as rough as it gets. I could say how younger people nowadays certainly would not rough it like that, but I prefer to leave the grovelling to Oseji-T. He is much better at it.

I mention a few good points to start off: the diligence of the Mitsubishi workers and the long-range vision of the company. Then I give a few opinions.

– Our company took over a year to decide whether we would be permitted to access the Internet. Other companies decided quickly that the new technology could lead to new opportunities but our company just waited cautiously. I think we have missed a few chances already and this is not the first time such a situation has occurred. One of my bosses who works in computer-aided design told me that when CAD first became available in the 1980s his managers decided it would be too risky and stuck with conventional ways until they saw how Hitachi and the others were making big improvements in efficiency. Mitsubishi is too slow in adopting new ideas.

Komon-H responds and the Administration scribes grab their pens again and write furiously.

– I understand the frustration you might sometimes feel, especially since you work in the laboratory. I would ask you to keep in mind the size of our organisation. Head Office has to make decisions that relate to all employees. It is difficult for them to cater for individual needs in different divisions of the company. And please remember we are market leaders here at home and in some cases worldwide for many conventional products. We are not doing too badly, are we?

Oseji-T then has his say and the administration staff sit back because he is only a T.

– I must mention my admiration for Komon-H and the difficult times he had when he entered the company, travelling rough to New York and not complaining. I am sure that such experiences helped him get where he is today. As regards the caution displayed by Head Office when embracing new technologies, I believe we must be patient. Otherwise, mistakes will be made. It is important to avoid mistakes. The opinions of our seniors are important and should be respected.

Give us a break, Oseji, I want to say. But he does not give any breaks. He continues with all the possible ideas he has to make Komon-H and the other senior managers feel important, and they are probably thinking what an exemplary employee, we must remember his name, he will be a good employee to use when we want to show what our company is like.

Kawaii-T announces that the honourable Komon-H will now talk about his long-range vision and his dream. She and her fellow scribes grab their pens and get ready for Komon-H's dream. I wonder if he really dreams about the company. But if he is important enough to be on the board of directors then I suppose he does. He probably has nightmares about being wiped out by Hitachi and Toshiba, although that is unlikely because they are good friends of ours as well as rivals. His nightmares are more likely about Samsung in Korea and Siemens in Germany.

– We are aiming to be not just a multi-national company but a trans-national enterprise, he says. We now have operations in thirty-four countries and outlets in over 100. We have to think on a big scale because Japan is just a little country. Our employees who have international experience have an important role in making this a trans-national company.

But Kawaii-T and the other two scribes do not seem to think the employees with international experience have an important role. They think that only Komon-H has, and they keep writing for a few minutes after he finishes talking. Who should I believe? I think I'll believe Komon-H. I'll believe I have an important role in making this a trans-national company because that is what I want to believe whether it is true or not. I've already reached the dizzying heights of manager class and I am now Muruta-KS. I wonder if Komon-H will fast-track me even further? There is a chance – as long as the scribes from Administration are not running the show. I'll hang on and hope for something good.

Wanabe-B joins us at the reception afterwards and introduces me to the manager of the computer division, Mueki-B.

– Mueki-B has a big plant, he tells me, but he always loses money.

Mueki-B grins and says things will be better in a year or two.

– Maybe they will close your division down, says Wanabe-B. But don't worry, Mueki-B. There will always be a job for you in our project. Isn't that right, Muruta-KS?

– That's right. But Mueki-B, was it your division that made those great laptops a while back? There was a really nice Mitsubishi model on the market, the thinnest and lightest available, better than anything made by Toshiba or even Apple, but I haven't seen or heard about it since last year. Has it disappeared or what has happened?

– The laptop venture? says Mueki-B. It wasn't my plant that made it. It wasn't our fault. I believe the plant down south was responsible. They had logistics problems. The suppliers couldn't get the super-thin battery quickly enough. Sales outlets got fed up of delays and finally it was decided to cease production. The computer business is too competitive. There are plenty of other more stable business sectors for us to focus on.

– What happened to the manager responsible for logistics? Did he get fired?

– No, no. He was moved to Head Office. He did his best and that is what counts, even if the product failed. I think he was promoted.

Promoted for screwing up big time? But he did his best and that is what counts. Mitsubishi is a gentle sort of giant. That logistics manager is probably a good company man, cooperative with Head Office and the managers in the factories, so he would not be demoted. Attitude and connections are more important than results.

– Now, Muruta-KS, says Mueki-B, what did you think of today's seminar?

– It was useful to hear different ideas. I still think Mitsubishi is too conservative. But will anyone act on the opinions offered?

– Well, that depends on the people involved. The administration department may be interested in your ideas.

– From the notes they took during the discussions, I think they are only interested in what Komon-H said. They wrote down every syllable he spoke. In triplicate. They won't be able to report any of what I said unless they have good memories.

– You might be surprised. You should look out for this month's laboratory newsletter. It will include a report on the seminar. Administration will send you a copy when it comes out in a couple of weeks.

– Okay. I will wait for my copy.

A month passes but no copy of the newsletter arrives. Administration must have forgotten. I could go looking for a copy, I suppose, but what's the use. They probably sent all their copies to Komon-H. I'm still a T as far as they are concerned.

9

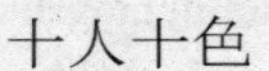

十人十色

Ju nin to iro

Ten men, ten colours

It is the biggest table I have ever seen: shining dark wood, oval at each end, surrounded by matching chairs with red upholstery and high backs, fit for kings, emperors or at least for some very important salarymen. Portraits of former illustrious company presidents look down from the walls, the doors are made of mahogany and mini-chandeliers hang from the ceiling. This is the inner sanctum of the corporation, a couple of blocks west of Tokyo Station and east of the Imperial Palace, the boardroom where grey-haired directors gather to plan the future of Japanese technology, or at least to rubber stamp the proposals from their subordinates in the factories and research laboratories. Someone tells me that this is where the *Kinyokai* takes place – the *Friday Club* – where once a month the illustrious presidents of the twenty-nine corporations in the core Mitsubishi Group gather to eat lunch and exchange opinions.

But today is Tuesday and there are fewer than twenty people at our meeting. We only get a cup of coffee to help us concentrate, no lunch. The table looks too big and most of us are not illustrious like the presidents who meet here on the second Friday of the month or the former presidents who look down from the walls. We are only going to talk about our Gnosis project with managers from the other companies in our consortium – trifling stuff compared to what normally goes on here. The first two years' research has produced several long-winded reports, thick enough to fulfil funding requirements and keep the Ministry men happy, complicated enough to keep the research managers busy, but with no clear results to apply in the factories, nothing to sell or market, at least not in the foreseeable future. We have ideas for customisable cars and self-organising factories where next-generation products will be produced using optimised configuration algorithms, but it is all a bit vague and two of the companies in our consortium are thinking about quitting. Fuji Xerox are restructuring their organisation and they just might restructure their participation in the project while they're at it. Nissan have let it be known that sales are down, losses up, and headquarters is scaling back all long-term projects. If Nissan leave there will be no car-maker left in our project because Toyota, Mazda and Honda are in different consortia so they certainly won't join us, and cash-strapped Mitsubishi Motors have no inclination to join. With only a few electrical and construction companies remaining, the consortium will look weak, especially to the Europeans and Americans. We have to keep Nissan and Fuji Xerox on board.

Wanabe-B decided that an impressive location would help convince them it is an important project, of vital interest not only to Japan but also to our companies and probably to ourselves as well. Wanabe-B even invited Socho-*sensei*, President of the University of Tokyo, the most senior academic in the country. I remember Socho-*sensei* from one of our project trips. We were on a plane about to take off from Paris for Tokyo. The business class seats on the flight were all taken, and Wanabe-B and I were asked to move up to first class. We didn't complain. Then Wanabe-B noticed Socho-*sensei* sitting down in business class on his way home from an OECD meeting. Would I mind swapping with the honourable professor? I picked up my hand luggage and Wanabe-B invited Socho-*sensei* to move up to first so that they could discuss vital matters, such as the state of the world, the OECD and, most importantly, the Gnosis project. But Socho-*sensei* said he was fine down in business class. The state of the world, the OECD and Gnosis could wait for another flight, and I stayed in first. I remember that flight because it wasn't every day I found myself a class above the top academic in Japan, nor was it every day Wanabe-B was told the state of the world, the OECD and our project could wait for another flight.

Back in the Mitsubishi boardroom, Wanabe-B stands up to greet everyone and give the agenda.

– At any moment I expect we will be honoured by the presence of Socho-*sensei*, who has been involved in promoting our project from the start. He will speak about the importance of our work.

Socho-*sensei* does not arrive and Wanabe-B keeps talking. He talks about the great potential our consortium has and about the great efforts being made by its members because it is polite to praise everyone and criticise no one. He talks about how we have come this far – which is not so far at all – and how much further we will go if the companies keep giving the support we need. He never runs out of words or breath, always finds something more to say, doesn't notice when people look bored or look like they want to say something themselves. Wanabe-B is not a typical Mitsubishi manager who would have few words and would be looking at his listeners to see how they react, making sure he is not imposing. He doesn't mind imposing his ideas on people when he wants to and maybe that's not bad for a change.

Shatai-*san*, the man from Nissan, finally raises his hand and asks to speak. Wanabe-B takes a break. Shatai-*san* says that things are tough in the car business. His company is looking hard at where to cut costs and the first place the budget cutters will look is at a project about virtual gadgets that depend on inspired knowledge from who knows where. How long will it be before we shift our focus from the future to the present and get some practical results?

– I appreciate the situation you and your company find yourselves in, says Wanabe-B. Indeed I believe Nissan is not the only company in this situation. To the representatives of all such companies I would say the following. Firstly, keep in mind that the Ministry of International Trade and Industry is backing our project. Their guidance should be respected above individual company preferences. Although the Ministry requires very detailed reports every year – perhaps too detailed, in my humble opinion – and although our companies pay high participation fees to the Ministry, we nevertheless receive much funding to help us carry out the research. Secondly, I would point out that we have many eminent university professors backing this project, giving us new ideas. Our academic mentor is a Todai professor. We also have foreign partner companies in Europe and North America. We must not let them down. Finally, as I have mentioned, today we will be privileged to have some words from Socho-*sensei*, President of Todai. Please listen to what he has to say.

A secretary enters the room and quietly whispers something to Wanabe-B, who loudly announces that Socho-*sensei* is about to arrive. Everyone stands up when he enters. He bows, everyone else bows and he takes the seat beside Wanabe-B, with the portraits of the illustrious Mitsubishi salarymen looking down from the wall behind him.

– Thank you all for giving me a chance to talk to you today, he begins. Although I cannot spend as much time as I would like with you, I will briefly give you some ideas about why your project is important, not only for your companies but also for our country. Let us suppose, for a moment, that you live in a simpler time many years ago and you wish to feed your family. You decide to grow some rice.

It is not the type of introduction we are expecting but we are all too polite to raise our eyebrows.

– To learn how to do so, what should you do? Study botany? If you did, you might understand how seeds left in the fertile earth sprout into plants if they have water and sunshine, but you still would not know exactly how to grow rice, how to protect it from the crows and insects, when to harvest it, how to prepare it. To know these things you would have to do many experiments, probably failing a few times. It would take a long time before you could become proficient at growing rice for your dinner table and by the time you did so, your family might have perished from lack of food. No, you would not study botany or carry out experiments. Instead, you would go to someone who knows how to grow and harvest rice. You would learn from someone who is good at practical things, not theory – from a farmer, perhaps, or from a book written by a farmer. In this case, the practical person who can teach you how to grow the rice is more valuable than all the theory and the scientists.

We are still paying attention because Socho-*sensei*'s lecture is different from the usual mid-afternoon talks that make everyone sleepy.

– Well, we Japanese are the practical people when it comes to making things. Not rice – I believe our agriculture is inefficient and our rice is the most expensive in the world – but cars, electrical products, even buildings. Up to now the Europeans and Americans have been more successful at basic science, at the theory. We may have inefficient agriculture and service industries, but I believe we are better at applying ideas and making things. Yes, we have borrowed the theory from foreign countries, but so far we have applied it better than anyone. And now some of the successful American manufacturers of cars and other products have borrowed many ideas from us. So have other Asian countries like Korea and Taiwan. Can you see where this leads us?

No, we can't. But we are listening.

– We can make a valuable contribution to the world by sharing our strategies about how to manufacture products. We can still make superior cars and electronics, but by sharing our strategies we can buy goodwill and open markets for what we want to sell. In the past we have been criticised for imitating rather than creating new ideas. Now we have a chance to contribute something. You do not teach the Europeans and Americans how to grow rice – I believe they prefer bread in any case. But you can share your experience about how to apply the basic ideas for making things. Your work in this research programme will help achieve this.

He talks about how we can put our practical knowledge into knowledge bases and share them with whoever wishes to learn. Then Wanabe-B announces that the honourable Socho-*sensei* has another appointment and will have to leave. Everyone stands up and bows. Before Socho-*sensei* reaches the door he is bowing in return and as he exits he bows again.

That evening a reception is held in the plush Mitsubishi Club on the fifteenth floor of one of the Mitsubishi office blocks. The Club was established by the K*inyokai* in the early 1970s to mark the centennial of the Mitsubishi Group. Its purpose is to provide high-class facilities for receptions and commemorative events. It is exclusively for the directors of the twenty-nine member companies of the K*inyokai* and even today its website requests that outside parties refrain from making enquiries about its use. We have no director at our meeting or in our project but Wanabe-B has friends in high places. He's the next best thing to a director.

We are guided into the thickly carpeted, mahogany-panelled reception room. Kimono-clad waitresses offer us *sake*, whiskey or beer – Kirin beer, because Kirin is the only beer-brewing company in the Mitsubishi family.

On the tables are plates of sashimi delicately laid out like cascading fans, with slivers of squid and salmon roe glowing orange under the chandeliers. The reception is buffet style to make it easy to mingle.

Wanabe-B says Socho-*sensei*'s talk was just what we needed to keep all the companies on board. Ueda-KS says these ideas about sharing our knowledge are all very well but we should be careful about giving the game away to our competitors, shouldn't we? Our lead in many areas is shrinking. The Americans are catching up. The Koreans too. We have to watch out.

– Still, you have to admit Socho-*sensei* has different ideas, says Shatai-*san*. There are too many people with the same ideas in this country. Or if they have different ideas they keep their thoughts to themselves; they don't want to disturb anyone with offbeat suggestions.

Shatai-*san* glances around to check that Wanabe-san is out of earshot, then continues.

– Even Watanabe-san is useful when he gives us some of his ideas. He may be hard to understand but he's not afraid to talk. He's not a typical salaryman.

When I think about it, I've bumped into quite a few non-typical salarymen in this NGP programme. Kiguchi-*san*, who is also at the reception, is one of them. Though he is now a research manager on contract in Todai, he veered off the usual career track a long time ago. He took a job in a development project in Indonesia, sharing his knowledge with the locals, as Socho-*sensei* is suggesting, except Kiguchi-*san* was sharing the theory, not the practical ideas. He married an Indonesian lady, settled down and almost stayed there for good, but not quite. One time when the political situation was unstable, he decided to return to his native land and was lucky to find work in the university. I would often see him at project meetings and he'd always be ready to have a chat, have a coffee, talk about Indonesia or about Gnosis, even in the middle of the working day when salarymen don't normally chat. Kiguchi-*san* must have picked up this habit in Indonesia. He makes me think that all of us salarymen should spend a while there to learn how to work in different gears, have a chat in the middle of the working day when everyone else is busy. At least I did my stint in South Asia, didn't I? I even learned about rubber time in Indonesia, where time is as flexible as rubber if you want it to be. Kiguchi-*san* knows about rubber time but my

Mitsubishi colleagues do not. They skipped that part of their education. Many of them don't even regret their misspent youth, wasted on study, work and doing what is expected. But I can't blame them. They didn't have the chances I had.

– You know something, Kiguchi-*san* says. Doing things differently doesn't always pay. In spite of everything, I'm quite a poor man now. I live in a two-roomed apartment in Yokohama, I take a crowded train to work each day, and when this project ends in four years' time they'll fire me.

– Fire you? Won't they give you a new contract?

– I'll be pushing sixty in four years, so they cannot give me a new contract even if they want to. I will have to look for another job to pay the rent. How is it in Mitsubishi? They look after you, I suppose?

– Yes, they do.

– I've always wondered if I would have been better off in a big company like yours. Sometimes it's good to be looked after.

– The problem is that we are *too* well looked after. We have health checks and surveys by company doctors or dentists several times a year. We get reports every month on all serious work or non-work accidents involving Mitsubishi employees, explaining how the accident occurred and how it could have been avoided. We have lectures about how to relieve stress and enjoy sports, even though the really stressed people are too busy to attend. We have all-day seminars about how to prepare for retirement. We have rules about how we should commute to work – motorbikes are not allowed unless there is no alternative and a bicycle is only allowed if we live between one and four kilometres from the company. We have safety awareness meetings and every month there's a safety patrol in the lab. The department manager and the safety officers put on their Mitsubishi caps and yellow *Safety Patrol* armbands and walk past every desk looking for something dangerous or untidy like a book that might fall or a jacket left hanging on a chair. I have to join the safety patrol myself sometimes. I don't like wearing the Mitsubishi cap, but it's nice to go for a stroll around the building and see what everyone has on or under the desk. We also have warnings about avoiding dangerous places if we go abroad. We are supposed to think everywhere is dangerous except Japan. We even have to report where we will be during holidays and give contact addresses and telephone numbers just in case something goes wrong. We wouldn't want our bosses to be worried about us, would we?

– Of course not. Keep the slaves safe and healthy, Kiguchi-*san* grins. And your company gives you a place to stay too?

– I have a company apartment. It's not too far from work and the rent is cheap.

– Give the slaves a place to sleep, close to the plantation. Like the farms years ago in Java.

– Except the wages are better than on the farms in Indonesia. The company doesn't feel like a farm. More like a big family. We are the kids and the important people, like Watanabe-*san* over there, are the parents. If we're good kids, they look after us well: subsidised membership of sports clubs and holiday resorts, cheap loans for buying a house or apartment, cheap tickets for baseball or football matches, allowances for children or family members who are ill. There's an introductory agency to help the young guys move on from the singles dormitory, and if you stay in the company a long time, you and your wife get a pre-retirement holiday to Hawaii or Australia, although it's only for four days.

– Nice and cosy, Kiguchi-*san* says. None of this individualistic stuff you get in foreign places.

– Yes, but maybe it's a bit too comfortable. Once you settle in, it is hard to leave, at least for my colleagues. I think I am freer than them. I can tolerate being pampered because I feel free to leave if I want to.

A couple of months later I see how hard it is for fellow employees to leave. One morning an unexpected email arrives on my computer screen:

Dear Group Manager,
For the reasons I explained to you yesterday, I wish to resign. I have thought it over and over last night, as you told me, but I have not changed my mind.

I ask to be allowed to leave for personal reasons and because I have reached the limits of my ability and energy. But you keep saying you will not permit me to leave and you do not say why. I do not understand or accept your refusal.

Once again, I repeat my desire to leave Mitsubishi. For personal reasons I wish to quit. I strongly request that you respect my decision.

Hiroki Yamakawa

I don't know anyone called Yamakawa and I wonder if the email has been sent by mistake. I check the addressee list at the top and see about fifty names – everyone in our department and in Personnel. Whoever Yamakawa is, he seems to have given up persuading his boss to set him free and is shouting out his frustrations.

– Why does the manager want him to stay? I ask Riko-C.

– A manager doesn't like it when someone leaves. It reflects on him in some way. Maybe it makes him look like a bad manager. And maybe Yamakawa did not have a good reason to leave. That is why the manager refuses.

– But this isn't a prison. You can walk out whenever you want, can't you?

– It's not so simple. Mitsubishi is a big, powerful organisation. If a salaryman resigns, he should do it as smoothly as possible and leave a good impression. If I quit I would do it properly. I would make sure to persuade my bosses beforehand so there would be no friction. Yamakawa did not plan things as he should have.

There is no follow-up email and no other information about Yamakawa. But after shouting out his frustrations to so many people he is surely not going to stay around and his manager is surely too embarrassed to keep refusing the papers he needs to leave, though it is certainly not a smooth exit.

When people leave for a good reason, they always mention in the final email that their parting with the company is an amicable one, agreed to by all sides, no friction, no problems, everyone happy, and I used to wonder why they say it is a smooth parting. Now I know that if they don't people will think it is a rough parting, like Yamakawa, and they will wonder who the bad guy was – the boss for not being able to keep his staff or the employee for being selfish and not listening to his boss.

There is one strange salaryman in the research lab. If he wanted to resign, I'm sure no one would try to stop him, but he doesn't quit. He comes to the company at ten or eleven every day and leaves well before five. When I visit the small company library he is usually there. He approaches me and starts talking in English.

– Excuse. How you think this paper? he says pointing to some technical article he has found. I look at him, then at the article and tell him I don't know how I think because I haven't read it and I don't plan to either. He starts giving me his opinions in English till I get bored and start giving my opinions in Japanese. He realises he will get no more free English conversation practice today. He goes off to another row of library shelves and I wonder why he's always reading articles in the library. Doesn't he do any work at all?

Riko-C says this guy had problems – mental stress or something – and never quite recovered. Now he comes to the company every day but doesn't do any work, just busies himself in the library. Being here is enough.

– Won't he get fired?

– No, most likely not. Mitsubishi would not fire someone like that. They would protect him. It's the human side of our company. It is true that if you get some illness the rules of employment only allow you a few months to recover, but in practice the company will try to bend them, rather than discharge you. And if they finally have to terminate your employment, there are some support funds available. The company would not abandon you.

Being abandoned by the company is not a good way to go because it would probably mean falling not only off the salaryman carousel but also society's carousel, and when you fall there's bound to be a hard landing because everyone just forgets you or ignores you. On the way to my local train station I often pass someone who has fallen off the carousel. He sits in the street watching the world go by, wrapped in an old overcoat, with his possessions stuffed into a cardboard box behind him. In the winter he moves to the underground passageway and sits there, holding a can of warm coffee he has bought from the machine nearby. Perhaps it's not a bad life when the weather is warm, no work, no overtime, no stress, no company. But when the cold weather comes, it is a different matter.

He sticks in my mind. He makes me remember what it is like to sleep out in the city. He makes me remember nights under the stars or the clouds far away and years ago, like that chilly autumn night on the banks of the Danube, hoping the rain would hold off and the police would not suddenly appear and tell me that sleeping by the river was not allowed in the Federal Republic of Yugoslavia. Or that park near the train station in Athens, waking up in the night to see my rucksack being slowly dragged away, grabbing hold of it and shouting, Hey, can't a travel bum get a proper night's sleep in the park without being woken up by an insomniac rucksack snatcher and would you mind leaving me alone so that I can get some rest because I'm hitching to Istanbul tomorrow? And he left me alone. But sleeping rough was an adventure for me and when the dawn came I'd be up and on my way to somewhere new. I wouldn't just sit there holding a can of coffee passing the hours, watching the world go by. I wouldn't be like that man near my station, sleeping out even when the cold wind blows and there's a hint of snow in the air.

As I head to work I wonder what the thousands of commuters think of him. Does he stick in their minds too? Does he remind them of times when they travelled light and rough, living on fresh air and freedom? I doubt it. The thousands of salarymen who pass probably don't think of him at all because he's not part of their world. They probably never travelled light and rough.

One February evening when the wind is colder than usual, I stop and talk to him. He has a scarf wrapped tightly round his neck and he wears old woollen gloves. I ask him how he manages through the cold nights – does he have anywhere to go when the cold comes? He doesn't react with shock when he looks up to see a foreign face. He's better at handling foreigners than many of the officials and shop assistants who go into semi-panic mode when confronted by an outsider. The old man tells me the underground passageway is good enough for him; he knows some warm spots where there's a little heating. He's not too cold, thanks for asking, and he doesn't mind living outside, the passageway is not the worst.

I talk to Miyuki about him. She drops by the local welfare office next day. They say, yes, they know about the old man. He used to stay in a shelter for the homeless but he didn't like it, moved out, would not return. He likes to live on the street and what can be done about that? But he has a little money too, they say, because he often buys food at a local 7-Eleven store. I expected that the welfare office would say it was not their job to look after people who didn't work. I'm surprised that at least they know about him and think about him.

He must have worked in a company at some stage. Maybe he was a salaryman, a long time ago, like I am now. Maybe he lost his job because people lose their jobs all the time in the small companies, even if they can never be fired in the big, powerful companies. Or maybe he just got tired of the salaryman life, decided he had had enough listening to Important People, enough talking to machines. Maybe it's better to talk to yourself than to computers and colleagues who don't talk back.

Out here in the Yokohama suburbs officialdom is laid-back about living on the street. His wishes are respected; he can stay in his underground passageway home and nobody disturbs him. It's different in Shinjuku, near Tokyo City Hall, where the important officials work and it is not laid-back. There used to be dozens of homeless people living in cardboard boxes in the underground passageway west of Shinjuku Station but the officials told them to move along and take their cardboard boxes with them to a shelter far away where they wouldn't disturb anyone, good riddance. The city officials wanted to build a moving walkway to help the commuters reach their offices more quickly in the morning and reach the station more quickly in the evening. When the cardboard box people refused to move, the police came with the riot squad in tow and the cardboard box people had to go. The walkway was built – by Sumitomo, not Mitsubishi – and now the commuters can reach their offices a little quicker in the morning, one, two or even three minutes quicker than before. The passageway on the west side of Shinjuku Station is clean and neat with a new moving walkway, no more cardboard box people, good riddance. But the same would happen in any country, wouldn't it?

10

七転び八起き

Nana korobi, ya oki

Fall down seven times, get up eight

Kaikaku-M takes over from Nishi-M as general manager. Like Nishi-M, he doesn't think much of the Gnosis project nor our research into next-generation products based on systematised knowledge. He believes we would be better off with fewer of these big-scale international ventures that only produce thick reports about what we can do and might do but little about what we did do. The reports might be useful to Mitsubishi sometime in the distant future when we have all retired, but then again, they might not. Kaikaku-M puts up with us and our project because of Komon-H in Head Office. Komon-H still likes our project and he is Kaikaku's boss. But during the fourth year of the project Komon hits sixty, the age when lifers get permanent parole, and we get ready for changes. One day Kaikaku-M invites the NGP Group members to his office for an announcement.

We troop down the stairs and across to the old building, wondering what's in store for us. The door of his office is open and he beckons us in.

– This meeting is to let you know about some organisational changes that have been decided by Head Office. Firstly, I would like to tell you that your work in the Gnosis project is very much appreciated.

Coming from someone who certainly doesn't appreciate the project, that sounds ominous. But no need to worry. We are all lifers so cannot get fired no matter what he thinks of Gnosis.

– Your project has some relevance to the company's long-term strategy, he continues. Your work gives indications of where we should be going in five or even ten years' time, although …

He pauses and purses his lips.

– Although it is not directly related to the products and business strategies of this lab, which I am trying to redefine and redirect.

This is the metaphorical glove removal and rolling up of shirtsleeves. Better get ready for what comes next.

– Of course, the laboratory appreciates your unflagging efforts – in particular, Watanabe-B for his international management skills, bringing over a dozen different organisations to work together, overcoming significant language and culture barriers, undertaking difficult technical research, travelling overseas at short notice and fulfilling the reporting regulations of the Ministry.

Wanabe-B nods in appreciation. He likes to have his linguistic and technical skills praised, though he probably doesn't want to be reminded of the Ministry regulations.

– The laboratory has duly noted the detailed reports of last year's work, the research papers written and the international meetings attended.

Come on, I feel like telling him. Get to the point. Just spit it out.

He reads our minds and spits it out.

– But for strategic reasons, it has now been decided to move the Gnosis project to the Osaka lab, where some practical application may be found for your work. The exact date for the move has yet to be fixed, but I expect it to be in about three months' time. As to the movement of group members – Watanabe-B, I believe you already know you are to be appointed department manager in this laboratory, so you will remain here.

Wanabe-B looks pleased with his new position – he will be a real class B manager now, not a wannabe anymore, but I'm sure he will miss the international project, flying here and there, with personal sidekick in tow. If Wanabe-B is moved upwards, who will run the Gnosis project now?

– Ueda-KS, you have been seconded from Osaka to our lab since last year. You will be pleased to hear you can return to your home lab in Osaka. You will take over running the Gnosis project from Watanabe-B and will be assigned the GR title. Finally, Riko-C and Muruta-KS – you will be given the option of moving with the project to Osaka or staying here and undertaking new work in Yokohama.

For a moment I wonder why I wasn't given the task of running the project because I was involved from the beginning and know it better than anyone. Perhaps it is because Ueda is a few years older than me. But at least I have the option of staying in Yokohama.

– Please do your best in your new assignments, Kaikaku-M says, and we head back to our desks.

Riko-C tells us he doesn't want to move anywhere. He will stay in Yokohama. Wanabe-B says Gnosis may be finished up soon. In spite of his best efforts, Nissan and Fuji Xerox have quit, and although Sumitomo Electric and some others have joined in their place, it is not what it was. With Komon-H retired, Mitsubishi has lost its enthusiasm.

Ueda is pleased to be able to return to Osaka and to be made GR. He tells Wanabe-B he will do his best, whatever happens, although it would be good if Muruta-KS moved to Osaka with him. How about it?

– Sorry, but no, I tell him. I really want to stay here. Kaikaku-M was serious about me being able to stay, wasn't he?

– Oh, yes. He means what he says.

– That's a relief. My wife's parents prefer that we stay here and she doesn't want to move either. She's expecting.

Our son arrives a few weeks later, a wad of dark hair on his head, but not black like the other babies, blue-grey eyes that would later turn to brown. We call him Eoin-Keisuke – Eoin because it is one of the few easily pronounceable Celtic names not already taken by older cousins, and Keisuke after the Japanese rock star, Keisuke Kuwata, whose tapes kept me going through the early years in Tokodai and still do. Miyuki stays in her parents' home in the western suburbs of Tokyo for a fortnight and her mother takes control, organising visits to the local hospital, preparing a baby futon, buying enough toys for the first twelve months and enough clothes for the first three years. I take a few days off to learn some baby management skills, then return to work. Riko-C tells me that from now on I should rush home at the 5 p.m. bell and forget about overtime and deadlines. He doesn't mean it, of course.

Wanabe-B moves to his new department and our group feels quieter than ever. Ueda-GR goes to Osaka for meetings almost every week. One morning he calls me to his desk.

– Yesterday's meeting was about relocating to Osaka. A question was raised about you. Do you wish to move?

– Move? No, of course not. No change. Kaikaku-M told me I could stay here, didn't he?

– Yes, he did. I need to know your decision because there will be another meeting in Osaka next week. Will I tell them you wish to stay here?

– Yes. For family reasons.

I'm wondering why all the questions. Perhaps he is hoping I will change my mind and move to Osaka to help him with the project. I know he'd like my assistance. But Kaikaku-M said I could stay and Ueda himself confirmed it.

A few more weeks pass. One day Ueda-GR comes to me and tells me a memo has arrived with details of the move. Boxes and computers are to be forwarded on 30 March and group members will move the following day.

– Well, it has been good working with you over the last year, I say.

– Wait a moment. The memo here says that two members of the current NGP Group are to move. The two members are, myself and … and Muruta-KS.

– What? Me? Is it a mistake?

– No.

– But did Kaikaku-M not tell me I could stay here?

– Yes.

– And didn't you give my answer that I was not moving?

– Yes.

– Then why is my name on the list?

– I don't make the decisions.

– But isn't there any explanation? I mean what is going on?

– Well, the situation seems to have changed. Kaikaku-M is no longer involved.

– But you can't just do things like that. I was told I could stay, wasn't I? Didn't you tell them that I decided to stay here?

– I conveyed your preference. But things do not always happen the way you want.

– This is too much. Look, if this is how things happen around here, then I'm outta here. I'm going to quit. *Sayonara.*

– Calm down, calm down. Take a little time to think it over. Think what's best for your career. You can't quit just like that. Remember you are a permanent employee.

– Can't quit? Oh yeah? I'll quit if and whenever I feel like quitting! My wife wants me to stay here, not 500 kilometres away. My wife's parents want to see their grandson.

Ueda-GR is looking a little uncomfortable now, as though I have suddenly become the boss and he is the naughty staff member who has screwed up. I take his advice and calm down. We've got on well up to now. Better think things over.

– Okay, okay, I'll think about it.

I think it over. I have a family now. I had better not make any hasty decisions. What about that meeting with Kaikaku-M? He probably wasn't telling a straight-out lie. He was trying to give the most optimistic scenario from what he knew at the time. It was a sort of short-term truth. If things changed later that would be a different situation, unrelated to the present. Or he may have assumed I would be treated specially, being a foreigner, but the planning department must have decided I was not really a foreigner. As far as they were concerned I was a permanent employee, a lifer, and had I not been given not one but two promotions in the space of a year and a half? Surely I couldn't expect any special concessions after that. Perhaps it was a case of one person or department treating me as a foreigner and another treating me as an ordinary employee.

At home that night, I discuss the situation with Miyuki.

– One option would be to just refuse the move. I wouldn't be fired. I'm a lifer, am I not?

– What would Ueda say to that?

– He wouldn't like it. He would have to tell the Osaka people that a senior member of his group was refusing to move. It wouldn't look good for him. That's why he is trying hard to persuade me. If I refuse, he will probably be down-ranked a notch or two.

– Well, you can't help that.

– If I refuse to move I will probably be sidelined with boring work, so I should be prepared to quit. But the Tokyo head-hunters I contacted don't seem to have anything on offer now, and there would be no use in applying to Toshiba or Hitachi. They would not appreciate defectors. I'd probably have to move out of Japan. But, you know, in spite of the work hassles, I still like living here.

– And my parents would prefer if we stayed in Japan for a while, even if we have to move to Osaka. At least they can come to visit their grandson once or twice a year. It might be best to do what Mitsubishi wants. They might return the favour by giving you a good position later. Why don't you talk to some other colleagues and then decide?

Next day I talk to Wanabe-B, who is settling in to his new department. He thinks I should accept the move.

– You know, Muruta-KS, this organisation is changing, becoming more internationalised. There will be a big future in Mitsubishi for people like you. You know the language, the ways of doing business, the working styles. You're the right type of foreigner for Mitsubishi. You should stay around. Stick it out and you'll see.

I go to Ueda-GR.

– Well, what is it to be?

– I'll move.

– A good decision, he says, and he looks relieved.

A week later, I receive a memo about the *jirei* ceremony, where the new appointment will be formally announced. The memo tells me to be in the lecture room five minutes before three on Friday afternoon. I should wear my company jacket and make sure my ID badge is attached to the left-side breast pocket.

About ten others are also receiving their *jirei*. Name cards on the desks tell us where to sit. Omiya-C from Personnel is there checking that everyone is present and making sure we are all in the correct seats, wearing our jackets with our ID badges attached to the left-side breast pocket. We sit in silence and I'm wondering why we always have to be five minutes early. Kaikaku-M walks in, flanked by two managers from Personnel.

Hey, Kaikaku-M, I want to shout, you didn't tell me the truth in that meeting, did you? Forgotten all about it, have you?

Of course he has. He is a busy man, managing several departments, organising people to do this and that, to go here and there. He would probably have forgotten he ever met me except that I'm the only foreigner in the division.

As Kaikaku-M steps up on the dais, Omiya-C shouts *kiritsu*, which means we should jump to attention. It's the army syndrome. I hate it when they go military. I feel like walking out. Deserters won't be shot. Or I could ignore the command, sit there as if I don't understand, but everyone knows I understand. I can't go back to being a real foreigner just when it suits me. It's probably not worth making a fuss over. I stand up with the others.

Omiya-C shouts *rei*, and everyone bows. I can skip the bowing. No one notices that I'm not bowing because they are busy bowing themselves.

– Please be seated, says Kaikaku-M. The *jirei* has come through. I will now announce the new appointments for those present. First, Sugai-T.

Sugai-T jumps to attention and shouts *hai*.

– You are assigned to the planning department in Head Office. You will move to Head Office at the end of the month.

Sugai-T bows deeply and sits down.

– Kunii-C.

Kunii-C jumps to attention and shouts *hai*.

– You are assigned to the visual display factory in Kyoto. However, you will continue to work in your present location till the end of the current financial year.

Kunii-C bows and sits down.

– Muruta-KS, he says. I stand up but don't jump or shout *hai*. That will have to be enough. I don't care what they think. I'm not into this militaristic stuff. It seems to be enough. No one tells me to shout *hai*.

– You are assigned to the industrial systems department in Osaka. You will support the Gnosis project as a member of the Cyber-Factory Group.

I nod and sit down.

– Ueda-GR.

Ueda-GR jumps to attention and shouts *hai*.

– You are assigned to the industrial systems department in Osaka. You will manage the Gnosis project and the Cyber-Factory Group.

Ueda-GR bows and sits down.

Kaikaku-M continues till everyone in the platoon has jumped to attention, shouted *hai* and been given orders.

– Please do your best in your new assignments.

Omiya from Personnel shouts *kiritsu*, then *rei*. We all stand and everyone – or almost everyone – bows as Kaikaku-M exits. Platoon dismissed.

The Mitsubishi employee rules state that I may take up to five days off for a move within Japan – two days for packing, one day travelling, and two days to put everything in order in the new place. It would have been enough when I was single, moving into that timber-framed, paper-walled place with the difficult neighbours and few belongings. Now with a family I need about five weeks, but the permitted moving time is fixed for everyone. There can be no exceptions. We start preparing three weeks in advance. Two men from the logistics department arrive at our apartment one Saturday morning, measure everything in sight and bring in 100 folded cardboard boxes from their van, fifteen rolls of plastic bubble wrap and fifteen rolls of sealing tape. They tell us they will be back with more boxes later and we prepare.

When moving day dawns the truck is waiting outside at 8.30 and they have everything loaded by midday. We travel to Osaka by train, in accordance with the regulations, spend a night in a small hotel and arrive at our new company residence in nearby Amagasaki at nine next morning.

It is a concrete building with an elevator up to the fifth floor and a view out over a little river that doubles as a storm water drain, a tiny park that is mostly paved over, and the asphalt labyrinths of north-west Osaka. The truck has already arrived, with five strong movers waiting for the order to unload. They place each box in the designated room and are gone by lunchtime. In the afternoon a man from the gas company arrives to check the gas supply; an electrician comes to fix the air conditioner units to the walls and install the standard toilet seat-heating and spray units; and the TV man adjusts the television to the local broadcasting frequencies. The telephone already works – we were given the new number two weeks before we moved. Everything seems perfect till we connect our light fittings to the ceiling sockets and discover that Osaka has a different electrical frequency from Yokohama. We manage without the main lights for a night and buy new lights next day. The apartment is smaller than the previous one. We use the window balcony as a storage shed and throw away any books, toys and kitchenware we don't absolutely need. It feels like we are going down in the world.

Then the paperwork begins. Tanjun-C from Personnel brings the forms to my desk and explains what has to be filled in. The housing forms ask for details of my family registry – which prefecture I was born in and registered in. I point out that, for reasons which should be obvious, I was not born in any Japanese prefecture and was not registered anywhere in this country except as an alien. Tanjun-C scratches his head and frowns. Just his luck to get an awkward employee. Never happened before. Why couldn't I be the same as everyone else and be born in some prefecture or other and be registered like every other employee somewhere in the country? He goes off to check the employee-housing regulations and returns with a smile.

– Your wife is Japanese, he says, as though this is the key to solving the complicated situation.

– Here is another application form. Your wife can fill it in. Her father can act as guarantor for your apartment and you will not need a family registry. Please return it to this office within three days.

I take the paper. It requests the guarantor's name and address, current employer, annual income and number of years in current employment.

– Wait a minute, I say. Why do my wife and her father have to be involved? This move is not for my own convenience. It was decided by Head Office for some unexplained corporate reason. I didn't need a family registry or a guarantor for the Mitsubishi apartment in Yokohama. Why do I need it here?

– The company housing you have moved into is not owned by Mitsubishi. The owner insists that all tenants submit their family registry to prove they have a reputable background. Otherwise a guarantor is required.

– But why can't the company act as guarantor for me? They did it a few years ago when I was renting a private apartment near Yokohama.

– You were a contract employee then. Exceptions can be made for contract employees but not for permanent ones. The company can hardly be expected to act as guarantor for every employee, can they? Please fill in the form.

I take it home and show it to Miyuki. She says it is just company bureaucracy and she will phone her father about it. He is a salaryman and will know what to do. She phones him. Even if he has been a salaryman all his career and is a department manager in NHK, he is not pleased to be asked about his salary and the number of years in his current employment in order to guarantee a company apartment for his son-in-law. He says that we should politely tell the man from Personnel where to get off.

I convey the message to Tanjun-C. He scratches his head and asks Ueda-GR what we should do.

– *Saah*, what will we do? says Ueda-GR. Can your wife's father not give us the information?

– No, he can't.

– But we need a guarantor because you don't have a family registry.

– I will accept a family registry if you give me one.

– Now, don't be silly. You can't have a family registry. You are not Japanese.

– If I am a normal Mitsubishi employee and have to accept the *jirei* whether I want it or not, I should have the same housing conditions as everyone else, shouldn't I? Look, I know what I'll do. I'll ask the general manager to be my guarantor. I'm sure he would just love to write down his salary and the number of years he has been in Mitsubishi so that he can help a hardworking employee get a roof over his head.

– No, no. Please don't do that, says Ueda. We cannot go disturbing the general manager for something like this. Let me have the paper. I will be your guarantor.

He fills in some details, leaving the salary section blank, and gives the form to Tanjun-C. Tanjun-C goes off with the form, pleased to have the awkward employee problems solved. Everyone happy.

Later I discover the probable reason for the family registry requirement. The apartment block is in a working-class area of Amagasaki, where many *burakumin* people live – the descendants of the *eta*, the lowest caste in feudal Japan, who were shunned by the other classes. Nowadays, conservative landlords still prefer not to rent apartments to *burakumin*, just as some businesses prefer not to employ them and conservative families prefer not to have a son or daughter marry one of them, although they are culturally and ethnically indistinguishable from everyone else. I heard people say you should not get into an argument with one of the *burakumin* because they are tough customers. But the *burakumin* I met later were as friendly as anyone. The Amagasaki city council has mounted various campaigns urging people to forget old prejudices, but cultural stereotypes don't disappear overnight. The owner of the apartment was probably less worried about having a foreign tenant than one of the *burakumin*. The easiest way of determining whether someone has a *burakumin* background is to request his or her family registry.

It is only a three-hour *shinkansen*-train ride from Yokohama to Osaka but the company culture is different. The Yokohama complex was half office, half factory. Osaka is mostly factory culture. The chimes and ding-dongs are the same, the exercise drill sergeant is the same, but they do not play the 'Tennessee Waltz' and 'Auld Lang Syne' as reminders to go home early on Wednesdays. Our building is rougher and older than Yokohama: the walls are faded beige without any colourful posters about quantum leaps in quality, although the company president's mug shot is still watching us. The ceilings are higher than in Yokohama, with water pipes running on overhead hangers and fluorescent lights dangling from chains with electric wires running between the lights. Thick water pipes are attached to columns in the middle of the building. Someone tells me these pipes caused a lot of problems when they broke in the earthquake a year earlier and sprayed water everywhere. But all was cleared up within a few hours of the quake.

In Yokohama I could cycle into the company complex, just stopping to show my ID card to the guards, but here I have to dismount at a white line two metres in front of the gate, walk my bicycle past the guard box as far as an inner white line, then remount and peddle off to my building. I don't mind stopping and showing my card, but why do I have to dismount and walk the bike through the gate? I ask Ueda-GR. He says that a rule is a rule and you cannot change that. I understand that it is discipline for discipline's sake, a bit of Mitsubishi schoolyard culture.

But if it is schoolyard culture, then I can play senior schoolboy, can't I? Some evenings when the guard doesn't seem to be watching and I have a cap on my head to cover my foreignness, I whisper to myself, *go for it,* and run the gate and peddle off home as fast as I can. Once, I hear a voice shouting after me, but I don't look back because if I do they will see my foreign face and I will surely be on the wanted list for breaking the gate rules and all the guards at all four gates, north, south, rear and main, will be on the lookout for me; they'll surely get their man one way or another because I'm a little different from the other 8,000 employees who pass through the gates every day. I might even find a note on my desk next day telling me that if I don't obey the gate rules my bicycle-parking permit may be revoked or even worse. But no one sees my face. It feels good to break a rule and get away with it.

I settle into the Osaka lab and think about that big future Wanabe-B mentioned, that future waiting for me if I stick it out a little longer. Besides running the gate a few times, I've been a pretty good company man. I've moved to a different part of the country, as I was ordered; I didn't complain about Kaikaku-M in Yokohama breaking his promise – well, not that much; I even put up with the militaristic *jirei* ceremony, except that I didn't bow and didn't shout *hai.* They won't get too many foreigners who fit in as well as I have, will they? I hope they will remember me when the corporate escalator moves up – not that I have strong corporate ambitions to be in charge of people. I just like to feel appreciated.

Ueda-GR is looking after the Gnosis project, receiving advice from a senior manager from Nagoya. He repeats much of what was done already because neither he nor the Nagoya manager know what went on in the early stages. It would be so much more efficient if I were managing things, but big organisations value tradition more than efficiency. Ueda says the project will be finished in a few months.

My new work is in eco-product design – how to make environmentally friendly air conditioners, refrigerators, undersea cables, satellites, mobile telephones and everything else that Mitsubishi makes, how to choose eco-friendly materials, minimise energy requirements and make all the marvellous Mitsubishi gizmos and gadgets clean, green and easy to recycle. That is a lot to do, but we have to start somewhere because we are behind the other companies, especially NEC and Hitachi.

I visit the Mitsubishi factories in Hiroshima and Kyoto. The buildings are not pretty – the usual cladding and concrete walls – but inside everything is neat, every piece of equipment in its place, not a speck of dust on the green-painted floors, every passageway marked with white arrows and lines to show where trolleys run and where employees walk, and signs on the walls with slogans about productivity, safety and quality. I visit a few non-Mitsubishi factories too. The Fuji Xerox model factory in Kanagawa is more than just clean and green – they have almost reached the holy eco-grail of zero emissions, zero pollution. I see we have a lot of catching up to do but that is normal. In Mitsubishi we are used to sitting around at the starting line till we see what the others are doing because we are a cautious bunch, different from those risk-taking, adventurous companies like Fuji Xerox and Sony. It is all very well being adventurous but, as the lady in Personnel told me when I suggested they consider employing foreigners from non-famous universities, just think of the risks, think of what might go wrong. In Mitsubishi it's always better to avoid risks. Wait and see what the others are doing and then follow. But once we get going, we'll catch up. And overtake. It's not my style, but I can't change Mitsubishi overnight.

I write up my proposals for the clean and green eco-friendly future that Head Office says is coming soon. Ueda-GR asks me to take charge of software development, overseeing programmers in another division. It has been a while since I was appointed to manager class but this is the first time I am really managing something and I feel appreciated again. I start off by organising a meeting with the programmers. I email Tani-KS, the supervisor, and ask him to come for a meeting, but he says he is too busy this week. I wait a week and try again but he is still busy. I telephone him but he has other work to do and cannot promise anything.

– I think Tani-KS is not interested in working for us, I tell Ueda-GR. Why did you suggest him?

– Because the department manager recommended him. Joshi-B gave me his name. Look, why don't I try to arrange the meeting?

Ueda-GR calls Tani-KS. Surprise. He is not busy after all. No problem. He can come for a meeting. Tomorrow will be fine.

I understand quickly that Tani-KS likes to do things through real native managers, not dubious foreigner-managers because who ever heard of a foreigner in Mitsubishi in a responsible position, in charge of a real project?

Ueda-GR attends the meeting with me and everything goes smoothly. Tani listens carefully and tells us he will have everything done on time, according to the specification, within budget.

– Good, says Ueda-GR. I will leave Muruta-KS to discuss the details with you.

I discuss the details but suddenly Tani is not so sure he can do all the work.

– I am afraid I will have to skip some parts because my group does not have the resources, he says, which means it is too much trouble and he doesn't want to go off learning new things just for me.

Okay, I'll accept a bit less than I originally wanted. We have a deal.

Two months later he comes back with a neat little program. Click the big yellow button on the screen, give the program some data and it draws pretty graphs and coughs up figures that tell whether the product – refrigerator, gas heater, washing machine or television set – is better or worse for the environment than last year's model and whether Mitsubishi products are environmentally better or worse than what Hitachi, Toshiba or Philips make. We think it is a good program because we can see that Mitsubishi products are the greenest. Well, not all of them – but a few are.

I tell Tani and his team they've done a good job for me. I organise trial data and the program is included in the lab exhibits in a laboratory open-day when we show off our wares and try to sell them to the Mitsubishi factories and development centres. Some visitors from Head Office tell me they like the program. Would I give lectures about it to the factory designers and managers in the corporate Institute of Technology and explain all the things we have learnt? Sure, I'll do the lectures. Ueda-GR is pleased. He thinks it will be an opportunity to promote our work.

– But do not give away much information about your computer program, he adds. If you tell them too much they will develop their own programs in the factories and they won't give us any funding for next year's work.

I prepare my lectures, making sure not to give away any of our classified knowledge. Being an official Mitsubishi lecturer in the Institute of Technology makes me feel important, although I wish the attendees wouldn't all stand up and bow before I begin my lecture and stand and bow again at the end, because it reminds me of that *jirei* ceremony. I wish the guys at the back would pay attention and wouldn't close their eyes and take a nap while I'm talking. I'm not a boring lecturer – honest – even if it is mid-afternoon, which is semi-official naptime during lectures in this country.

I give out free sample versions of the computer program and a few of the attendees who didn't take a nap are happy to try it out in their factories. It works for some of them but for others it has too many buttons on the screen, needs too much data, and when they click the wrong button at the wrong time with the wrong data, the program stops being a neat little tool and becomes a crotchety piece of techno-trash.

I go back to Tani and tell him we have a problem: the program crashes big time when someone presses the wrong button with the wrong data. It should just give a warning, shouldn't it?

He scratches his head.

– It's not my group's fault. It's really Microsoft's fault for making a bad operating system. Besides that I am not used to working with a foreigner. But I will fix it if the lab pays for my time.

No use asking what the hell being a foreigner has to do with it and why it is only a problem when the program crashes. I wouldn't get a good answer. Working with a foreigner probably means extra stress because he has never done it before and the stress only becomes noticeable when someone finds problems with his work.

I talk to Ueda-GR and Joshi-B. They agree the lab will pay for Tani's time. We're not tough bargainers and maybe we appreciate the stress that Tani feels, having to work for a foreigner, even if the documents are all in his own language. Tani fixes the program buttons that don't work. But then I find another bug and the factory people find more problems. The weeks are going by, deadlines are being missed and soon we are all pointing invisible fingers at one another. The only thing we can agree upon is that it is Microsoft's fault – they're mostly foreigners too, aren't they? But we cannot get Bill Gates to rewrite his wobbly operating system for us and Head Office wants the bugs fixed and quickly too. Finally I give up on Tani and his team. I fix some of the bugs myself and get a local non-Mitsubishi company to do the rest. They don't complain about Microsoft or about foreigners. They fix everything and they even charge less than Tani. Head Office is happy again and the factories that want to make eco-friendly products are happy. We're slowly catching up with the other companies and not taking any risks – perfect Mitsubishi business strategy.

At the end of the year a notice arrives in my in-tray telling me I am to be awarded one of the laboratory prizes. Well, what do you know? Someone appreciates my work after all. That program probably has some bugs hidden where no one has looked yet, but still, I deserve a pat on the back, don't I? Especially after all that hassle with Tani and his men who were so stressed by working with a foreigner they couldn't do the job properly and delayed everything by six months. At least Head Office considers my work useful. They like to see proof that we are an ecologically responsible company. But please don't compare us with Fuji Xerox. We're not that good. Not yet.

I go to the main hall for the prize-giving ceremony, five minutes before starting time, wearing my jacket with my ID badge over my left breast pocket, keeping my hands out of my pockets. I can obey the rules this time. I sit down with the handful of other prize-winners. Behind the dais are two large flags – the *hinomaru*, or red sun flag of Japan, and the Mitsubishi red diamonds. The two flags match, red symbol on white. There is some low music being played in the background and I listen for a moment. *Dum-dadum-dadum* … Could it be? After all these years? Yes, they are playing our song, the company employees' song. It's the first time I've ever heard it. I can tolerate the heavy lyrics for once, O*h-oh techno-life, Mitsu-bishi wu wu wu.* Thank God we don't have to sing along.

The general manager arrives, makes the usual speech – let us build on the good work we have done this year and scale even greater heights next year – and he calls each prize-winner in turn. He says, *shocho hyosho hyoshojo*, which means General Manager's Commendation, Certificate of Merit. It is quite a tongue twister but he never stumbles and he repeats it for every prize-winner. When my turn comes I go up, give a little bow and accept the certificate. The general manager tells us that unfortunately, with the way the economy is, the cash prizes will be small this year but look out for them in next month's salary slip, and sorry, but they will be taxed at source. Congratulations to all.

Back at my desk I look at my certificate of merit. In spite of all the problems with that program, things seem to have worked out. Perhaps I was right after all to accept the *jirei* and the move. Perhaps I was right to hang on.

11

貧乏暇なし

Bimbo hima nashi

The poor have no time for leisure

In springtime, before the cherry blossoms bloom, before the children set off for their first day at school, before the young men and women set off for their first day at the company, the thoughts of many a salaryman turn to one of the more important things in life – the *shunto*, or spring labour offensive. It is the time of year when, for once, unions and senior management don't agree about everything. Positions are staked out, wage demands drawn up, meetings planned and the annual spring offensive is on.

It's not just our union in Mitsubishi. All the manufacturing, transport and service industry unions join in the *shunto* because it is an annual rite and without it the labour movement might lose its zest for life. The rest of the year the unions are quiet, content to issue the odd bulletin of percentages and slogans, organise meetings between business divisions, and give us rank and file a corporate shoulder to cry on, should we have work or family problems. The unions do get a little noisy on May Day with colourful gatherings in the parks, but only a few, mainly left-leaning, members attend. They wear red headbands, wave red flags, raise their fists in unison at the end of the speeches and shout, Power to the unions, the workers or something or other, while the TV cameras are watching. Then they go off for a picnic and a chat. But the *shunto* is different. The *shunto* is serious business.

This year the export market has picked up. The American consumers have been good to us and the Europeans and Asians haven't been so bad either. Profits are up in Mitsubishi. We can expect management to look kindly on us hardworking minions and give us a reasonable raise.

But we expect too much. This year management are being stingy. They are keeping the corporate purse strings tight because they say the Americans might not keep buying or the yen might start rising again, and a year of plenty must provide for the lean years that may follow.

Our union does not agree. The union bulletins tell us that we workers have done our bit, we deserve more and if more is not forthcoming, then, yes, the union is prepared to consider using the ultimate weapon, a weapon to put fear into the top brass, a weapon that even the most radical of workers would hesitate to use – the union is prepared to call a strike. I'd never have dreamt it possible here in conscientious, hardworking Japan. It is so foreign that no native word exists to describe the concept. Instead, the English word has to be used, with some adaptation, and an awkward, four-syllable *sutoraiki* is theoretically possible. It's so awkward that it is often abbreviated to *suto*. But things would never go as far as a real *suto*, would they?

The union sets up a ballot and we prepare to vote. A slip of paper is left in my in-tray one lunchtime:

Do you approve of giving the union the power to call a strike, Yes or No?

Yes, yes, yes. I'd love to see what happens in a real *sutoraiki*, see how the top brass react. I'm careful not to spoil my vote because it is the only chance I get to vote in this country. I mark the slip, fold it in two and place it carefully in the box set out on a table near the stair landing. I tick my name on the list beside the box so that the union can confirm I have exercised my rights and the union rep won't be running to my desk in mid-afternoon to shake the box under my nose. Most of my colleagues also seem to have voted yes because a few days later the union announces that they have been given the mandate by us rank-and-file members to resort, if need be, to the ultimate weapon and call a *sutoraiki*. They will, however, continue to do their utmost to find a solution and will negotiate in good faith with management right up until the end because officially no one really wants the ultimate weapon to be used. Privately, of course, many of my colleagues wouldn't mind a little strike. None of us would mind seeing the ultimate weapon used a bit, just to see what it is like.

Wanabe-B is visiting the Osaka lab for a meeting and we go for a drink after work to share stories. He tells me Riko-C has quit and started a little company of his own, writing software or fixing hardware, he's not quite sure. It is a big surprise. Cherry trees can blossom in December, after all.

– Really? That's great, I say. Or I mean it is a pity – for the company.

– Maybe it's as well he quit. He was not a real Mitsubishi man. Too hasty. But if he is prepared to take the risks, then let him. Now tell me, how is Gnosis and our inspired knowledge?

That project is still dear to his heart, even if he has moved on and up in the world.

– As you guessed last year, it is being finished up soon. I think it was a bit heretical for management here. Too futuristic. It was all right for Yokohama but this is Osaka, where only practical stuff goes down. The general manager here said he thinks the project should be completed and Ueda-GR just said yes, sure. He always agrees with what the boss says. He has asked me to edit the final report.

– The wrong people running the wrong projects. That's what often happens, says Wanabe-B, reflecting on what a good project manager he was himself – how he got his strategic ideas across to so many people in different companies and continents almost unaided, how he grasped all the finer points of the new technologies we were proposing as long as they were explainable with pictures, and how he travelled far and wide, with trusty sidekick in support, tolerating business class on Japan Airlines, reluctantly accepting first class only when there was no alternative. He tells me the Gnosis project was useful because it made management think about where we are headed.

– And if I may say so, top management need a bit of shaking up, he adds.

– They might get shaken up soon enough. Did you hear about this talk of a strike?

– I heard. But you know, a strike might not be a bad idea. Nowadays everyone is too damn satisfied. A strike would liven things up. It might make people think why they are working, make them value their jobs more.

Wanabe-B is a radical sort of manager. He is right that a strike would liven things up. Even talking about it might liven things up. But it's strange because he is a department manager. Department managers are not in the union and cannot go on strike even if there is one. He is a radical sort of manager.

– The strikes we had long ago were useful. Shook everyone up, so they did.

– How long ago was that? The nineteenth century?

– No, not that long ago. The last one was in 1980 and there were lots of strikes in the seventies. Hard to believe, isn't it? The union was much stronger than now, our salaries were low and we had that fire in our hearts. We didn't overdo the strikes either. One lasted, let me see, an hour, others a bit longer, half a day or more. And then, as I recall, we did have one endless strike. A death match.

– Was it that bad?

– I mean it went on till one side gave in. I forget who gave in but someone did.

– And the death match lasted longer than half a day?

– Yes, much, much longer. Maybe a week, or more. That was the best strike we had, all those years ago. Exciting times we had back then. Nothing like it since. I will tell you something. I really think a strike this spring would be a good idea. A few hours or perhaps a day would be enough. But do you know what I think?

– What do you think?

– I think the union no longer has the guts to do it.

A union meeting is called at lunchtime. Two union men from our lab stand on a dirty-white podium dragged out of the union storage shed for special occasions like this. The podium is in the middle of the company road between our building, B3, and the factory building, K2. We won't be run over by the trucks and vans because they all stop for lunch and the drivers are probably attending their own union meetings a few company blocks away. Our union men have white headbands with the characters for *faito* written in black to show they're ready to *fight-o* for their demands. I know one of them – Kuroda from the sensing department on the fifth floor. He delivers the union news bulletin. He's always quiet, never says anything. He just puts the bulletin in the in-tray and leaves. I don't think he is really the type to *faito* about anything. The other union man looks tougher and looks like he might be ready to *faito* if necessary. He is the important one because he's holding the loudspeaker as if to say this is my show and I am raring to go.

– Good afternoon, fellow union members, he shouts. My thanks to you for taking time from your precious lunch break to come to hear what I have to say. I can announce that management have refused to increase their offer. We plan to continue negotiating till the deadline on 31 March. If negotiations fail, we will call a strike on 1 April from 8.30 a.m. Detailed instructions about the strike will be given to each employee by the department union representative.

He talks about how the negotiations have gone, who said what, why this year is the year to act, what we should expect if the ultimate weapon has to be used, let us hold firm for our demands, let us see this through. I seem to have heard most of it before. I leave the meeting and go for my lunchtime walk down the company road between the lab buildings and the factories, past the fit-looking guy who has a skipping rope he takes out every day to skip quietly for ten minutes, past the factory workers who have finished their union meeting and are getting ready to play mini-tennis with mini-rackets from the union shed, using the white lines painted on the company road specially for the mini-tennis; I walk by the Shinto shrine, bigger and rougher than the one in Yokohama, where the manufacturing gods are probably scheming against the union, then past the guy who practises his trumpet near the warehouse, finally past Nonbiri-KS from our lab, who swings a baseball bat at lunchtime to keep in shape – no ball, just a wooden bat, whoosh, whoosh. He is one of the friendly guys who likes to chat. Sometimes he puts on a scary grin when he sees me and pretends he's going to hit me, a friendly bash on the head, and I keep away from the whoosh, whoosh. The swinging bat and the scary grin scare me just a little. You never know what a stressed-out salaryman might do by mistake. Sometimes he stops whooshing, no scary grin, and we have a chat about Mitsubishi or about the union.

– The union won't do anything, he says. The union likes it the way things are. They like the *nurumayu*, the lukewarm water. The managers are the same. Everyone is content, like being in a lukewarm bath. Why leave it for the chill outside?

He starts swinging his bat again, whoosh, and I move away before he gives me his scary grin. See you later, Nonbiri-KS. I go back to my lab, up the stairs, the right-hand side of the stairs, which has arrows on the floor pointing downwards, telling me I'm on the wrong side, but who cares about the stair rules when no one is watching? I wonder if Nonbiri-KS is right about the union and about Mitsubishi. I wonder if we are too comfortable in the lukewarm water, the *nurumayu*. Or would our union really use the ultimate weapon? Imagine having a real *sutoraiki*. We might have an interesting few weeks ahead. But then again we might not, because the chances that agreement will be reached are high. Nonbiri is probably right because he has been in the company twenty years.

Three days before the 31 March deadline, our department union rep gives a short speech at lunchtime in the passageway between the partitions of our floor. He has no podium nor loudspeaker, which would be overdoing it in our quiet and sometimes silent department, but he shouts as loud as he can so that the people at the far end of the floor can hear him. I'm sitting only a few metres away and I wish he would keep it down but he doesn't. We always eat at our desks because we have no canteen here in the Osaka division, just a lunch box delivery service. A few people look up from their food and computer screens of solitaire or noughts and crosses and pay attention to what he is saying but most just continue eating lunch and playing solitaire. They are not really interested because they like the *nurumayu*, the lukewarm water.

– Management have increased their offer, the union rep shouts. But it still falls short of our demands. Negotiations are continuing.

Then he shuts up and it is quiet again.

The TV news announces that some of the unions are taking it to the wire this year. Discussions are expected to go on into the night if necessary.

A strike is a possibility, but unions and management will do their utmost to come to agreement.

March the 31st. In mid-afternoon a special announcement is made over the public address system. Management and union have come to an agreement. The offer of 1.2 per cent is accepted by the union and the *sutoraiki* is called off.

I feel let down, disappointed. What are we paying them the high subscription fee for if they won't grab the chance and have a strike even once?

I see Nonbiri-KS at lunch. He stops whooshing his bat and says, What did I tell you? They are too comfortable in the *nurumayu*.

The union does more than prepare for strikes that never happen. Every year, union and management in each department have a formal meeting, the *shoku-kon*, to discuss work and worries, solutions and improvements. Two months before the meeting we fill in a long questionnaire, a bit like the annual health check except that it is about the health of our department, so it does not ask surprising questions such as whether we have bad breath, in other people's opinion, or if we dislike our personality. The questions are sensible:

What problems do you have with your work? Do you have suggestions for improving efficiency? Does your manager show adequate leadership? Does he explain requirements to you? Is there a shortage of personnel or of equipment? Do you feel there are barriers that make it harder to carry out your work? Do you have suggestions for making our department a better place to work in? Can safety, hygiene, welfare or training be improved? Can overtime be effectively reduced? Please feel free to make proposals and requests.

It seems like a good system and I enthusiastically put together my wishes and requests – the first year, that is, before I know better. I write my requests and submit them to the union.

1. *My desk is not large and I have two computers, two storage drives, one scanner, one telephone, an in-tray, several books and many journals on it. Additionally, in this lab I have to eat lunch at my desk. I know space is a precious commodity but I would respectfully request some more elbow room. It would make life easier and would surely make me more efficient.*

2. *It is very hot at my desk some days in the summer. My keyboard and my desktop feel sticky with sweat and the upholstered chair is uncomfortable to sit on because I am too far away from the air conditioners, when they are switched on. Can we please switch those air conditioners on according to how we feel, rather than according to calendar dates, and can we set them below 28 degrees Celsius?*

A few weeks later the *shoku-kon* report comes through, a half-dozen pages of discussions and conclusions, and in there I find the answers to my questions – not the answers I would like, because the company lab is not meant to be a holiday camp, is it?

Please try to use your assigned desk space as efficiently as possible, discarding old books and hardware when no longer needed. Please note that the desks will have to be moved later in the year to fit the relocation of the kitchen. This will make things a little tighter so let us all try to reduce the space we use. In the Osaka division lunch is normally eaten at one's desk, making sure not to drop any food or disturb colleagues.

Operation of the air conditioners is decided for the laboratory by the environmental management committee. Air conditioners may only be switched on after 1 June, if and when the room temperature goes above 28 degrees, and the temperature must be set no lower than 28. Please understand that this is to conserve energy and the rule must be strictly applied.

I see. I shouldn't have asked. I know it's not a holiday camp, but it sometimes feels like an army camp. Next year I won't make any awkward requests. If it gets too hot I will follow the example of Tsume-T in the row next to me. He doesn't have too many books or computers on his desk and there is space for a little electric fan that he bought in the company shop. He switches it on in the hot summer months and it blows air at his face, helps him stay cool in the hot office and probably helps him concentrate and work more efficiently. I suppose I could buy a little electric fan like Tsume-T and work more efficiently and comfortably, but I have no space for it. Instead I make do with an old-fashioned paper fan for the really hot days. I swish the fan back and forth; it's cool and the desk is almost tolerable, till I get tired swishing. I buy a straw mat for my upholstered seat to keep my backside from getting hot, and I keep an ice-pack in the kitchen freezer that I take out in the morning and hold on the back of my neck for a few minutes or sit on when the straw mat is not enough – a bit of cool luxury in the summer swelter and the company lab almost feels like a holiday camp.

Tsume-T also has a good solution for the winter when the air is dry and it is easy to catch cold. He has a little electric humidifier on the floor next to his desk to blow humid air. He never gets colds so it must be worth it. He looks after himself well. He even keeps his fingers in good shape for typing because every few weeks he takes out his nail-clipper and clips away for a few minutes. The clips are really loud in our quiet department. I'm sure everyone can hear them but no one seems to notice. They are used to people keeping their typing fingers in shape. In any case it's quieter than the Yokohama lab, where one of the senior managers used to clip away for such a long time I wondered how many fingers he had. One day I sneaked a look into his alcove and I understood. One sock was off and lying on the floor beside his shoes and he was just pulling the other on. The Osaka managers would never do that.

It is my second year in the Osaka lab and the next *shoku-kon* questionnaire comes around. I won't make any awkward requests like last year inviting sod-off answers that made me feel I was stupid to even ask. But before I get a chance not to ask awkward questions, Nitta-C, the department union rep, comes to my desk.

– Muruta-KS, we are organizing the union reps for the year. It appears that the other senior members of your group have already done their rep duty. Would you mind being rep this year?

To tell the truth, I would mind. I don't want to attend boring meetings, prepare long-winded questionnaires, listen to management's politely phrased sod-off answers to awkward questions, write them up and send them back to probably disappoint the question-askers. But it would be selfish to just say no, refuse rep duty and force Nitta-C to find someone else. I will do my bit for the union. It might even be useful to see how it works, just this once.

– No problem, I tell him. I will be rep this time.

The first meeting for all six reps in the department is held one lunchtime. Nitta-C distributes the proposed questionnaire, which will be mostly the same as last year. We add a couple of headings about current projects and Nitta-C says we can submit it for approval to the company. I wonder why we need approval. Does that not take away our freedom to ask what we want?

– We have to get approval, says Nitta-C. It is a company rule.

There are no sections inviting potentially awkward questions because Nitta-C knows what can be asked and what cannot. Everything is duly approved. I make copies and distribute the sheets to everyone in our group, collect them a few days later, write a summary of the main points and forward them to Nitta-C. I hope that is enough because I have plenty of other work to do.

Nitta-C emails me a week later. There is a preparatory meeting this evening at seven to discuss all the responses to the questionnaire and decide what to include at the big meeting. All group reps are to attend.

Could he not give us more notice? He thinks evening meetings are normal because he works till nine or ten every night. I like to go home before seven. I send an email telling him that I will not be able to attend and I ask if this meeting is really necessary; if so, could we not hold it during work hours?

Next morning his reply is waiting for me: yes, this meeting is really necessary and, no, union meetings cannot, for any reason whatsoever, be held during normal work hours. It is a rule. He would like to emphasise that the *shuku-kon* is not something to be treated trivially. It is an important chance to improve things just a little in the department. Each year the department reps hold several meetings lasting three or four hours in the evenings in preparation for the *shoku-kon*. They do not complain about how it might interfere with work or family matters. If I am not prepared to offer that sort of commitment to the union, I should find someone else from my group to take my place.

I'm not prepared to offer that sort of commitment, but I don't want to go looking for someone else to do my job either. I attend the next meeting because it is the last one before the *shoku-kon*. We re-double-check the final list of questions.

– Everyone agree with this? asks Nitta-C.

Everyone agrees.

– Then we can submit it to the union executive, who will submit a copy to the department manager. Next we will confirm the procedures for the *shoku-kon* as described in the *shoku-kon* rule sheet.

We confirm the order in which we will speak, who will ask the questions, how many questions can be asked by each union rep (two), how many answers the company are allowed (two), who takes the minutes, who sits where, everything except the colour of the seats. That is all. See you on the day. Do not be late.

We're early. We gather in the reception area of our building six minutes before the starting time, even earlier than the instruction sheet tells us because we want to be squeaky right, at least at the start. We walk out of our building together, looking very serious, cross the company road to the new B4 building and take the elevator to the executive meeting room. The department manager, Joshi-B, and group managers are seated on the side of the table away from the door, in order of decreasing seniority from the centre to the ends of the table, with the union secretary at the far end. Our seats are nearer the door. We know our place, even if we are asking the questions today and the group managers are in defensive mode. There is no small talk today. This is serious. Joshi-B opens the meeting. There is no bowing, no military stuff like the *jirei* ceremony and I'm glad about that.

– On behalf of management I wish to thank everyone in the department for their efforts over the past year, he says. I believe the work done in this department has contributed in no small way to the improved financial situation of the company. In today's *shoku-kon* I urge you to frankly express your opinions and requests. The managers will try their utmost to respond positively and promptly to all matters. Please look at the schedule I have distributed. Does the union agree to the schedule for today's meeting?

– The union agrees, says Nitta-C.

– Good. Now I would like to hear the union members' opinions on management policies and current work. In particular I know there is concern at the amount of commissioned work you do for the factories and the consequent lack of time you have for basic research – the breakthroughs. My answer is that the factory commissions will lead you to the breakthroughs, so please keep this in mind. Now, let us move to the first question.

We look at the sheet listing the questions for discussion.

– We will begin with Ota-KS from the Factory Controller Group.

– Thank you, says Ota-KS. The first point I wish to mention is that we believe our team motivation has recently become weak. We feel this is due to the lack of strong leadership. Furthermore, our group members think that lab policy news and planning information are slow in reaching us. We would like to have group meetings more regularly.

Just as well I am not in Ota's group. They like meetings. Maybe it means they want more mid-afternoon breaks for having a little doze as the manager rambles on about the latest pronouncements from Head Office. Or maybe they don't care about the meetings and they are just trying to sound diligent after criticising the boss's leadership.

Motoda-KS, the manager of Ota's group, does not seem to mind the criticism. He glances at his notes and begins to answer.

– The work of the group has changed considerably over the past year. It is natural that team members find it hard to motivate themselves at the beginning. These are problems that occur with new projects and are not, I believe, due to leadership issues. I request the group members to wait another six months and see if they feel the same way about team motivation and leadership. As to the meetings, we will hold them more often from next month.

– Is that sufficient? says Joshi-B.

– We would request that the meetings be held weekly. Also we would request that the motivation issue be considered sooner than in six months, says Ota-KS, who is a tough negotiator, which is probably why he is still on the door-side of the table and not sitting next to Joshi-B.

– Okay. We can have weekly meetings, and I will consider the motivation issue soon, says Motoda-KS.

– Now, anything else from the Controller Group? says Joshi-B, looking directly at Ota-KS because I think he has used up his quota of two questions and, according to the rules, is not supposed to ask any more.

– No, that is all. Thank you.

– Then let us move to the Cyber-Factory Group. Muruta-KS, please go ahead.

– In our group we feel that some of our specialist areas are being covered by other research departments. As a result we feel we are competing internally for work from the factories. We would like to see some more coordination among departments to avoid internal competition. Another point is that senior members of the group would like to have the authority to independently select subcontractors.

The second point is my own. I want to quietly remind Ueda-GR and Joshi-B that it was they who told me to use Tani and his men, who were unable to finish the programming for me, whether that was due to foreigner-induced stress or not.

Ueda-GR, sitting next to Joshi-B, glances at his notes and gives his answer.

– I realise there seems to be some internal competition with other labs and development centres. Solving this issue involves coordination at a higher level. I will make the concerns of the group known to the general manager. Regarding the selection of subcontractors, we can allow preferences but decision-making is ultimately with the department manager.

He is telling me politely that Joshi-B still calls the shots. I don't mind. I have made my point. They know what I am thinking.

– Does that answer your question? says Joshi-B.

– Yes, thank you.

– Then let us move to the Car Navigation Group.

– The members of the Car Navi Group are concerned because what are clearly the manager's tasks are being thrown to the senior group members. Can the roles and responsibilities of each member of the group be clarified?

– I understand the group members' concerns, says the manager. I admit that some unforeseen problems resulted in delegation of tasks to group members who are KS-class. I will clarify roles for the year ahead. Also, I would point out that certain members have high-level expertise in certain areas. It is not easy to avoid passing on tasks to our experts. In the coming year, however, I will do my best to clarify roles and responsibilities in advance.

– Is that adequate? says Joshi-B.

– Yes, it is adequate.

The other groups in the department ask their questions and get their answers.

– Any other matters?

– We have some general topics, says Nitta-C. The locker room has a bad smell in the summer. We request that a fan be installed. Secondly, in order to cut electricity costs we have been instructed to turn off all lighting at lunchtime. Some departments turn off the lights but ours does not. We request clarification on this matter.

I think Nitta-C prefers a bit of darkness at lunchtime because he often folds his arms on his desk, lays down his head and has a little nap. I myself prefer the lights on so I can see what I am eating.

– About the locker room, says Joshi-B, yes, I have noticed the smell. I believe we can install a fan. And I will request clarification from the general manager regarding the lights. This is related to our lab maintaining its ISO 14001 certification for environmental management. As you know the assessors gave us an excellent rating when they visited our laboratory.

It's true the assessors were impressed to see the lights out at lunchtime. They were also impressed that all employees had environmental management cards and could answer their questions when they did a spot check.

We knew the answers because it was part of the laboratory environmental plan to prepare for the assessors' question:

What measures are being taken to improve the environmental performance of the lab?

Answer: We turn off the lights at lunchtime; we separate the rubbish into combustible, non-combustible and recyclable waste; we save paper by implementing two-sided copying and printing; we set the air conditioners to a temperature of 28 degrees Celsius and we only switch them on in mid-summer.

The environmental assessors were clearly not interested in the ten or twenty trucks and vans that park outside the gate with engines idling for forty-five minutes every day at lunchtime, nor were they concerned at the waste of resources in the annual transfer of hundreds of employees, either alone or with their families, to various parts of the country for unknown corporate reasons and sometimes back again within a year or two. The assessors were only interested in the formalities, which we are good at obeying.

Nitta-C says he has one final point to make.

– We would request that the senior managers take more of their assigned vacation days. This would make it easier for the rest of us to take our annual leave.

– We understand. As far as it does not interfere with work, I encourage all of the group leaders here today to take at least half their twenty-five vacation days. This can be achieved without the need to take a long break. A day or two every couple of months or a few days when the factories close in August should be possible.

– The union thanks management for their cooperation at today's *shoku-kon*, says Nitta-C.

– The management thanks the union for their unswerving commitment to the company, the workplace and the welfare of the employees, says Joshi-B.

We take our papers and leave while the managers stay to write up their impressions. We go back to the union room. Nitta-C thanks us for our efforts.

– And do not forget our *shoku-kon* reflection meeting next week. Please bring a summary of the answers given today.

I learned a bit from my union rep duties. Behind the Mitsubishi ritual, the meeting was useful. If you ask the right questions in the right way and avoid offbeat topics, you can get some information from the senior guys. You can even push them in the direction you want. There were some tough questions asked that almost made the managers feel uncomfortable – although nobody really wanted to go that far. I think they will try to do the things they said they would do. People in Mitsubishi always do what they say they'll do, as long as it is in the rulebook. But it is no use straying outside the rulebook with awkward questions because if you do you'll just get sod-off answers like I did the previous year.

12

地震、雷、火事、親父

Jishin, kaminari, kaji, oyaji

Earthquake, lightning, fire, father

A fire has broken out on the fourth floor of our building, we are told. It started near the smoking room and has spread to the middle stairway. Hayami-T of the Factory Controller Group is first on the scene. He immediately informs his manager, Motoda-KS, who contacts the safety officer, Nonaka-C, who rushes to press the big red button on the wall near the meeting room to sound the alarm, which is a loud, high-pitched siren, so different from the everyday dings and dongs. When we hear that high-pitched siren we know what to do. We pull our white helmets out from under our desks, put them on, snap the chin strap closed and get ready to evacuate.

But wait! Nobody moves. We sit and wait for the order.

Motoda-KS switches off the coffee maker and the lights. Sato-C closes the windows. Tsume-T takes the first aid kit and waits at the emergency staircase for orders. Osaki-KS leads the fire-extinguishing unit towards the stairs and the fire.

Yoshida-KS, the floor safety manager, shouts that the emergency exits and stairs are clear. Joshi-B, the department manager, has now got the evacuation order from Administration.

– Evacuate! Everyone evacuate!

The first group in our department walks quickly towards the emergency staircase, following the department manager, who is holding a placard with the department name high above his head and carrying the bag which contains a portable radio, flashlight and important documents. The second group follows, then ours, then the rest.

The stairs are full of people, full of navy blue jackets and white helmets stamped with the three-diamond Mitsubishi logo, all descending silently. Out into the cold air we go, everyone walking briskly away from our building to the wide company road where no vehicles are running. Two fire engines are parked nearby: the small company fire truck that has a water pump and extinguishers but no ladder, and the big city fire engine. The company firemen stand watching, ready to support the city firemen, who are unravelling hoses and extending ladders. By now there are hundreds of blue jackets and white helmets lining up behind placards held high by the department managers. It's like the parade of countries at the Olympics except there are no flags and the uniforms are all the same. I catch sight of our placard and Joshi-B, and I squeeze my way in his direction, looking for our group leader, Ueda-GR, but it's hard to find him. Everyone looks the same from behind. Ueda-GR taps my shoulder. A foreigner is always seen, even from behind: it's the brown hair sticking out from under my helmet, or perhaps just the foreign vibes that I can't hide.

– That's everyone in our group accounted for, he says, ticking off my name on his chart. He goes to pass the list to Joshi-B, who collects all the group lists and passes them to the chief safety officer, who collects all the department lists and passes them to the general manager.

A shout goes out from the front and we all squat down, like the elementary school classes I often see waiting in the school yard for the teacher's command. More people evacuate from our building and the other buildings nearby, and soon there are 1,100 navy blue jackets and white helmets hunkered down on the company road under the grey sky in the cold January morning, waiting in silence.

The general manager appears and walks briskly to the front. He stands on a temporary platform and shouts into a loudhailer.

– Good morning, everyone. Thank you all for taking part in this year's emergency drill. It is cold today so I will not talk too long but I would like to make a few points.

– First, as you know, today is the anniversary of the Great Hanshin Earthquake of 1995, which brought tragedy to some of our colleagues and to many thousands of our neighbours. Though only a few years have passed, it is surprising how people quickly forget about great tragedies, so let us remember today.

– Second, the last few years our emergency drill has assumed an earthquake has taken place. This year we decided to have a fire drill instead. Fires often break out after earthquakes so we must prepare for any eventuality.

– Third, the emergency drill committee manager tells me that today's drill has been carried out efficiently. It took exactly 17 minutes and 15 seconds for all 1,167 members of the Osaka research laboratories to evacuate and be accounted for – a little slower than last year, but we had fewer employees then. Although our evacuation was planned in advance, I want to emphasise the importance of the drill and how it can help us be prepared for a real fire or earthquake.

– Finally, as you may have noticed, the city fire brigade are cooperating with us this year. They are about to run their ladder up to the roof of the main building, over there to your left, to rescue two volunteers from Administration. Please watch them. I will tell you when the drill is complete and you can all return to your warm desks.

We watch the ladder rise slowly from the fire engine, up to the roof of the five-storey building. An electric cradle with a fireman inside glides up the ladder. The fireman climbs onto the flat roof, clips a safety harness onto the first volunteer, helps him into the cradle, gives a signal and the cradle glides slowly back down to earth. He repeats the performance for the second volunteer and I suddenly want to clap and shout, *Banzai*, way to go, fireman Sato! But I know the general manager would not be amused because this is serious business and I've been in the company too long to even think about it.

The general manager thanks the city fire department, and all 1,167 of us file back to our buildings, up the stairs, take off our white helmets and put them under our desks till next year.

We write our opinions, if we have any, and send them to the emergency review committee, who forward the results to everyone a week later. A few people comment that it is too cold to have us all standing outside listening to speeches on a chilly winter's day. Why not have our drill on a warm spring or autumn day, as the factories do? The committee's answer is that even if it is a chilly winter's day and even if someone might catch cold, we should still carry out the drill on 17 January in remembrance of the Great Hanshin Earthquake of 1995. How the factories carry out their drills is their own business.

Someone thinks it strange, to say the least, to have to wait patiently at our desks for the order to move if there is a fire. Should we not just go as quickly as we can? And can we not leave the lights on? What happens if there is an emergency at night when it is dark? It's dangerous to have a rule about switching off the lights. The committee will consider these points before next year's drill.

Someone asks if it is really necessary to have speeches? Yes, it is – the general manager has important things to say. Someone else says that other companies do not have an emergency drill so why do we have to? We know what to do, so can we finish with the drills? No, we cannot. Just because other companies are lax about safety does not mean we should be. Please be aware that next year we will revert to the usual earthquake simulation practice. Please remember to crawl under your desk while you wait for the evacuation order. Always maintain sufficient space under your desk – no storing of books or spare computers. The monthly safety patrol in each department will check that all employees have space to take refuge under their desks. You never know when a quake might hit.

Winter is safety season and we have at least one and sometimes two safety awareness meetings. Osaki-KS is the safety officer and he chairs the safety meeting for our group. He shows us a cartoon drawing of a car approaching a set of traffic lights with a couple of cars parked nearby.

– Please look at this picture. Can each person point out at least one danger?

Tsume-T says the car in the street should slow down because the traffic lights might change suddenly. Machiya-C says there might be children playing around the parked cars. Kanda-T has to think hard to come up with something different. He says that, well, the traffic lights look like they might not be working properly so the driver should be extra careful.

Everyone laughs. Suzuki-T says the driver might be late for work but he should not speed. I say there are too many cars and the drivers should swap their cars for bicycles. Everyone laughs again. Safety school can be fun, boys and girls, can't it?

Osaki-KS tells us we must think about safety in the workplace. Each of us must give an example of something dangerous we have come across in the lab and Osaki-KS will note it in his group safety awareness meeting report.

– Group Leader Ueda, can you begin?

– Let me see – when was it? A couple of weeks ago I was about to go into the toilet when Nishida-T pushed the door open and almost hit me in the face, so … so we have to be careful of toilet doors that open suddenly in our face.

– Fine, that's one item, says Osaki-KS. Who is next?

– I was filing loose pages the other day when I cut my finger with a sheet of A4 paper, says Tsume-T. Just a little, but still … I suppose we should be careful of the sharp edges of A4 sheets of paper.

– I didn't think paper could be dangerous, says Osaki-KS. But there you go. You never know where safety issues crop up. Now, Muruta-KS, do you have anything?

– Yes, I have something. There is a loose drain cover just outside the rear entrance to our building. It's hard to see it these dark evenings and I almost tripped over it last month. It should be fixed before someone gets hurt.

– Sorry, says Osaki-KS, that's no good. It has to be something *inside* our building.

– Even if it's more dangerous than toilet doors opening and the sheets of A4 paper?

– Yes, that's right. Now, anything else we can put in our report?

We try to think of other dangerous things in the office, as dangerous or even more dangerous than the sheets of A4 paper that might cut our fingers or the toilet door that might open suddenly and hit us in the face, but we cannot repeat anything that has already been said nor mention anything outside our building no matter how dangerous it is, and we most certainly cannot say, Isn't this all a load of bullshit? because we know this is an official safety awareness meeting in a world-class Fortune Global-500 corporation.

Osaki-KS says he will write his report listing the points we have mentioned. Thanks for your cooperation. Oh, and don't forget your homework!

Tsume-T rolls his eyes. Me too. We don't want homework! We don't want homework!

– I think you have all received notice about drawing your commuting map, haven't you? says Osaki-KS. Everyone should submit a rough map showing the route taken to work each day, pointing out at least three dangerous places such as road crossings and intersections. And do not forget the slogan – please write some short phrase that will help you stay safe. No imitating other people's slogans, all right? Please submit your safety homework by Friday.

I do my homework by Friday because I don't want Osaki-KS coming to tell me the safety committee is waiting. I draw a colourful map with several lines going this way and that, because I take different routes to work, depending on my mood, the traffic and the weather, and also because I'd like to confuse the map reader and see what happens. My slogan says, *Life in the fast lane is fun.* I write it in English so that I can plead it is an internationally recognised slogan that doesn't really mean what it seems to mean, just in case anyone from the safety committee calls me up and says, Are you trying to be awkward or something? But no one calls me up to ask about the coloured lines, what I mean by my foreign-language slogan or if I'm trying to be awkward. I think no one even checks the homework.

The next year I take over as group safety officer from Ozaki-KS. I decide to skip the safety awareness meeting. No one in my group seems to notice, but Motoda-KS, who is now department safety inspector, tells me I have to submit a safety awareness meeting report. I use my imagination and write a report as good as Ozaki-KS would have done, except I don't mention any dates. Motoda-KS glances at it when I give it to him. I think he knows I made it up, but he doesn't say anything.

The annual safety awareness meeting and the colour-me-in homework are not so serious, but the annual performance evaluation meeting is. We are called one by one for a chat with the boss or sometimes, for KS-class employees, the boss's boss. For an hour or so he talks about how we have done over the year and what is expected of us in the year to come. It is serious but not nerve-racking because he restricts his comments to positive ones and, of course, we are all lifers. The worst that might happen is a transfer to some distant city. Normally, you know you have done well if the boss heaps praise on your work or tells you the department is indebted to you and would be in dire straits without you; you know you have not done so well if he says your work was satisfactory. Rarely, there might be a hint of criticism – let's try a bit harder next year – but that would be the worst you could expect. It is a civilised sort of performance evaluation.

I sit in the meeting room facing Ueda-GR, who has copies of my performance review sheet and my personal data sheet.

– This year, he says, you have worked on the eco-design project, managing the revised version of the computer program. Your work is appreciated. You are now testing the new version, I believe. The tests are important, in view of the problems with the earlier version. Please continue to test and ensure its usefulness for the factories. And please continue to give the eco-design lectures to the factory designers and managers. Your contribution there is also appreciated. Now, what else? Yes, you have completed a couple of research reports this year, one patent application and one conference paper. Please continue your work on patent ideas. Our department has not reached its quota for the year yet. Now, any questions you would like to ask?

Oops, I'm thinking. He is being pretty restrained about the praise this year and I'm not sure why. I decide to throw a difficult question at him.

– Yes, I was wondering about the new salary system. It is supposed to be performance-based, right? Last year I had no patent application, only wrote one research report and, as you know, there were many problems with that computer program. This year things went better, much better, and company profits are up, yet my salary has gone down. Do we now have a reverse-performance-based system or what is going on?

– I agree with you that the new performance-based salary system is a little hard to understand. You have to keep in mind that there is more involved than just your output. Our department is also evaluated and so is the laboratory. Only below the department level is individual performance considered. So your salary reflects department and laboratory performance as well as your own output. Is that okay?

– But do you not think the traditional seniority-based pay system might be better than a complicated performance-based one where your salary may go down if you do more, and may go up if you do less?

– *Saah*, it is a difficult problem, he says, and I know he doesn't want to get into a complicated discussion because it might lead to talk about who gets the most and the least brownie points within our group.

– Yes, it's a difficult problem, I say and leave it at that.

I think I know what's going on. There are only so many brownie points to go round in our group. The robotics project for the Kyoto factory is getting high priority and I know Osaki-KS is doing good work there, bringing in mega-yen, and he does plenty of overtime. I'm sure he has more brownie points than me with my eco-design program, which only brings in micro-yen, and I don't do much overtime either.

– Let us move on to your personal sheet, he says. Healthwise, you have no problems. Good. Your family are well, I see, although your parents and those of your wife are not in the best of health. I hope their health improves this year. And I see that you still wish to move back to the Tokyo–Yokohama area. Is that correct?

– Yes, the same request as last year and the year before. For family reasons. It is difficult to visit two sets of parents every summer. You remember that my wife prefers to live closer to her parents while our boy is small.

– Yes, I remember. I believe Personnel are aware of your preference.

– Any chance of a move?

– Not that I know of. The company cannot satisfy the preferences of every employee. Please keep this in mind. Any other problems?

– No. Everything is fine, I say, because it is no use asking for more desk space, more transparency in decision-making and more brownie points for projects that only bring in micro-yen.

– Please do your best next year. Can you tell Tsume-T to come in now?

My evaluation for the year is over. I don't like some parts of it but that cannot be helped. All the Mitsubishi salarymen have to accept the same system and I'm no different from any of my colleagues.

◆◆◆

Ueda-GR treats me the same as the others in most things. I have to write my weekly report like the others, attend the same group meetings, and when Ueda is away I sometimes have to take his place at the department manager's meeting, which is about budgets, what Head Office is planning and what we can do to promote our department. Each October I have to propose research plans for the following year – new projects we should start, old ones that should be extended. The research plans usually include the latest buzz words from America but there has to be some useful idea in there too. Some years my plans are adopted, some years they are not. It depends on what the department manager, the laboratory general manager and Head Office want. Sometimes there are political decisions involved – the laboratory has to maintain good relations with the factories that make money and provide us with research funding. We don't need to cultivate relations with factories that don't make money, unless Head Office tells us to.

I hate the weekly reports. We have to send an email to everyone in our group, stating what we have been doing during the week, what meetings we have attended, what patents we are working on, what reports or papers we're writing, and, most importantly, we have to list the names of people we meet from outside our group. Meeting people to discuss our work always sounds good. Our report also has to mention the things that do not sound good, such as plans to take a day off. But it is rare to plan days off and tell everyone in advance. Normally, we just call in sick when we want to use a day from our annual leave: *I've a bit of a cold today, I'm not feeling the best.* That sounds much better than saying I'm taking a day off, even if everyone knows what *a bit of a cold* means. The concept of sick leave does not exist as in Western companies. If we are really ill, we use up some of our annual leave. We don't mind this because with twenty-five days' leave per year we always have plenty of days to spare that will eventually be discarded. Visits to the company doctor, dentist or pharmacy during work hours sound okay in our report because it means we are only taking an hour to go to the company clinic, not a half-day or more to visit a hospital.

The reason I hate the weekly reports is because Osaki-KS always tries to sound so diligent and hardworking in his. He always seems to be writing a patent, though when I look at his old reports I notice he was writing the same patent three, six and even eight months earlier. He knows that people don't usually check old reports and that working on a patent always looks good. Tsume-T, Machiya-C and the rest of us don't want to sound like slackers. We too have to sound diligent and hardworking and it becomes a contest to see who sends out the best-looking report. When Osaki-KS finds a book about the work he is doing, he writes in his report that he has purchased a new book and is currently studying it. He brings it to the group meeting to show everyone. Ueda-GR tells him he can claim expenses but he says, no problem, he will pay himself, so that Ueda-GR will think, What a zealous employee he is. Sounding diligent in the weekly reports may be a good long-term strategy for getting promoted, but I don't like it. I feel the weekly report business is a silly contest and sometimes I don't bother to send off any report. Ueda-GR doesn't say anything but Osaki-KS notices right away and sends me a reminder message that I cannot ignore. Occasionally, he is out of the office and I can get away with skipping my weekly report.

Outside the company, at home in the Mitsubishi housing block, I'm different. I'm the foreigner. Everyone in the block knows what time the foreigner goes to work and what time he comes home – you can hardly miss the brown hair and foreign face in a quiet street in suburban Amagasaki. They know he cycles to the company in the winter and takes the train in the hot summer, which is sensible, but rumour has it that he sometimes jogs home in shorts and T-shirt with what must be his proper clothes in a little backpack. Still, it's not surprising because foreigners do all sorts of strange things. It's probably the way they do things in America, England, Germany or whatever country he comes from. The neighbours know which of the plastic rubbish bags is his and which letterbox is his because of the non-regulation sized envelopes that sometimes stick out. There can be no secrets when you're the only brown-haired salaryman in the block.

If I was living alone I would never know about the rumours nor hear what the neighbours think, but with a native wife who chats with the others, the rumours and the gossip get back to me. Someone saw the foreigner going for a walk with the baby in a baby-carrier on his back, someone saw him go jogging, and someone else put the pieces of information together, added a little to spice up the news, and the latest rumour is that he goes jogging with the baby on his back, the poor baby, probably bouncing up and down as he runs along the river without a care. Amazing what foreigners get up to – the rumour is out so don't try to deny it. It's probably normal in those funny foreign places like America, England or Germany. Another rumour is that he is responsible for the abandoned bicycles that are taking up so much space in the common bicycle area – at least that is what the apartment caretaker thinks because the abandoned bicycles look big and foreign, and she asks the housewives if they belong to the foreigner, because a foreigner is likely to do strange things. She also asks the housewives if the rubbish left out on the wrong days is the foreigner's. It is no use pleading innocence, because the rumours take some time to go around and by the time I hear them they are part of the Mitsubishi apartment block history and you can't rewrite history and what could you expect from someone from a funny faraway place like America, England or Germany. But I don't mind. I don't mind giving America, England or Germany a bad name.

At the beginning we have little contact with our neighbours. It's hard to strike up a conversation with people you only see once a month in the elevator, but Eoin is soon two and then three, old enough to go playing outside and he quickly gets us in contact with people we never knew before. He drops stones from the second floor on Ochiai-*san*'s car and we get to know Ochiai-*san*. He pisses through the fifth-floor railings onto Inoue-*san* walking below and we get to know Inoue-*san*.

Ochiai-*san* is not a car fanatic, fortunately, and he doesn't mind a dent or two in the roof of his Toyota – just don't let it happen again. Ever.

Nice guy, Ochiai-*san*. I'd like to invite him in for tea but I think he'd prefer to keep a neighbourly distance from the international couple with the stone-dropping kid.

Inoue-*san* lives on the ground floor but she comes up to the fifth floor one day to tell us our boy seems to be playing with water on the balcony because water fell on her as she walked by. We apologise and tell her we will certainly stop the little fellow playing with water on the balcony – wherever he got the water from, we don't know. But we make a quick guess and I think Inoue-*san* also knows where it came from, but she doesn't want to go into the details just before dinner. When she's gone we explain to the little fellow that it is not polite to piss on your neighbours. He understands.

He grows quickly and never pisses on the neighbours again. Soon he has a little brother, Brendan-Naoyuki, who doesn't introduce us to any new neighbours we had not met before. Time goes by and Brendan sets off to kindergarten on a colourful kiddies' bus every day to paint pictures, make paper toys and splash about in the kindergarten pool. Eoin moves on to primary school, where life is tougher than in kindergarten. One day he comes home with special homework to do: he has to draw a map showing the route he takes to the school, pointing out the danger spots. He doesn't have to write a safety slogan. That's only for the senior boys like me.

We wonder if he will have any problems with bullying because his hair and skin are lighter in colour than the others. Most of the time it makes no difference, but one day he gets into an argument with the class toughie, Uemura, who calls him *gaijin*. Eoin does not like being called a foreigner and decides to rub Uemura's little nose in the schoolyard dirt. While he is doing so, the teacher arrives, separates them and makes them both write an essay about being polite to your classmates. Uemura doesn't call him a foreigner again.

We think he is envied by the other kids and mothers more often than looked down upon. All the mothers would like to have bilingual kids without paying a fortune for extra classes and they'd like to be able to go abroad every year like that international family in the Mitsubishi block. Some of them think it's cool to have a kid with light-coloured hair that is not dyed and who is tall for his age. The mothers in the Mitsubishi block say he's tall because his dad's a foreigner and foreigners are always tall, aren't they?

There is another international kid a few streets away from us and I feel she has a harder time. Her mother is Japanese but the father is never around. The little girl has dark skin and fuzzy hair. I get the feeling the local mothers don't envy her.

On weekends I take our kids to a small park where there's a swing, a sandpit, a slide, a short grassy lawn, though the grass doesn't grow well, and a bench where I sit reading the newspaper. After a few Sundays I begin to know some of the other parents who come. A few of them chat with me about the kids or the weather, although others prefer to keep their distance. One day an old man hobbles into the park, stops, surveys the scene, notices the foreigner on the bench and shuffles over. He sits down beside me, which is strange because people here usually keep their distance till they know you well.

– Nice day, isn't it? he says.

– Yes, nice day.

– By the way, where are you living? Over in that block, if I am not mistaken.

– Yes, on the fifth floor.

– Thought so. I thought I'd seen you coming and going. I still know what is going on. I still see the comings and goings.

He looks at me and says, How old do you think I am?

I glance at his creased face and sparse grey hair. He looks about eighty.

– Sixty-five?

He looks pleased.

– I am seventy-seven years old! I don't look it, do I? That's because I go for a walk for an hour every day. Summer, winter, rain, wind. I go for my walk and that's why I'm in such good condition. Is that your son over there?

– Yes, it is.

– Thought so. Yes, I thought so. Hair is not as black as the other kids. And where are you from, yourself?

I think he doesn't want to go into geographical details, so I say Europe.

– I see. There used to be some Americans near where I worked. With the army or something. But that was a long time ago. I wonder where they went. Must have gone back to America. Never spoke to them. Come to think of it, never spoke to a foreigner before. Today must be the first time, even if I'm seventy-five.

– Seventy-seven.

– Oh yes, seventy-seven. You speak the language. That's useful. No use trying to talk if you can't speak the language.

I like his easy-going style, no inhibitions, no hang-ups about foreigners, even if it is his first time to talk to one. I ask him about his family.

– Wife passed away a few years ago, he says. Children grown up and living in Osaka, but they don't have much time to visit. Just at holiday time. I could go and visit them, but it's troublesome getting trains. I like it here where I know everything. Yes, I know this place. Well, I'll be moving along now. Have to walk another thirty minutes today.

And he moves on.

Miyuki's mother takes the train down from Tokyo to see the apartment and the grandkids for a few days. When she leaves we go to the *shinkansen* station at Shin-Kobe and see her off. Miyuki and the kids go shopping and I decide to take a walk up the mountain path behind Shin-Kobe, where there's a view over Kobe and a waterfall that should be pretty in the autumn with the maple leaves turning red. But I'm not sure which road to take. I look around for someone to ask and see a policeman standing outside the station. He seems to have nothing to do. He looks friendly. He's probably there to help people find their way.

– Excuse me. I'm looking for the path to Nunobiki Park, where the waterfall is. Can you tell me which way it is?

– You take the underground passageway down that stairway, he says, and then quickly adds, Where have you come from just now?

I'm surprised. It's not a friendly enquiry. It seems he's checking me out. Perhaps there has been some incident in the neighbourhood – although he seemed to be just standing there with nothing on his mind.

– I've just come from Osaka. With my wife and kids. They've gone shopping.

– Can you show me your passport?

He is really checking me out! There seems to be no reason for his question and for a moment I feel like just walking away. Then I remember that non-Japanese are supposed to carry a passport or alien card at all times and I don't have mine with me now. Strictly speaking, I'm breaking the law. I'd better be nice to this alien-baiting lawman. If I don't he might just say, Come with me, alien-*san*, and I'd have to go with him and be his guest in the police station till someone could find my alien card and bring it to the station and get me released – that is, if I am allowed to make a telephone call.

I start looking through my wallet and apologise. A few strategic apologies should get me out of trouble.

– Sorry, I must have left it at home today. Will my company card do?

He doesn't change his attitude. And I was only asking for directions. Bastard.

– Let me see the company card.

He examines my Mitsubishi card closely. He asks me for my home address, telephone number, where I work and what I do and writes it all down.

– Was there some incident? I ask, wondering if there is a reason for the mini-interrogation, but he doesn't answer. He just says that foreigners are required to carry their passport or alien card at all times and I am allowed to go. I should be thankful, I suppose – thankful that I controlled my anger and had my Mitsubishi card. I wonder what would have happened if I had a Middle Eastern or Chinese face.

I walk up the mountain path to the waterfall thinking it over. Was my question polite enough? Yes, I'm sure it was. I've been asking questions here for more than fourteen years. I know how to ask a question politely. Perhaps he thought it strange for a foreigner who looked like a tourist to be fluent in the language. Perhaps he had nothing else to do and here was a foreigner he could hassle in his own language for a change. If I had spoken in English or broken Japanese I think he wouldn't have bothered me.

I feel I should do something, make some complaint, because this happened not in a dark alley on the bad side of town but on a quiet Sunday afternoon in the international tourist-friendly city of Kobe just up the street from the glistening Oriental Hotel. There would be no use in a foreigner complaining to the police about a policeman. Instead I write a little article and send it to the *Asahi Shimbun*. They probably won't publish it, but I'll try anyhow. Surprise. One of the editors telephones me at work a few days later. He would like to expand it a little and publish it. He will send a cheque later but first he wants to verify the details. He suggests the word I used – *iyagarase* (harassment) – might be too strong. Would I agree to *fuyukai* (unpleasantness)? I agree. A few colleagues in the company see the article and tell me it's great to get something in a newspaper like the *Asahi Shimbun* and it's a pity Kobe has cops like that in the tourist area on a quiet Sunday afternoon. I don't hear anything from the police department. Maybe just as well. They might not be pleased to be complained about in a prestigious newspaper, especially by an outsider, and they might cause me further problems. But I have made my point. And I've learnt something too. I've learnt that in spite of having a native wife and kids at the local schools, in spite of being a Mitsubishi salaryman and being polite when I asked for directions from the policeman at Shin-Kobe Station on a sunny Sunday afternoon in November, I'm still an immigrant and that policeman thinks immigrants should be kept in their place. The *Asahi Shimbun* and I don't agree.

13

雨降って地固まる

Ame futte ji katamaru

The rain falls, the ground hardens

In the late 1990s the Japanese economy is in recession and several of the Mitsubishi companies fall into the red. Our corporate cousins in Mitsubishi Motors and the two Mitsubishi banks are in even worse shape than us. The car company is losing market share and the banks are saddled with huge debts – the legacy of speculative loans made during the bubble economy a decade earlier. Mitsubishi Motors get desperate in their efforts to stay within sight of Honda, Nissan and Toyota. When design faults are discovered in their vehicles, top management conceal the truth in order to avoid costly recalls. The cover-ups are discovered after a spate of accidents, some fatal, and eventually, in 2004, the former president and top executives are arrested on charges of professional negligence. This is a big blow to the Mitsubishi companies because Mitsubishi Motors have a high public profile and many people identify the group with the car-maker. As I read the newspaper headlines I wonder how the other Mitsubishi companies will react. Will they cut their losses and embarrassment and encourage Mitsubishi Motors to dissolve and sell off its divisions to other car-makers? No, they wouldn't take such drastic action. The Mitsubishi presidents have an emergency meeting and make a decision: when a fellow Mitsubishi company is in dire straits the old family ties come into play. The wealthier corporate cousins – the Mitsubishi banks (in spite of the bad loans), Mitsubishi Corporation, Mitsubishi Heavy Industries and others – do a whip-round, put a few yen in the prodigal son's hat (150 billion, for starters), tell him not to do it again and remind him of the old Mitsubishi principles of integrity and corporate responsibility to society. No doubt they suggest reissuing the *Corporate Ethics Manual*, which probably exists in Mitsubishi Motors as it does in our company. Even after 130 odd years, the Mitsubishi name and the three-diamond symbol still mean something.

But back at the turn of the century, many of the big corporations are forced to implement restructuring and cutbacks. The newspapers are full of articles about downsizing and the end of lifetime employment, but they exaggerate. No salaryman in any of the large corporations is directly fired because we are all lifers and life means life. Instead, overseas factories are shut, foreign staff at the overseas offices let go and their Japanese supervisors reassigned. At home, salarymen approaching fifty are given enticements to go on permanent parole and transfers to subsidiaries become more common. One of my senior colleagues is transferred to a national research laboratory three hours by train from his home. He accepts the transfer, of course, and tells me it will only be for three or four years. But he is over fifty and we know he won't be back.

Although the number of employees in our company group is steady at around 100,000, the number in the core organisation decreases to less than half that total. Transferring staff to low-cost subsidiaries is one way to improve the balance sheet. The other simple way is to reduce salaries. All of us take a cut, with top management showing the way: bigger cuts at the top, smaller at the bottom. Top management sometimes do it right. We work harder, or so it seems, and the balance sheet swings into the black, with record profits. We haven't caught up with Sony and we don't know how long we'll stay profitable, but we get an unexpected 2001 spring bonus anyway – a corporate pat on the back to make us feel good about ourselves and Mitsubishi. It's not a bad old company after all.

The difficult times don't go away and soon our company is living dangerously once again. Ueda-GR calls an emergency group meeting one evening in February 2002 to announce an all-time record loss of 78 billion yen and further salary cuts. Senior management in the Osaka research laboratory react by proposing a one-year campaign to be known as *Change Mind 21* – an English title to show how international we are, even if we're not. I think it's a strange title. I ask Ueda-GR if it means we should change our minds twenty-one times or change because it is the twenty-first century. He smiles and says he is not sure. He only knows we should change our minds about something. The emails from above tell us to change our minds about many things: about wasting energy with too much air conditioning in summer and heating in winter, about long meetings and working inefficiently, about selfishly claiming payment for overtime instead of trying to improve the company's balance sheet, about unhealthy lifestyles and smoking too much, about not doing the morning and afternoon exercises, about not following the safety rules at work and on the way to and from work – like cycling in the rain while holding an umbrella in one hand, though I cannot see how cycling with both hands on the handlebars will make up for the 78 billion yen loss, in the short term at least. I wonder what will happen if we change our minds about working overtime and decide to focus on more important things like having a life outside of work and getting home for dinner with the family, or what will happen if we change our minds about always doing what we are told and decide to be naughty employees and walk around with our hands in our pockets. Surely senior management wouldn't want us to change our minds *that* much.

No, they would not. As the months go by, we see that we don't really have to change our minds about anything unless we want to – it's a voluntary change-your-mind campaign organised to keep Administration busy because they have nothing else to do in these tough economic times besides think up silly slogans in foreign languages. The only thing we have to do is sit through a group meeting about how to implement the Change Mind campaign and forward a report to Administration. The best report will receive a prize. I find an excuse to go to the library when the meeting is on.

Senior management are the only ones who take the Change Mind campaign message seriously. They change their minds about budgets and projects, which they slash or cancel altogether. My eco-design work is recycled into factory support. I start writing software for a disassembly line in a factory where old TVs, washing machines, refrigerators and air conditioners are to be dismantled by robots. It's another Ministry-sponsored project but it finishes after a few months because the robots seem to get all flustered when asked to pull apart old, dirty things instead of putting neat, new things together, and they are soon retired to the warehouse. Humans do it better. The whole eco-business is downsized because there is not much profit in it and we have already done enough to give the company that cosy ecological feel, with green procurement, clean manufacturing and other eco-buzzwords to put on the company webpage to show how squeaky green we are.

When the next round of corporate musical chairs takes place, I'm moved to a project writing Internet applications for one of the Nagoya factories – an interesting change and maybe a good one because my colleagues in the project are friendly, helpful and not at all stressed by working with a foreigner. But when I sit down and think about all the job changes, I wonder why I'm always moving sideways, never up. I sometimes think my career is permanently on a horizontal Mitsubishi walkway rather than an upward escalator, whether spiral or straight. Maybe I'm beginning to change my mind about the company. Just a little.

Since our Gnosis project finished, all my work has been within Japan. I have no problem with that. I still enjoy being simultaneously culturally and technically challenged, and I can now accept the company rules because after all these years they seem almost normal. But I don't enjoy being forever moved sideways, in spite of having the semi-prestigious KS-title, the only Westerner promoted to manager class in the company. Sometimes I feel there is a phantom boss looking over my shoulder. The phantom boss thinks a foreigner should not really be in charge of locals in a traditional company. It would make the great Yataro Iwasaki turn in his grave – whether he was cremated or not. Maybe the phantom boss *is* Iwasaki himself, hovering around the company, checking that traditions are not being lost. I realise that the proper way for an outsider to enter a traditional Japanese company would be at the top, through a financial buyout – like Carlos Ghosn, the star CEO sent from France to rescue Nissan. He would never have got far in Nissan if he had joined as an ordinary employee.

I think I would be better off not working on local projects. I'd be more useful to the company in some international position. I'd even take an assignment overseas if it were offered. Miyuki would not mind it now that the kids are a little older and her parents would agree that if we cannot get moved to the Tokyo region, we might as well be overseas. It's surprising that senior management have not put me in some international position before, but on reflection it is not surprising at all – everyone in Mitsubishi keeps their nose to the ground or their desks, struggling quietly with the problems at hand, no need or time to think about unnecessary things. I will have to push for an international career myself. I start by asking Nonbiri-KS. He is putting into practice the Change Mind 21 campaign. He has changed his mind about whooshing his bat at lunchtime and has taken up cigar smoking instead. The smoke helps him concentrate, he says, makes him more efficient in his work, better than whooshing a bat.

So what does he think about getting onto the international career track?

– It's like I told you. Everyone is satisfied with the lukewarm water – the *nurumayu.* The managers are content with the way things are. They don't want to risk putting a foreigner in charge. But you could try asking Joshi-B. He is a good guy. Or maybe you should start lower down with Ueda-GR, even if he prefers the *nurumayu.*

I talk to Ueda-GR.

– *Saah,* he says, which he always says when he's not sure what to say. In my opinion, it might be difficult for you to do international work. You would have to do different tasks and perhaps even move to a new division. That would be difficult.

– Hey, Ueda-*san,* did I not get moved to new departments and divisions about six times already?

– That was different. That was decided by very senior people. It is not the same thing when you want to move yourself. You would need approval from above. I'll tell you what. I will mention it to Personnel next time we submit the employee reports. How about that? See if they come up with anything. Please wait.

– Okay, I'll wait.

◆◆◆

We get occasional newsletters about employee education courses in the corporate Institute of Technology. Up to now I've only paid attention to the eco-design lectures I give three times a year, but among the non-technical courses there is one I had not noticed before. It's held every three months for employees who expect to be put in charge of international business or sent overseas. It includes intensive study of English, advice on how to conduct meetings with foreigners and tips on how to survive in culturally hostile environments far from the safety of home. The course even teaches how to understand *the mind of a foreigner.* Heavy stuff. I wonder if I will have to graduate from this course in order to get on the international career track or will an exception be made for me. I still remember how to speak English, I know how to conduct meetings with foreigners and I believe I can survive in culturally hostile environments far from home, wherever that is. Haven't I been working in a culturally hostile environment for the last fifteen years? I'm not sure how *the mind of a foreigner* works but I have a good specimen close at hand should the need for study arise.

The months go by and I don't hear anything from Personnel. I ask Ueda-GR.

– Any feedback?

– No, I'm afraid. Nothing. As I told you, it is very difficult to get an international position if you just apply yourself. Personnel have your file. That is all we can do.

– If you ask me, they're not looking too hard. But I have an idea. How about me taking that company course for employees who expect to be put in charge of international matters? If I do it, my chances of getting an international appointment might improve.

– What course is that?

– The one where you study *the mind of a foreigner* and how to survive in culturally hostile environments.

– Now, now, Muruta-KS, there is no need to go making silly suggestions. Look, to be honest, I cannot do much for you and I don't think Personnel will either. Why don't we talk this matter over with the department manager?

We go for a chat with Joshi-B. He understands my situation. He knows

Mitsubishi is not the most flexible organisation in the world, especially for the only foreign lifer in the whole place. But he will see what is possible over the next few months.

One day he calls me to his office.

– The general manager is looking for someone to represent our corporate laboratory overseas. The posting would be based in Europe and would involve quite a bit of travel – visiting companies and university research centres – but I think it would be an important job. Would you be interested?

– I'm interested.

– Good. To be frank with you, I think your background makes you just the person for this. You have the PhD and you know a few of the languages they speak over there. I think you could also help Head Office because they often have problems understanding the Europeans. I will let the general manager know that you are interested. It will take a month or two before a decision is made. Please keep this confidential for now.

Two months later Joshi-B calls me for another chat.

– Top management in the lab have made their decision about the new appointments. They would like you to act as liaison between our department and Europe. You won't have to move anywhere and this job will not interfere with your current work.

Liaison for the department? This sounds a step down from being the European representative for the corporate laboratory he mentioned two months earlier.

– What about the lab representative?

– Oh that? The general manager decided Higashi-B would be best for the job. But I'm sure you can assist him if necessary.

– But did you not ask me to be lab rep two months ago?

– Perhaps you misunderstood. I was just asking about your general interest in the position.

– Okay. Perhaps I misunderstood, I say, although I know I didn't misunderstand anything and Joshi-B himself knows I didn't misunderstand anything. It is clear he thought I should be appointed as lab representative and it is clear he was overruled by the general manager or someone more senior than himself. Still, he probably did his best for me. I'm thankful for that and I don't want to press him on it or make him feel guilty. It's not his fault.

– See how the liaison work goes, he says. It may be more important than you think.

So Higashi-B will be the lab representative. I know Higashi-B. He is capable enough, although he is not the hottest at understanding foreign ways because he comes to me now and then to have some document translated. He has never lived abroad and I wonder if he will do that course about how to survive in culturally hostile environments and how to understand *the mind of a foreigner*. But that is not important. What is important is that he is a department manager, is over fifty and has good connections with the general manager because he rubs shoulders with him at meetings every month. The current general manager is not the type to do any mind-changing and would not dream of appointing a foreigner as official lab representative. It would raise too many eyebrows in Tokyo and the directors would be frowning and wondering what is going on in the labs. They would be thinking to themselves there's far too much changing of minds going on – Change Mind 21 notwithstanding. Better choose a black-haired, dark-eyed Mitsubishi man even if he doesn't know how *the mind of a foreigner* works and doesn't know anything about surviving in culturally hostile environments.

I go on one trip to Europe as liaison for the department, visit a few research institutes and write my report, but no one back home is really interested in the contacts I make. Joshi-B tells me to hang on there, the liaison job might still be important and there are always new projects starting, but I think he's an eternal optimist. I feel our general manager is more in line with Mitsubishi culture than Joshi-B. The general manager is intelligent but docile, wouldn't say boo to anyone, never do anything that Head Office wouldn't approve off, and that's how he got where he is and why he always takes the cautious approach. But for surviving in culturally hostile environments, somehow I think I'd be better than Higashi-B. I know my way around, and if, just if, my wallet was stolen – as happened to Higashi-B on his last trip to Europe – I'd even know how to sleep in the park, wouldn't I? I don't think Higashi-B could get a good night's sleep in the park. He wouldn't know where to put his suitcase.

I do a little more mind-changing. I contact a couple of foreign companies to see what is available, although I'd want something culturally as well as corporately challenging. An offer comes through and I quietly let Ueda-GR know that one day soon I might move on, up and out.

– Wait, don't rush into things, he says. Let's talk it over with Joshi-B.

Joshi-B tells me he really thinks there is important work for me to do here. Please reconsider, or at least wait a few weeks. He will investigate what is possible.

Whenever I talk about quitting I suddenly become an important person in the department. The threat of leaving is a powerful one because the bosses seem to think I'm still useful. Or perhaps they think I'm one of the family and it would be a traumatic experience were I to head off into the sunset, never to return. It might also be a traumatic experience for myself, trying to get used to a foreign company. I put off my decision for a few weeks.

Joshi-B calls me to his desk.

– I have discussed your situation with some people from Head Office. They would like you to move into the intellectual property department. The job will be based in the Osaka city office for a year or so, after which you will return to the lab. It will involve more than just translating patents for the US and Europe – there is also important decision-making involved. I think you would have an important role in helping the department. Will you take the job?

It seems a reasonable offer: work with an international flavour and a change of office scenery for a year; I won't be managing software engineers who get stressed when working with foreigners; and I won't have to study *the mind of a foreigner* or do the course about how to live in hostile foreign environments.

– Yes, I'll take the job.

◆◆◆

I move to the new position in the autumn. It's a long bicycle commute into Osaka now, but the office doesn't feel like Mitsubishi anymore. There are only a few people remaining at their desks after 5.30 p.m., there are no chimes and bells dinging and donging for this and that, no exercise sergeant shouting out the drills twice a day, no arrows on the stairs telling us which side to walk on, nobody wears the uniform and people actually chat with one another during the working day. It feels so relaxed after the hard life in the labs, I stop and ask myself if I've reached the salaryman's nirvana, a place up on the seventh floor where all good salarymen go after working their ass off for years in the labs and factories. I guess it's as close to nirvana as I'll get in uptown Osaka, even if it is only for a year.

The managers see that I'm good at translation – have I not been doing it every day for fifteen years now? They ask me to act as supervisor. Most of my colleagues in the section are easy to work with, but there is one senior salaryman who doesn't like being supervised by a foreigner, especially one younger than himself. It's a delicate situation. I let the senior salaryman know I'm just an assistant supervisor, not really in charge of anyone – this is Mitsubishi, isn't it? He's happy enough with that and we can have tea and chat as we look out over the streets of Osaka and pretend that Mitsubishi is a great place to work.

As I get used to the relaxed atmosphere in the Osaka office I start asking myself some questions. Do I really like being a salaryman? Why have I stayed a salaryman so long? Perhaps it's because I wanted a different sort of life and Mitsubishi just happened to turn up. Or perhaps I stayed because I learned to tolerate the oppressive company culture and because I met many good colleagues in Mitsubishi. They have to put up with strange decision-making for much longer than me and I know that some of them don't like it. They may enjoy the security and the honour of working for a huge and powerful organisation, but the company culture is something else. I remember that talk with Sano, Nagai and Nakamura when we were preparing our presentation for promotion to become *nominal* managers. They would move out if the chance came. But all three of them are still working away in the lab. They're sensible, I suppose. They stay for the security and the salary.

Riko-C was an exception. He managed to set up on his own and is doing well, I hear. I think I'm more like Riko-C. I start thinking about moving out, about working for myself, not someone else. I'll be happy to be finished with the Mitsubishi culture, but it will be hard to leave my salarymen colleagues behind – the ones who don't grovel to managers and don't mind working with foreigners, who work hard while still keeping their individuality, even if that means they'll probably never become senior managers.

Through the Osaka winter I cycle the fifteen kilometres to the office each day. The commute takes me along the Kansaki River, where it is peaceful in the morning, just the grey river moving slowly down to Osaka Bay, a barge or two floating by, the noisy traffic and crowded trains far away. On chilly December evenings I can see the lights of the city to the south, the silhouette of Mount Rokko and Kobe to the west and high above a few stars shine through. Sometimes I can make out Orion, faint but just about visible, and when I do, I remember another time and place, those nights long ago when I used to watch Orion and a million stars above, and for a moment I'm back riding the waves of the Atlantic, feeling the spray, waiting for my watch to be over, waiting for daylight to come, thinking about finding a more settled existence when I reach the other side, somewhere, anywhere, as long as it's different I don't care. Well, I found my settled existence, didn't I? But what a settled existence I found – a salaryman in Mitsubishi! As I pedal along I ask myself if I've really come this far. Have I really become a lifer in Mitsubishi? No, not a lifer. Not me. I've stayed this long because the Mitsubishi life is weird, tough and almost fun at the same time. And I found the salaryman's nirvana on the seventh floor in uptown Osaka. It'll do for now.

EPILOGUE

Epilogue

過ちては改むるに憚ることなかれ

Ayamachite wa aratamuru ni habakaru koto nakare

In mending your mistakes, do not hesitate

That corporate nirvana in uptown Osaka didn't last forever. I fell to earth the following year when I was moved to an affiliate company in Tokyo. The Mitsubishi culture still shone through and, if anything, was even more pernickety than before. Our time sheets had to specify how long we spent cleaning the office, taking part in safety patrols, listening to announcements over the public address or the boss's pep talk at the *hiru-rei* call-to-arms, taking tea-breaks, smoking, visiting the company clinic, going to the lavatory and even the time spent writing the time sheets. The personnel department, as always, were busy worrying about our health. They organised a month-long competition where employees who walked around the one-kilometre company block at lunchtime could compete for healthiness prizes, such as a Mitsubishi flashlight. Groups of workers – those who wanted the flashlight and those who always did what Personnel advised – changed from office slippers to walking shoes after lunch and diligently walked the walk each day. But when the competition was over they put away their walking shoes and returned to spending spare lunchtime moments as before: head rested on folded arms on their desk or sitting upright squinting at a bright computer screen in the dark office, lights switched off to save energy.

There was an annual department trip to Okinawa: two company-subsidised days in the sunshine, getting to know your colleagues, buying presents for all known relatives, partying as loudly as the boss would permit, then back to Tokyo, refreshed and ready for work – or nursing a hangover, depending on your constitution. Almost all the salarymen went, accompanied by a few brave OLs. I would have liked a freebie to Okinawa but not on a salaryman tour. I found something better to do that weekend.

Since my work now consisted of translating into English, I had some authority in the department. A few of the employees did have experience of working abroad but seemed to have remained within the cultural safety of the Mitsubishi compound and had learned little, besides how to communicate long distance with the office back in Japan.

Hayakui-KS, who had spent some time in France, often arrived at my desk or sent emails with questions and I provided answers. One day he had an idea.

– Why not have English classes during lunch break?

– Sure, I said. We can talk as we eat.

– No, we should not mix eating with talking. It is too difficult to do two things at once. We eat first, then talk.

– But we could eat slowly, couldn't we? Didn't you notice that in France lunch can take up to two hours?

– Not in the Mitsubishi canteen. Eating quickly is more efficient.

So we ate first, then talked – or tried to find something to talk about. But even with empty mouths, full stomachs and minds loaded with technological facts and figures, there was little to discuss, besides work. A couple of decades as a Mitsubishi lifer does not broaden the mind.

Something surprised me about these conversation classes. Japanese people are normally very grateful for any help or favour received and feel an obligation to return in kind – especially in the case of a visitor or someone higher in the social order. In his book, *The Japanese Mind,* Robert Christopher describes how during the post-war US occupation he had casually given some calcium tablets to a Japanese assistant who could not get milk for his pregnant wife. Although he thought nothing of it, he was later presented with gifts far more expensive than the man could afford. Christopher explained that he had saddled the man with what were felt as debts that must be repaid. I myself had often received little gifts or at least a warm *thank you* for something I had done for someone, so what surprised me about the lunchtime classes was that I didn't hear a single word of thanks. The positive spin on this would be that it showed I was accepted as one of the bunch, no need to say thanks, that I wasn't just a permanent visitor, treated well because I was an outsider. The negative spin is that after being *upgraded* from visitor to one-of-the-boys status, my place in the local hierarchy was low.

Sometimes I felt the more I was accepted as part of the family the lower my position in the hierarchy, and it even applied to competency in English. One of the senior employees, who had spent some years in Edinburgh and spoke English with a Scottish-Osaka accent, took it upon himself to correct my English, whether it needed correcting or not.

– In Mitsubishi we say a laser beam is *wobbled*, not shone or radiated, he told me one day.

I said he should be careful of using *wobbly Mitsubishi Engrish*, but he didn't see the humour because juniors should not talk back to their betters.

– Are you trying to make fun of our Mitsubishi English? I'll have you know that *wobble* is a very fine technical word.

When I spoke to Hayakui about the matter at lunch, he said not to worry, I should just do as I was told by those who know better than me.

– *Go ni itte wa, go ni shitagae* – when in the company, obey the company. Muruta-KS, you have been in Japan a long time. Perhaps you forget your English.

Somehow I resisted the urge to clobber him with the biggest *Oxford English Dictionary* I could find.

◆◆◆

To improve their translation skills, my colleagues attended a series of after-hours classes at company expense. I waited until a conference more relevant to my work came up and then asked my boss, Katai-B, if the department could look after the attendance fee.

– No, I'm afraid not. 25,000 yen is too expensive.

– But didn't the department pay 65,000 yen for each of my Japanese colleagues to attend night classes?

– The budget allocation has been decided. I cannot change it.

– But I've been supporting the department a lot over the last year, supervising the translations and assisting my colleagues. And that is on top of my own work. I've saved the company a large amount of money, haven't I?

Katai-B hesitated. No doubt he was also aware that my salary was lower than most of the others, since salaries were age-related in this department.

– You can wait for some cheaper conference to come up. You do not fit into the same category as your colleagues. You do not need the same training. That is why you are supervising their work.

– Look, if I'm not treated the same as the others, I'd like to stop the supervising. From now on I want to do the same work as the others.

– That would not be feasible. I want you to continue the supervision. This is not a matter of personal choice. It is my decision. Do you understand?

I looked at him for a moment and decided an argument would not be productive.

– Okay, I understand, I said and returned to my desk.

What I understood was that if a manager wants his staff to do a good job, he shouldn't piss them off. Although the conference fee was only a small issue, this was not the first time such a problem had occurred. I decided there and then that it would be the last. I would be an ex-salaryman soon enough.

In theory the company should have been glad to see me go. The lifer system was beginning to break down and Personnel were promoting voluntary retirement. Since the concept of getting rid of employees before the official retirement age did not fit the company ethos, they came up with a positive-sounding title for the scheme: *second life*. In company newsletters and seminars the personnel managers explained that permanent parole was there if we wanted it and that there was indeed life after the company; you just had to organise yourself and, provided your bosses approved, the company would give you a generous good-riddance package.

When I told Katai-B that I planned to quit within a couple of months

– plenty of time for him to reorganise – he didn't make any comments. He put on a serious face and told me to say nothing to anyone until Head Office had been informed and had approved. I think he also wanted to keep the news quiet till the last minute so that there would be less talk with colleagues about why I was leaving, and he knew he was at least part of the reason.

I expected it would take some time before approval would come through, but early next morning two senior managers arrived from Head Office and I was called for a chat. Fine, I thought, things are proceeding quickly. We entered the small private meeting room. I sat on one side of the table, the managers, looking very serious, on the other. They took out pens and notebooks, and began to ask questions that would continue for almost two hours. It felt like an interrogation. Why did I want to resign? Why now? Why not wait a few more years? Would I please reconsider? I was a very important person in Mitsubishi.

The latter point was news to me. I smiled and told them Mitsubishi would survive without me. And were there not good corporate reasons for leaving? Wasn't the personnel department trying hard to promote the *second life* program to reduce employee numbers? Surely they would welcome my quitting.

– Personnel have their own strategies, the managers said. We have ours.

Big organisations are nothing if not inconsistent: Personnel pulling one way, Head Office, the other. I realised the issue was not a corporate problem, but one of face-saving. Head Office didn't want to lose employees assigned to the project I was involved in. And they may really have believed I was a useful person to have around.

I thought hard about other reasons for quitting, not wishing to sound too negative. I told them that I honestly needed more time to visit relatives overseas. When I requested two weeks' holidays the previous July to visit my mother, who was not well, Katai-B told me I should wait a few weeks because it was the department custom to take holidays in August. Presumably I should tell my relatives to time their illnesses to coincide with Mitsubishi holidays. When another boss found out I was taking two weeks off in July he complained about me taking *long term leave* – even though I had almost fifty untaken leave days.

– In Mitsubishi, holidays are a privilege, not a right, he said, and family matters should not take precedence over work.

The managers from Head Office listened to me and agreed those bosses had gone over the top.

– We will see to it that such problems do not happen again. Now, will you reconsider your decision?

– Sorry, I've made up my mind.

They wrote everything down, asked a few more questions, then left with glum faces to report to their superiors.

An uncertain week went by. While no one could stop me from leaving, Head Office could, if they felt so inclined, refuse the *second life* package. Being a foreigner would make this even easier to do.

The following week I was summoned to Head Office near Tokyo Station. I sat opposite the managers as before. They talked about the background to my case, referring both to their strong desire that I remain but recognising the problems I had encountered. Then they announced their verdict: my request to resign had, after some deliberation, been approved. I would be given an honourable discharge.

I breathed a small sigh of relief. I would get the *second life* package which would tide me over till I started working on my own. On this occasion Head Office did play fair. And I seemed to have handled the negotiations well: not overdoing the complaints, finding an acceptable reason for leaving.

In the final two weeks I planned to take things easy and take a couple of days off but Katai-B pushed me to get more work done before leaving. He said I could take all the holidays I wanted after quitting. Holidays are a privilege not a right, remember? Colleagues said they were *surprised* that I was leaving – the polite way of avoiding expressing approval or disapproval, although a few of them quietly congratulated me, saying it was a good decision. I think they envied me.

◆◆◆

With the company gates behind me, I intended to get busy with preparations for working on my own, but after so many years as a salaryman the sudden freedom was overwhelming. I took off for a few days, cycling across

Yokohama, not worrying about getting to the company, not worrying about working up a sweat in the spring sunshine. One day I rode down to Shonan – the beaches that could be the Japanese Waikiki or Bondi, if it wasn't for the dirty grey sand and the murky water washed down from Tokyo Bay. A few surfers bobbed about among the waves, waiting for the big one that never came. They were the *freeters* – the Japanese slang for easy-going freelance – who prefer part-time jobs and fun to being lifers in the big corporations. But some of them will probably end up as salarymen in a year or two and settle for weekend surfing. Everyone has to compromise sometime.

When the first edition of the book came out, I went on a short promotional tour. A London radio station wondered if I could sing the company song. (No.) In Dublin one trendy radio station wanted to know whether there were machines in Japan that sold lady's undies. (I didn't see any near the Mitsubishi plant.) Are the zany Japanese TV game shows broadcast on Western media really that bad? (About as bad as the zany Western TV game shows broadcast on Japanese media.) After the book was featured in the Japanese edition of *Newsweek* magazine, a few former colleagues called to congratulate me and said a book like this might encourage the company to become less mono-cultured. But would it?

Mitsubishi have been employing foreigners in Japan since the late 1980s but always with the assumption that they are temporary, never with the idea of encouraging them to stay and aim at senior management. The foreign hires are assigned, as I was, to traditional departments where they are required to fit the existing company culture; they are not expected nor permitted to propose changes and if they do, they will be reminded of their place. This strategy doesn't achieve much except short-term international exchange followed, in most cases, by frustration and disappointment.

Would it be different if the foreign employee fits in and *goes native*, corporately speaking? As in any company, following the local rules is important – although the good thing about Japan is that *appearing* to follow them is usually enough. But becoming fluent in Japanese can be a double-edged sword. While in some situations it is either necessary or extremely useful to be good at the language, I occasionally noticed colleagues who felt uncomfortable with a foreigner speaking their language. They didn't quite know whether I should be treated as a local or as an outsider. A Westerner who speaks and reads fluently is sometimes treated as an oddity – like a talking robot: amazing, but does it really understand what it is saying?

What surprised me was how attitudes in the company changed as I gained fluency. When I was at the beginner level, people often praised my stumbling efforts, but as I got better the praise stopped. It was as if I was trespassing into some off-limits territory where I didn't belong. Many highly educated Japanese are proud of the fact that they can communicate with a foreigner in his or her language and feel slightly disappointed when that ability is made redundant.

When a foreigner has some professional expertise, he (assuming a male in this case) may be more highly regarded and receive better treatment if he speaks little or no Japanese. On the other hand, if he is fluent the issue becomes more complicated. After generating some initial surprise and perhaps admiration, he may find himself compared with Japanese peers more easily and may be found wanting; to older Japanese, who believe a foreigner should behave like a foreigner, he may appear to be getting uppity; some people may assume that greater abilities in the language imply reduced abilities in specialist expertise; and an outsider who speaks fluent Japanese will surely have lost some of that foreign *cachet* by going native, linguistically speaking. It might be compared to a French *cordon bleu* chef who arrives to work in England. Having a strong French accent and displaying French body language would emphasise his French-ness and might make him more highly regarded. If, however, after a few years he picks up the local ways and begins to speak and act like an Englishman, his perceived professional value may go down a few notches, even though he might be a better chef.

One solution to this would be to separate one's professional interactions into categories and carefully select those where acting foreign is an advantage and those where it is not. With outward-looking bosses in a corporate research laboratory, for example, one could emphasise one's foreign side in proposing new technical or business ideas: whether good or bad, they will probably get more air time at meetings if they are introduced as being non-Japanese. On the other hand, when it comes to implementing those ideas among the ordinary workers, going native might be best.

◆◆◆

With the rapid greying of Japanese society and the record low birth rates, demographics will force change in the big Japanese corporations. They will begin to tap the abundant human resources of China and other Asian countries, and the chances of them doing so successfully are greater than with Westerners because of the larger salary differentials between China and Japan: when you know you're being paid much better than in your home country, you can tolerate more. Chinese brain power and business sense combined with Japanese organisation and work ethic could allow an east Asian economic zone to match the US and EU, were it not for the political and cultural friction that keep them apart. At the very least, however, it seems clear that non-Japanese Asian employees will become more common at technical and commercial levels in the big companies, if not in upper management.

Most foreign employees working in the large corporations of Japan encounter inconsistencies and unfairness that would rarely happen in the West. The fundamental problem is that the managers making the decisions have no experience of anything other than the company they work for: they have spent their careers inside a corporate box and cannot think outside it – they don't even realise their decision-making leaves much to be desired. Colleagues often said that the company wasn't used to foreigners, that they need a little more time. I heard this first in the early 90s after I joined Mitsubishi, but I was still hearing the same thing thirteen years later. No doubt the big corporations will slowly grow more multi-cultured. But I won't hold my breath.